Fletcher's Gang

Fletcher's Gang

A B-17 Crew in Europe, 1944–45

Eugene Fletcher

UNIVERSITY OF WASHINGTON PRESS

Seattle and London

Copyright © 1988 by the University of Washington Press
Printed in the United States of America

All rights reserved. No part of this publication may
be reproduced or transmitted in any form or by any means,
electronic or mechanical, including photocopy, recording,
or any information storage or retrieval system, without
permission in writing from the publisher.

Library of Congress Cataloging-in-Publication Data

Fletcher, Eugene.
  Fletcher's gang: a B-17 crew in Europe, 1944–45.

  Bibliography: p.
  1. Fletcher, Eugene. 2. World War, 1939–45—Aerial operations,
American. 3. World War, 1939–1945—Personal narratives, American.
4. World War, 1939–1945—Campaigns—Europe. 5. United States. Air
Force—Biography. 6. Flight pilots—United States—Biography.
I. Title.
D785.U6F57   1988   940.54'4973   87-32289

ISBN 0-295-96604-1

Dedicated to those who anxiously waited,
and especially to Alice and Sherry,
the former who thought it should be
recorded and the latter who made it possible

Contents

Foreword

Written while the author was in combat crew training in the United States and later flying combat missions in Europe, Eugene Fletcher's letters to his beloved wife, Sherry, capture faithfully the joys and sorrows of a typical bomber crew during World War II. With varied backgrounds and interests, from different sectors of the country, Fletch's crew of four officers and six enlisted men were thrust together for only two months of training before being sent to England to engage in air combat just after D-Day.

On the one hand, Fletch documents the challenge and seriousness of his task in molding an effective team of young men; on the other, he reveals his sense of humor in writing about such incidents as their goof when they became lost on a training mission.

As one of their instructors at Ardmore, Oklahoma, and later as their squadron commander in England, I well remember Fletcher's crew as one of the most dedicated and professional of those I had the pleasure to lead. He and his crew served their country exceptionally well under the stress of repeated missions over Germany in a high threat environment, knowing that each time they took the risk of being shot out of the sky. Reading Fletch's letters covering that combat period, one detects his realistic acceptance of such hazards while at the same time one notes his attempts to reassure Sherry that all would be O.K.

For those who would like an insightful documentation of what it was like to be on a U.S. bomber crew in World War II, this is well worth reading. My compliments to Fletch for having written the letters and to Sherry for having preserved them for history.

James O. Frankosky
Maj. Gen. USAF Ret.

Author's Note

This narrative is not intended to be a saga of the Battle of the Air during World War II. Many authors have already documented the thrilling air battles and the heroism and danger inherent therein. It is a study of the mood of the times, and what went on in the minds of the people who were caught up in this crucial struggle. Some stories of combat must be told to provide a setting for the documents, and to justify and explain certain references in the letters.

It is well to point out that on any base in the combat area there were two different groups of people. The Permanent Personnel were there for the duration. If they were extremely lucky, they might get a furlough home for thirty days and then return, or they might be transferred to Higher Headquarters. But most would remain on the same field until the war was over. These people had their own living area, their own mess halls, and their own circle of friends.

This narrative is about the men of the replacement flight crews. They were assigned to a group, flew a tour, and left, if they survived. These were temporary people, "Pipeline Personnel." They had their own living area and combat mess halls, but they shared the clubs, post exchange, and theater. The two groups lived in two different worlds, and their worlds were not of their own making.

If you find people and their thoughts as interesting as deeds and battles, perhaps you will find this chronicle to your liking. The events that are detailed are true. The letters are authentic, but they have been edited for spelling and punctuation, as well as deletion of personal messages and other extraneous and repetitious material. Deletions are marked with ellipses.

Our crew was reunited in late July 1985 at Boeing Field in Seattle, Washington. The nine living members of the ten-man crew were present along with their instructor from Ardmore, Oklahoma, who later became their squadron commander in England. They were privileged to meet Ed Wells, the man who designed their airplane, *Knock Out Baby*. The crew and commander flew one "Last Mission" for KING-TV in Seattle. This documentary has been aired several times.

The reunion coincided with the fiftieth anniversary of the Boeing B-17 Flying Fortress, and the reunion of the 95th Bomb Group, plus numerous other groups of the Eighth Air Force. The occasion gave impetus to the recording of the life and thoughts of this crew in accordance with the time in which these happenings occurred. Thus it was that the idea for the book began.

In regard to the participants: their biographies will unfold as the story goes along. The one exception who needs a special introduction is the recipient of the letters. They were written to my wife, Evelyn. Her sorority sisters of Alpha Chi Omega gave her the nickname of Sherry, which was derived from her maiden name of Sherrod. We met on a blind date while attending Whitman College in Walla Walla, Washington. Sherry was an honor student, a music major studying piano, with plans of being a professional accompanist. She was a lovely young lady with a bubbling personality and a host of friends. I felt extremely lucky and fortunate that the dates were continued, even though many of them were study sessions.

My college and working life was interrupted when I received a notice that I would be drafted into military service on July 1, 1942. Since I was a licensed pilot and desired to choose the branch of service in which I would serve, I enlisted as an aviation cadet in the Army Air Corps on June 22. With the war dominating our lives and our desire to be together growing we were married August 25. Sherry was able to accompany me through my flight training as we moved from field to field. However, when I received orders in March 1944 to report to Ardmore, Oklahoma, for combat crew training, a task which would require all of my time, we decided that Sherry would return to live with her parents in Tekoa, Washington, until we could be reunited.

The crew consisted of the following members:

Pilot	Eugene R. Fletcher	1st Lt.	Dayton, Wash.
Copilot	Myron D. Doxon	1st Lt.	Enumclaw, Wash.
*Copilot	Billy Bob Layl	1st Lt.	Piggott, Ark.
Navigator	Robert C. Work	1st Lt.	Urbana, Ohio
Bombardier	Frank S. Dimit	1st Lt.	Steubenville, Ohio
Engineer	Edward W. Brown	T/Sgt.	Weir, Kan.

*Copilot for last fifteen missions.

Radio Operator	George W. Hinman	T/Sgt.	Pinkneyville, Ill.
Ball Turret	Kenneth C. McQuitty	S/Sgt.	Ardmore, Okla.
Waist Gunner	Robert L. Lynch	S/Sgt.	Muldrow, Okla.
Waist Gunner	Joseph J. Firszt	S/Sgt.	Chicago, Ill.
Tail Gunner	Martin J. Smith	S/Sgt.	Milwaukee, Wis.

Bear in mind that these were young men, ranging in age from eighteen to twenty-eight years. Some were still college students or just out of high school. Others were working, and two had just finished college. To me they were men who had been trained to do a special job, and what they did in the future was of more concern than what they had done in the past. What I knew of them will be revealed in the letters.

While this is the story of my crew and associates, it could have been any heavy bomber crew, on any base, of any group, of the Eighth Air Force.

Acknowledgments

The author would like to express sincere thanks and gratitude to Professors Tom Pressly and Maclyn Burg of the University of Washington History Department and Glen Adams, printer from Fairfield, Washington, for their timely advice and encouragement to keep going with the project. May they know that their support and critique were truly appreciated. To Paul Andrews of Vienna, Virginia, for information provided from the archives of the 95th Group, a very warm thank you. A note of appreciation to Roland Byers, Professor Emeritus of General Engineering, University of Idaho, for his continued interest and helpful advice. And a very special thanks to Lane Morgan for her editing expertise.

Although my name appears as the author, this book could not have been written without the material supplied by the crew members: Robert Work, Myron Doxon, Frank Dimit, and Robert Lynch.

Fletch

Prologue

Operational Training Unit

Ardmore, Oklahoma

Eugene Fletcher, November 1943

March 8, 1944

Dear Sherry,

Well, here we are at Ardmore. I don't know where to begin, so I'll just start out rambling. We have just about settled down. After reporting in, processing, and assigning crew positions aboard the ship, I gave the boys the old pep talk to get them on the ball. We sure have had our hands full.

Here's what we're doing now: going to school eight hours a day for two weeks. After that we will fly for four weeks, two more weeks of classes, four more of flying. Then our little stay here will be over.

We could live off the post but the field is eighteen miles from town and with no more time than we have off it pretty much discourages that. Those who are trying it are finding that it isn't so good. Besides, they are neglecting a lot of little things in order to have time off. I know we were right in having you not come.

Cap and Sis wrote me a letter and I think they are coming down soon to visit for a little while. It will be swell if they do. Now about my crew: they're really a swell bunch of fellows and I'm proud of them, my flight engineer in particular. His name is Brown and he's a staff sergeant, an old Army man. He has been Staff since '42. You can tell him something and you don't have to worry about it again because you know he'll do it and it will be done right. Right now he's my right arm and worth his weight in gold. As time goes on I'll tell you about the rest of the crew as I get to know them better.

P.S. I almost forgot to tell you that I'm now a flight commander—pretty fancy name for just a go-between.

3

Leonard Patton, nickname "Cap," brother-in-law, married to my sister, Leora. He enlisted in the Army Air Corps for glider training. When this unit was disbanded he was transferred to the Aviation Cadet Corps. Upon graduation he was assigned for training at Central Instructor School, Randolph Field, Texas, while I received B-17 Transition Training at Roswell, New Mexico. Cap and I received our wings and were commissioned second lieutenants on the same day, but in different flying training commands.

When I was at Ardmore, Cap was teaching cadets to fly in basic trainers at Coffeyville, Kansas. Before I left he was transferred back to Randolph as an instructor at the Central Instructor School. Before the war's end he was flying B-24s.

March 12, 1944

Here it is Sunday evening about 9:30. Being Sunday I took the evening off and enjoyed a show here at the Post Theater. It was The Uninvited Guest—*not too bad.*

By the way, if you can't read this it is because I'm trying to write on a stationery box which I am holding on my knee and it doesn't seem to be working out so good.

Sis and Cap came down Friday morning and stayed until this morning. We had a nice little visit. I went to classes all day but could see them at night. Cap went to a couple of classes with me Saturday. They were pretty dry and I had a hard time keeping him awake. Then we went out to look over the B-17. After we finished he decided the BT was big enough for him. . . .

It sure is lonesome here. Poor old Larry [Gassman] and me! When we get down in spirit we go look the other one up and moan together for awhile, then we get back in good spirits again. Larry called Izzie the other night so I had to get my two cents worth in. We are just about bosom pals here. Misery loves company they say. Since we're in the same boat we just hang together.

Oh yes, I almost forgot to tell you that Flores got a telegram yesterday. You remember that he's the guy from Alamagordo. Well, he's now the proud father of an eight-pound baby boy. Boy, is he swelled up and happy! We just about have to hog-tie him to keep him from going over the hill. Tonight he called the hospital where his wife is and they let him talk to her. Then they brought the baby out so he could hear it cry over the telephone. He just about went wild over that!

We have really been busy since arriving here—doing just routine things but they have sure kept us on the run. Oh yes, we have started P.T. [phys-

Sherry Fletcher's photo that Fletch carried with him

ical training] again. Everybody has more aches and pains than we ever thought possible. But I guess after a couple of weeks we'll get used to that again. . . .

March 14, 1944

Here it is Tuesday, my day off, so Larry and I are making full use of it by writing letters. Here's the setup: Larry has a table in his room and I have two chairs in mine so we got together on a little compromise. I bring my chairs over to his room; then we divide the desk in half and start writing letters. So far we've been doing good. I'm on my fifth letter of the day and Larry is on his fourth. We've been writing like mad all afternoon. You know me and my letter writing—one package of cigarettes and an hour and a half to each letter.

I made out an allowance of $225 which will be sent to you each month starting with April's pay. That should leave me my flight pay to have over and above the other allotments like board and insurance. I think I can get by here on $75 a month. If not I'll have you send me some occasionally. The reason I made it for that much is this: Allotments are paid every month regardless of whether I sign a payroll or not. This means that if something should happen that I can't sign the payroll you would still get the money. The pay would still continue indefinitely if I were missing in action or pris-

oner of war, or anything of that nature. Although I don't think I'll miss the pay formation it's just an added precaution. . . .

The Major explained the little article in Bombs Away *that I sent to you about a furlough when we finish here. Well, he says it doesn't apply to us so not to get our hopes up. He said it applies to those who are now graduating from cadet schools and pertains to their leave after graduation, like our ten-day delay-enroute. He also said our commitment date to the staging area is June 4. So about the only way we can get a leave is to finish here ahead of schedule and maybe get a delay-enroute. I don't know how it is going to work out—nobody does. But I'll sure be disappointed if I don't get one. . . .*

Here is a little verse I gave my copilot to make him feel better when the going gets rough.

You Lucky One You

For nine long months
　I've toiled in the sun
Just dreaming of flying
　A P-51.

Then came that great day
　Our sweat wasn't in vain
To think that now
　We would fly a hot plane.

But out of each group
　Some will get screwed
And just sure as hell
　I was one of those few.

My fighter pilot dreams
　Have gone up in steam
I'm now a co-pilot
　On a B-17.

The job is exciting
　Oh, the thrill that one feels
When the pilot says, Now,
　You may pull up the wheels.

I let down the flaps
　And keep the cylinder heads cool

I call off his airspeed
But hell I'm no fool.

I'm now in my glory
In my highest esteem
I'm second in command
On a B-17.

Author Unknown

March 17, 1944

I haven't written for a couple of days so I hope you'll understand. Of late we've been having quite a few examinations. Consequently we have been studying a little of evenings, reading technical orders and what not. Last night I was going to write but I had a crew meeting instead which lasted until about nine. Lately that has been my bedtime so I turned in instead of writing. These classes sure wear me out. After eight hours of it I'm dead tired. I guess I just got so lazy in Salt Lake that it will take me a little while to get over it.

I sure get a kick out of my crew. I really lay the law down to them. They are a good bunch of boys and probably wouldn't get out of line anyway. But I just don't take any chances. You see, if one of them gets into any trouble the first pilot takes the blame and the disciplinary action from Headquarters. Then he, in turn, comes back and chews out the whole crew for the actions of one man. They are our whole responsibility. We give them their passes, their promotions, have the privilege of breaking them, and, in general, control all of their disciplinary action. But we, in turn, have to answer to Headquarters for the whole crew. So if one guy messes up it's a black mark on us. We suffer from Headquarters, so the rest of the crew suffers from us. That's just one reason for keeping them on the ball. There are lots of others which I'll tell you about some day.

Larry and Bud both said to tell you "hello." They always ask about you every time I get a letter. I always tell Bud it's none of his business how you are and any interest he might have in my wife he can confine elsewhere. But he knows I'm kidding and always has some wisecrack for an answer.

March 21, 1944

Yesterday was our last day of classes. We start flying tomorrow. It looks as if we'll get our eight hours in okay. But if it should weather in and we don't it will be all right because we will get paid for back flying time whenever we get the hours in, regardless of the three-month period. At least that's one thing in favor of Ardmore. I forgot to tell you we didn't draw any travel pay coming down here. We had to pay for our own meals on the way, but that didn't make any difference—we just got rooked.

Today was supposedly our day off but I ran around more, trying to straighten out a few things, than I would have on an ordinary day. I had to exchange some flying equipment, draw a new oxygen mask, exchange a Mae West, get helmets fixed for the new mask, and draw a bunch of books and notebooks, papers, pencils, maps, computers, and other incidentals. That was this morning.

Then this afternoon my copilot, engineer, and assistant engineer went down to the line with me and looked the ships over, going through procedures and locating things on board the ship. This was voluntary, just an idea of mine to get the boys acquainted with the airplane before we fly together. We have been doing that occasionally when we have had spare time. I think it's a good idea myself and they are willing to do it.

Then later on this afternoon our bombardier and navigator reported in. We now have a full crew and I've met all the fellows. The bombardier's name is Dimit and the navigator is Work, both are from Ohio. I'll let you know what I think of them later, as soon as we get better acquainted. Right now I think they're both pretty good fellows.

I don't like my navigator so much, though. I'll tell you why—he just left on a ten-day furlough along with all the other navigators. I guess I shouldn't be too bitter because he has just graduated from Cadets and this is his graduation leave. Besides, we can't use him here for a couple of weeks anyway. But I'd sure like to have a furlough too!! Incidentally, neither of these two is married.

March 24, 1944

I was checked out for day flying a couple of days ago. At first we used only a skeleton crew, but now all the enlisted men have been checked out. I checked out my copilot, too, so we are all flying together. We get along swell. It looks like everything will be okay.

I have been getting up at 6:30 and reporting at 7:30 for Link trainer [a training system for instrument flying]. Two hours of that, then bomb trainer at 9:30 for another two hours. That makes it 11:30—we have forty minutes to eat, change clothes, and get to the line at 12:10 for briefing. After briefing we take off at about 1:30, landing at 7:30. Then we fill out all our required forms and have another briefing. About 9 or 9:30 we get back to the barracks, eat, and go to bed. So you can see they have really been rushing us. . . .

Crew photo taken at Ardmore, Oklahoma. Back row, left to right: Kenneth McQuitty, Robert Lynch, Martin Smith, Joseph Firszt, Edward Brown, George Hinman; front row: Eugene Fletcher, Myron Doxon, Robert Work, Frank Dimit

March 26, 1944

The last couple of days we have been flying nights. I received my final night check last night in time to get back and take the rest of the crew up for their first night ride. They enjoyed it no end.

Oh, yes, I was going to tell you about the boys. Starting first with the copilot: Myron Doxon is his name and he's from Tacoma [Washington]. He's twenty-eight years old, married, and has a daughter fifteen months old. His wife and daughter are coming down sometime next week, I believe. He is a little taller and a little heavier than I am—blond, blue eyes, and smiling all the time. He's quite a character, has a good sense of humor which keeps everybody laughing. But, at that, he has a wonderful sense of responsibility and can be trusted to do things, and do them right. He really likes the B-17 and is eager to learn how to fly it, so I don't have to worry about him. I know he can do his job and also do lots of things for me.

Now the bombardier and navigator: Well, the navigator is still on leave so I guess we'll have to skip him as I haven't had time to get acquainted with him. He's single, though, and a college graduate so I would imagine he's probably twenty-four or twenty-five years old. He is dark and would probably weigh about ninety-eight pounds soaking wet. At least he's smaller than I am so I know he won't cause me any trouble. If he can just navigate we will get along okay.

The bombardier is from Ohio, single, and quite a bit larger than I am. I imagine he weighs about 170 pounds, nineteen years old, fresh from Cadets and still glamorized by the gold bar on his shoulder—I know the feeling. He has a good personality and is easy to get along with—more than that he knows who the boss is so that's well taken care of.

Next comes the flight engineer, Brown. His home is in Kansas and I believe I have told you all about him, so will just say I still think as much of him as I did before, and pass on to the radio operator, Hinman.

I can't remember right now where his home is, but it's some place here in the West. He's married and has his wife here. I've met her and she seems very nice. Hinman jabbers at just about the same rate at which he takes code, which is twenty words a minute. I have quite a time keeping him quiet sometimes, but, nevertheless, he is a good radio operator and that's what counts.

Next is the assistant engineer or assistant radio operator. He is trained for both jobs and can take over either. His name is Firszt—brown hair, brown eyes, and fairly tall. His home is here in Muldrow, Oklahoma. Another good boy.

Then comes the armorer gunner, Lynch. Wait a minute—my mistake—Lynch is from Muldrow and Firszt is from Chicago. I don't want to get my farmer boy and city boy mixed up. Lynch is a slow easy-going Oklahoma farmer, a little slow to catch on, but once he catches on he doesn't forget. He is about 5 feet 6 and has blond hair and blue eyes, quite young, but very quiet, well-mannered, and knows his job.

Now comes the real character, the ball turret gunner and turret specialist, McQuitty. He's about my size and just as light as I am dark, always laughing or smiling at something. He's the one that somebody is always pulling jokes on. His home is Kansas City, Missouri. Every time I think of him I just have to laugh. He can screw up more things in the shortest length of time than any guy I've ever seen. He can listen to a lecture and come out with everything just backwards of what it should be. His mistakes aren't anything serious—just comical, that's all.

The tail gunner, Larson—I am not very well acquainted with him yet. He is still in the hospital with scarlet fever. But he's older than the rest of the boys. He's real quiet, never has anything to say, and is from Baker, Montana. He's quite conscientious about his work, though, so I know he'll be all right.

All in all I think I have the best all-around crew on the field. Of course that's just my opinion, but they think I'm a pretty good guy—they don't know me yet—so I'll stand behind them all the way.

Last, but not least, is the pilot. His name is Fletcher and his home is *almost anyplace in the State of Washington. He is short, dark, and deeply in love with his wife. His wife is a blonde whose home is in Tekoa. He surely does miss her—probably a lot more than she knows. Also, he's going to be a proud papa and he's all puffed up about that. So he really has a lot to work for, and believe me, he's doing his best.*

Well, so much for the crew. I can't describe them very well, but that will give you an idea. You really have to see them, work with them, and know them before you can appreciate them.

We now have all our flying time in for flight pay and my pay vouchers have already been turned in. By the time you receive this I should have been paid.

I'll have to buy some new clothes this month. After the first of April suntans will be optional and after the fifteenth they will be compulsory uniforms. And me without a suntan to my name! So I guess I'll have to break down and buy some. It's okay, though, because right now I have only one pair of pants that I can wear. I broke the zipper on my greens the other day so all I have left is a pair of pinks. . . .

Now then, about my job as flight commander. You know how it was in Cadets—at all the formations the flight commander stood out front and issued commands, took the roll, informed the Group of anything new, and in general was a go-between between the Squadron and the Tactical Office. It's the same way here.

We have fifty-six crews in Section "A" and Section "A" is divided into five Flights with eleven crews to the Flight. I'm the first guy in Flight 4 so I think that's how I was picked. Anyway, within the Flight are three Elements: two four-crew Elements and one three-crew Element. Each Element has a leader and I had to pick the Element Leaders. Gassman is head of Element 2, Flores head of Element 1, and Gosewisch head of Element 3. All the fellows in my Flight are Roswell men and the same goes for Flights 3 and 5. That's all the dope on that. We don't do much except take the chewing out for the whole outfit.

March 28, 1944

There isn't really much to tell you. It's the same as usual—Link trainer, bomb trainer, and flying. Today we were caught out in an overcast and I thought for a while we would probably fly up to Tulsa to land, as that was the only clear spot. But they got us back to the field just in time to land before the ceiling dropped to the ground and the field was closed. We were anticipating the bad weather, however, so everyone was in fairly close— there was no trouble at all.

I'm becoming more attached to my crew every day. It's really a pleasure to fly with them—if flying can be a pleasure.

April 1, 1944

Yesterday I received a nice long letter from you and also a wonderful box of cookies. They sure are good! Gassman and Flores and I have been sitting around eating them and chewing the fat. They wanted me to be sure to tell you how good they were.

Today we got a break. "C" Section, that is, what is left of it, had some formation flying to do so they took all the airplanes. Consequently, we didn't have to fly. They told us last night we wouldn't have to, so I figured I would just sit down last night and catch up on all the letters I had to write.

I didn't even get started before Gassman came over to see if I would go to town with him since it had been over a week and a half since either of us had been off the post. I decided it might not be too bad an idea because I was getting pretty well fed up with the base myself. So we chased off to town. We met most of our crew in town—just walked around and shot the bull. It was about nine o'clock when we got there so it wasn't long until the last bus left for the base at twelve. We put our men on the last bus, went over to the hotel, got a room, and slept in a good bed all night. We got up this morning in time to catch the ten o'clock bus to the base. I guess I really should have stayed home and written my letters as I'd planned, but, dog-gone, it sure seemed good to get off the post and just forget things for the night.

My copilot's wife and baby arrived yesterday. I haven't met her as yet but talked with her on the telephone today. She seems nice, but why not, she's also a Washingtonian. I guess I didn't tell you there are seven fellows in my barracks who are from Washington and I don't know how many scattered around the Field. Our section commander on the flying line is also from Washington. We sure have a good representation here.

Yesterday was pay day but our vouchers won't come through until Monday. They had better hurry up and get here as I have to buy some clothes. The guys on the crew have been kidding me about having only one pair of pants to wear.

The payoff came yesterday afternoon when the radio operator, Hinman, came up to the B.O.Q. [Bachelor Officers' Quarters]. He said he wanted my green pants as his wife had already bought a zipper for them. She was just waiting for him to bring the pants in so she could fix them. I played it cagey—I argued with him a little, but he wound up with the pants, so it won't be too long before I'll have two pair again. The guys are sure on the ball and looking out for me all the time. I have a lot of little funny things to tell you when we are together again about my crew and the things they do.

The last few days I haven't felt any too good. One of my wisdom teeth has been hurting so yesterday I had the dentist look at it. He doctored it up and it is feeling a lot better now. As soon as I get time, after all the soreness is gone, I'm going back and he's going to yank it out.

My navigator is supposed to get back either today or tomorrow. Most of the others are back now, but mine hasn't arrived yet. He's probably stretching the time just as long as he can, for which I don't blame him.

Oh yes, you wanted to know if the last class here had leaves. I don't know whether they did or not, but I do know that they now have five missions over Germany to their credit. That was of a week or so ago—probably have a few more by now. We'll know more about the leave deal when "B" Section leaves here. We should get a fair idea of what will happen to us by seeing what happens to them. I can assure you I have my fingers crossed. Maybe it will work out so we can get a short leave anyway.

April 4, 1944

I mailed you a little Easter package today which I hope you'll receive by Sunday. Sure had a lot of fun looking around for it. The wrap job was done by my radio operator's wife. She works in the place where I bought it. She spent almost the whole morning showing Gassman and me the contents of the baby department. We prospective fathers have quite a time. . . .

Yesterday I had to stand retreat (formal retreat) with all the enlisted men in my Flight. Boy, did I look sharp dragging that bunch around behind the band. It would be nice if I could just remember which one is my left foot! Oh well, we got through it and didn't encounter any serious difficulties.

I went to town first thing this morning so I could have breakfast off the post and not get in a rut. Besides, I wanted to get some Easter cards, and Doxon, my copilot, wanted me to meet his wife and baby. So I paid my duty call there.

Then Brown, my engineer, has his girlfriend here and he wanted me to meet her this afternoon and place my stamp of approval. So I spent most of the afternoon with them. They want to get married and wanted to know whether I thought it best they should—and all about it. So Old Pop Fletch took care of that little detail. I gave them the real lowdown. After all, why should he be single and happy when the rest of us are married! Now she's going home to quit her job, tell her folks, and live happily ever after. In the meantime Doxon and I got stuck with the check for dinner for the whole crew!

I'm really finding out what troubles are. I used to think I had enough of *my own, but now any time one of the fellows has anything happen, wants some advice, or wants to do something he comes to me and we hash it out together. Just call me the Chaplain!*

As soon as my tail gunner gets out of the hospital we're all going to have a picture made of the whole crew so you can see what they look like.

April 12, 1944

It has been quite some time since you've heard from me and I hope you haven't been worrying. Everything is okay. I have just finished about the busiest nine days I've ever put in since being in the Army.

About a week ago we had some bad weather and that, coupled with a lack of airplanes and being assigned some that weren't flyable, resulted in our getting behind on our flying hours and number of missions completed. Consequently, we have been going night and day to catch up. We aren't entirely caught up yet, but have made a good gain. The ceiling has been low most of the week and, as a result, we're behind on bombing missions. But with a couple of days of good weather we might very easily catch up.

We have done all types of flying the past week, including formation, instrument, low altitude bombing, instrument calibration, and air-to-ground gunnery. My gunners get a kick out of that! They're pretty good at it too. I would surely hate to be anywhere in range and have them pumping away at me!

The box of cookies you sent came the day before Easter. Needless to say, they're all gone. . . . Any time you want to send some more just go right ahead. . . . You don't have to wait for holidays—just send them anytime. Sis also sent me a box of cookies for Easter but they're all gone too.

Your Mother said they had a padlock for me and wondered about the size. Tell them it's okay. I can use it.

April 13, 1944

Went to a show here on the post this evening. First one I've been to for a week and a half, I guess. The name was Up In Arms—*slapstick comedy all the way through so I enjoyed it immensely.*

This is our day off so I'm holding down the barracks alone. Most of the fellows have gone to Fort Worth, Dallas, or someplace. But not this kid. I decided now was a good time to catch up on a lot of things which I have been letting go. I have been filling out a bunch of forms which I want you to have. I haven't fnished them yet, but when I do I'll send them along with a few other papers which I should have given you when we were in Salt Lake. By now you should have received a power of attorney form and a will which I filled out. If not, let me know and I'll see what is holding them up.

I haven't been back to see the dentist yet about my wisdom teeth—have been just too busy to make it. I hope I have time before we leave here but it looks dubious. I don't expect to be here as long as I told you at first. Could be wrong, but have good reason to believe that within the next five weeks Ardmore will be a thing of the past as far as I'm concerned. . . .

Cap didn't come down last weekend as the weather was bad at both ends of the line—and it was Easter Sunday. I'm sure he had a better time in Coffeyville. He intends to fly down, though, one of these weekends before I leave. We'll probably have quite a time when he comes. I hope to take him on a regular mission in the B-17. I know he would enjoy it because it is quite interesting to those who don't see it every day.

In my last letter I asked about the padlock. Well, it came this morning so now I'll have you thank your folks for me. It will work okay—just the thing I've been looking for. Another thing I could use if you can find one—I can't—is a flashlight. . . . Have been looking for a good steel hunting knife too, but, as yet, have not found one that is worth anything. I did find a good Boy Scout knife. It wasn't worth the price but it will do okay.

It's hard to be apart but if we're just brave enough to see it through I know we'll be repaid for it in the near future. It won't be long until we'll be back together and all this will be just a dream of the past pushed into the dusk by happiness and joy that will light up our lives forever. As I look outside I can see only a short distance along the ground because of the darkness of night. But as I look upward I can see the stars and the moon, a distance immeasurable. So it is with our lives. If we look only a few days ahead we see nothing but emptiness and loneliness. But if we look upward to the stars and the moon we can see clear to eternity showing us our life ahead and the pathway of happiness we'll walk together.

April 15, 1944

Here we go for the daily report: We flew from 6:10 p.m. last night until 2:30 a.m. this morning after our day off. I finally got to bed about 4:30, but that was cut short by the fact that the dentist wanted to pull my wisdom tooth at 7:45 this morning. He was quite definite about it so I didn't argue. Besides, I was so sleepy I didn't know what was going on until the novocain started wearing off. I spent most of the morning with the dentist, with him taking x-rays and picking out splinters. From 12 until 2 this afternoon I had Link trainer and bomb trainer from 2 till 4. We were supposed to fly again at 6:10 this evening but the flight surgeon grounded me for lack of sleep and the fact that I had a sore jaw, and was still full of dope. Good thing he did because I sure didn't feel like flying.

   I had some real fun last night. My navigator went with another crew on a cross-country and I, supposedly, on a bombing mission. Well, we missed the target and got miserably lost. When I finally located myself we were over Shreveport, Louisiana. So in the long run I guess I took a longer cross-country than the navigator! Everything worked out okay, though, as we had enough gas to get home. This is nothing unusual for we have no radio beam here or anything to locate the field. Usually one or two get lost every night. Some have to lay over and refuel and get into all kinds of trouble. I guess it was just my turn and I was lucky at that.

   I received two letters from you today and also the box of fudge. It would come on the day I had my tooth pulled! I have it hidden, though, where the vultures can't find it and I intend to enjoy it when my jaw is better. . . .

The truth is that we took off at 6:10 p.m. for a practice night-bombing mission. Our briefing hadn't indicated any particularly bad weather, but the wind was blowing pretty hard at the time. We were airborne after dark and started out to find the bombing range, which was supposed to be marked by flare pots. They were to be placed in a cross, the center of the cross being the actual target.

After approximately an hour of flying time we still hadn't found the bombing area. About that time we received a message from the base telling us to return as the mission had been called off. The weather had turned bad—a front was moving through—and the flare pots at the target had all been blown out, or were never ignited, which was probably the reason we didn't find them. It was also possible we didn't have enough wind correction in and would have missed the target anyway, since the winds were far in excess of what we had been told.

I was on the tower frequency and received the message to return. I tapped my copilot on the shoulder and told him on the interphone that we were heading back to the base: "If it appears on your side of the ship let me know." He nodded his head a couple of times, although he didn't say anything. I assumed he had received the message because the copilot was supposed to remain in interphone contact with the crew.

We made a 180 degree turn plus a correction for what I thought the cross-wind might be, which, in retrospect, was not nearly enough. We flew for about an hour and fifteen minutes. Then Doc motioned to me to switch to interphone and said, "What's going on? Where are we going?"

I said, "We're returning to the base. I called you on the inter-phone and asked you to tell me if you saw the base. Up to now I haven't spotted it."

"Oh," he said, "we passed the base quite a little while ago. It was on my side of the ship."

"Why didn't you let me know?"

"I didn't receive your message."

To which I replied, "Yes, you did. I tapped you on the shoulder and when I finished you nodded your head 'yes.' " He said, "When you saw me nodding my head I had Jan Garber on the radio—on commercial radio—and I was listening to his program. I was keeping time to the music."

At this point the copilot's job was to monitor the interphone system and my job was to monitor the tower frequency. But it was also my job to make sure the message had been received, which it hadn't.

We made another 180 degree turn and started back. Unbeknownst to us we were drifting farther east because of the severe winds and our lack of sufficient correction. There was no problem—we had been out before at night not knowing where we were. You just tune in a commercial radio station or a military beacon, identify them, turn on the radio direction finder (RDF), and get a bearing to the station. With two stations you can get a fix. Your approximate location is where the two lines of position cross when plotted on a map. There are all kinds of ways to locate yourself with these aids. Another procedure would be to start a "square search." In this you fly in a square and each time you come around you lengthen the leg a little bit and eventually you're going to get back to your home base—providing you have enough fuel. A square search takes a long time as you have to fly these elongated legs to eventually get back around.

We kept searching for something that would give us an indication of where we were. The static was so bad on the radios they were absolutely useless—we couldn't get a bearing on anything. I finally called the radio operator and told him to check in at the NET at our base. NET was a radio receiver and transmitter that was kept open so the radio operators could gain experience in their job. If anyone was out and having trouble he could call the NET. It was done through the radio operator's equipment in code and it had long-range capability. It gave him practice, but in this particular instance, I felt we really needed help, not practice, because the lights on the ground had long since disappeared. We apparently were over the top of an overcast and there were several thunderheads in the area which were causing a lot of electrical interference.

After probably a half hour the radio operator contacted me again and said, "I can't get into the NET. I think they must be shut down for the night. No one will answer me and we're certainly well within range."

We hadn't been able to reach anyone. We couldn't even pick up a commercial station. We had set up a square search, but this wasn't helping anything because of the undercast. Even if we had flown over our base we wouldn't have seen any lights. There were no radio beacons. Actually, there was a light line leading to the base that came from the Gulf Coast—through Fort Worth, Dallas, and on up to Ardmore. With the lights on and a clear sky it was no problem to fly up that line.

Realizing by now we were thoroughly lost, I called the radio operator again and told him to send out an SOS signal. "Why not let me send out PAM signals?" he asked, referring to an international distress signal of a lower grade which did not require a written report. "If I send out an SOS you will probably be filling out reports long after we leave here—if we ever get out of here." So I said, "Roger. It really doesn't make any difference." After all, a PAM signal was a good signal. It had the next priority under an SOS—anyone responding to an SOS would certainly respond to a PAM. So he sent out his signals—no response.

In the meantime we set up a long-range cruise condition—low manifold pressure and low rpm on the engines to conserve fuel. After a while we abandoned our square search. It wasn't doing us any good. I couldn't even make a guess as to where we were, but I knew we were someplace we shouldn't be!

After what seemed an eternity the radio operator called back and said, "I wasn't able to get a QDM [a code name for a bearing to the station] which you requested, but at least I did get an answer and a bearing away from the station at Shreveport, Louisiana." I grabbed the map and plotted the bearing on it, realizing then that we could be out over the Gulf of Mexico, depending on how far out we were on this line of position.

We turned around and started toward Shreveport, flying the reciprocal of the bearing they gave us, plus a correction factor for what we assumed the wind drift would be. Eventually we began to pick up a little bit on the radio. After what seemed like forever our radio direction finder indicated that we were passing over the station, so we started tuning in other radios heading west. It wasn't long until the sky broke clear—we could see the ground lights of Dallas and Fort Worth below us, and there was the light line heading north to Ardmore.

We'd located ourselves. We knew how to get to the base. We could fly the light line home, but another problem was starting to develop. Our fuel supply was almost depleted.

We knew we were getting close to the base but had not yet spotted the airport beacon when the red light came on for the #3 engine. This indicated we had roughly ten minutes of fuel left on that engine. So I called the engineer and said, "Brownie, can you transfer some fuel—it looks as if we're going to lose #3. Can you take some out of #1 or #2 tanks, come across the center line and into #3?" He answered, "Better yet, maybe I could pull a little out of #4 as it indicates more on the gauges." This meant he'd have to dump from #4 across the center line of the ship into either #1 or #2 and then back again. I said okay.

As soon as he started to pull a little out of #4 and put it into #2 the red light came on on #4. So then he turned around and transferred what little extra he had put in #2 back to #3, which turned the light out on #3. But about the same time the #4 engine, starved for fuel, sputtered and quit. We feathered #4, and at this point I didn't have any desire to try to transfer any more fuel.

Just as we feathered the engine I told him that if we didn't see the field in a few minutes he should alert the boys for bailout. At this instant I saw the field lights, and as he looked out the window he said, "Isn't that the base up ahead?"

"Yes, it is, but we're short of fuel, as you well know, and I don't know if we can make it. It may be that we will still have to bail out, so let's be ready. But we're going to try to make it in."

I called the tower and was informed we were cleared to land, but to hurry up because we were the last ones out. Obviously they were irritated and tired of waiting for us. We left for a two- or three-hour flight and now we had utilized the full tanks on the B-17. By this time we had flown eight hours.

They told us to make a straight-in approach, which is what we were going to do anyway. I told Doc not to lower the landing gear until we were sure we could make the field. A belly landing would be preferable if we fell short. Just as we touched down on the runway we lost another engine. By this time we had red lights on all four—two engines out—but we were on the ground and still had two engines to taxi back to the line. People weren't—well, in a way, I guess they were overjoyed to see us—but they were rather put out that we had kept everybody up for so long. We went on home, as by now it was early in the morning.

At 7 a.m. I was ordered to come down to the Operations Office to make a report on why I was so late the night before. Of course we knew what we had done was wrong. The mistake on my part was that I should have received confirmation from the copilot that he understood my message that we were returning to the base. There was also the factor that he was on the wrong channel listening to commercial music when he should have been monitoring the crew efforts. But these boo-boos were not mentioned in my report. Be that as it may, the squadron commander and the operations officer wanted me to understand that they were unhappy with what had happened.

I wasn't happy either. My only defense was that here we were with an aircraft worth a considerable amount of money, we had a crew on board without a navigator, and we had bad weather, bad enough for them to cancel the mission. Yet when they canceled the mission they also closed the communication NET. I assume this is the only thing that saved me. I made a point of the fact that had they left the NET open after they contacted us to return, we could have been in.

Apparently they didn't really want to break up a bomber crew just to discipline me. It was just a stand-off.

"Have you learned a lesson?" they asked.

"Yes," I replied, "I've learned several lessons." I enumerated what they were and this seemed to satisfy everybody as nothing more was ever said.

Clearly, at this stage of our training, we were a greater danger to ourselves than we were to the enemy.

April 19, 1944

Things are running about the same as usual—they couldn't get any worse. We're still flying just as hard and long as we can and putting in all the ground school and trainer time possible. We haven't averaged six hours sleep a night for the past week. But we still have to keep at it or we won't be able to finish here by the 18th of May. All our days off have been canceled and we're on a straight schedule.

I can say one thing, though, we have really learned a lot since we've been here, both from books and experience. It seems as if every time we go up something goes haywire. We always have a malfunction somewhere. If possible we try to fix it. If we can't we improvise some way so we can do without it and keep on going. We get experience all right—if we could just separate the good from the bad everything would be okay.

I've sure been having a time. My tooth hasn't healed up yet. My cheek is still puffed out and my jaw sore. Every day we go to high altitude and you should see me when I try to poke my face into the oxygen mask!

That's enough gripes for now. I must get to bed and get all the sleep I can, for tomorrow I have to fly high altitude formation to Galveston, refuel, fly a gunnery mission over the Gulf, refuel again, and fly high altitude formation back. We'll probably be in the air at least twelve or thirteen hours. Allowing a couple of hours for refueling we'll have quite a day ahead.

We went out on a daylight mission. We were given ten bombs to drop, giving Dimit a little practice. This was no problem. It was broad daylight. We found the bombing range, we had the practice bombs in the bomb bay, on our first pass over Dimit made his drop, and he made a good drop. We were using the Automatic Flight Control Equipment (AFCE), auto-pilot. On the bomb run, when you are on AFCE, the bombardier actually assumes directional control of the aircraft through the Norden bomb sight. The pilot maintains the altitude and the airspeed as requested by the bombardier, and it has to be accurate, as he has preset this information into his sight. However, if you have a malfunction in the automatic pilot you can always disengage it and fly manually using the Pilot Direction Indicator (PDI) needle. Things were working fine and we were letting him control the aircraft from the IP (Initial Point at which the bomb run commences) to the target each time.

On our second pass around we set up another good run, and there was no doubt that Dimit was a good bombardier. He dropped this one and we came close to getting a bull's eye. But on our third bomb run the radio operator said the bomb did not release. Brownie checked the electric bomb release mechanism and found a fuse had blown. We had some extra fuses on board so I told him to put another one in and we would try again.

We then made another run and the bomb went away. Frank again made a good drop. At the same time the fuse blew again, so Brownie said he'd make the switch. In the meantime I called the tower at Ardmore and told them what our problems were. With our being lost in my mind from the time before, I decided this time we had better communicate with our people and get their okay on what we were doing. They asked if we were experiencing any difficulties other than blowing fuses. I said no, as near as I could tell there was no danger to anyone or to the aircraft. There was never any smoke. It was just that each time a bomb dropped we blew a fuse. If we replaced the fuse we could drop another bomb.

"How many fuses do you have left?" I answered, "Three." "Roger, drop three more bombs and come home."

That sounded good. On our next drop the bomb released. Again the fuse blew. This time Brownie called me and said that when the fuse blew it welded the end of the fuse into the fuse block. "I'll have to try to pry it out of there, but when I touch it with my screwdriver we get sparks everywhere. If you can pull the power off of the buss I'll go ahead and pry it out and put in a new one."

"Okay, there's a procedure for this and it'll take me a couple of minutes, but I'll get that system isolated for you."

Well, Doc was still pretty new to the airplane and its systems, but he was learning fast. Our copilots came direct from twin-engine flying schools. This was their first experience with the B-17, and at this point they had had very limited ground school. He said, "Oh, just a minute. I'll solve the problem for you." I started to say, "Wait, Doc"—but by that time his hand was already forward and he pulled the master switch.

Believe me, you can't imagine how quiet it is in the aircraft when all four engines quit! The props are still windmilling, but it is extremely quiet, and it does shake you up.

In this situation I needed to get the manifold pressure control turned down or else the engines and props would run away. Luckily, the aircraft had an electric system with a single knob for the manifold pressure on all four engines. Many of the aircraft had four manual levers. Each engine had to be adjusted individually, and this took time. But just as I reached to grab the manifold pressure knob and spin it back, Doc pushed the master switch back on. All four engines roared back to life as I was still hollering because I didn't want him to turn them on until I had the pressure turned down.

As luck would have it I got just enough twist on the knob and the batteries on the airplane activated the control. The props did not overspeed, and the waste gates which direct the exhaust gasses down through the superchargers held. It is possible to blow them out, and this was what I expected would happen. But we were lucky that day.

When an engine goes into overspeed it means a mandatory engine change, and even in those days that Wright Cyclone engine—not to mention the labor to install it—was not cheap. The thought of buying four of them just didn't appeal to me. Most people didn't realize that in those days damage to aircraft that was caused by pilot error or ignorance could be charged to the pilot, and it took a long time on the installment plan to get even. I had friends who were already paying for wing tips damaged in taxi accidents, but the tips were trivial compared to this. This type of thing was frowned upon during the training stage. A pilot could and would be "washed out" for using poor judgment.

But we were very fortunate. Brownie turned white and I know I turned two shades of white because we both expected all the problems that go with an overspeed condition. Needless to say, we had had enough. We didn't want to try to drop any more bombs. We felt we had got out of that one—our engines had been restarted, we did not exceed the manifold pressure, and the props didn't run away. Not desiring to push our luck any further, we headed back for the base.

Doc was quite embarrassed and felt bad. He said he really thought that the master switch turned off everything on the aircraft except the magnetos, which would keep the engines running. I said I was sorry I hadn't pointed that out to him before. The master switch kills everything on the plane, including the magnetos. In the event of a crash landing or a wheels-up landing, you pull the master switch just before touch-down and it kills everything electrical on the plane, reducing the fire hazard.

Again it appeared that we were our own worst enemies.

April 21, 1944

Here it is Saturday and I still haven't made the trip to Galveston. The weather has been so bad on the Gulf that even the ducks are grounded, but we have managed to keep on flying. We have been flying lots of big ship formation at high altitude. They're trying to get us in shape for the big contest we have coming up next Saturday. We have challenged the fellows taking OTU at Dyersburg, Tennessee, and those at Alexandria, Louisiana, to fly formation with us. We'll probably have twenty-four ships from each field. Our group has been chosen to lead. The idea is we'll have a formation the size that they use in combat, then we all fly to our objective, which will be some large town down there, and we'll camera bomb it. The Big Shots will be stationed along the way to judge the formation and the bombing films will be exchanged. So the competition is not only formation but the accuracy of the bombing. It might turn out to be fun but right now it looks like a lot of work. Oh yeah, they've also arranged with a Fighter Transition School to give us fighter escort, and other ships to be enemy fighters. We'll use blank ammunition in our guns and also cameras. It will, no doubt, be a harum-scarum affair with all kinds of shooting and noise and airplanes scattered all over the Southwest.

Thursday evening I had quite a pleasant surprise—Cap and Sis dropped in. They were on their way to Randolph Field, Texas, where Cap has now been stationed as an instructor. It was just by luck that they came by after

I had just finished flying. They stayed overnight in Ardmore so I was able to visit with them four or five hours. I enjoyed their visit but was so tired I could hardly stay awake to talk. . . .

Boy, am I having troubles. First, I was fined five dollars yesterday because the ball turret slipped when we were coming in for a landing. It let the guns point straight down at the ground. If the tower hadn't notified us and we'd landed that way we would really have torn things up. Then bright and early this morning they tell us that there are only three first pilots out of fifty-six crews who will make 1st lieutenant while we're here. At first they said at least twenty-five percent would make it. So everybody has been working like the dickens to get in that class. Now we see that we have been disillusioned. Even that wouldn't be so bad, but no, I've taught my copilot too much, so now I think they're going to take him away from me and send him to Transition. If they send any copilots back at all he'll be among them because he heads the list. As you can see I'm slightly disgusted. Oh well, I have to tell my troubles to someone and you're the only one who will sympathize with me.

We have been working like hell to get someplace and it seems that the harder we work the more things go against us. If it weren't for all the old buddies here going through the same thing and the thoughts of what we are working for this place would be unbearable. We thought we were having a rough time coming through Cadets, but I'm convinced that was child's play compared to this. Several fellows have been dismissed from the service here already for some of the darnedest reasons, dishonorably, of course. None of them were from our outfit, however.

Ran into Gassman while at the chow house and he gave me some of the latest dope. It seems, according to him, that the Donkins and Gosewischs are expecting. It must be something in the Oklahoma air that did it because I don't think the fellows have had enough time off to do the job. That's just my opinion, though. . . .

Must close—we fly at 4:30 in the morning. Incidentally, we leave here May 18th.

The incident with the ball turret deserves further comment. We had been out on a combination air-to-ground practice gunnery and bombing mission. The gunnery phase was completed first and we were well into the bombing phase when I decided to let the ball turret gunner leave the ball turret. The ball turret is probably the most uncomfortable place in the airplane. Since the mission was about over it would be a good time to let him get out, stretch his legs, and get the blood circulating again.

For the ball turret gunner to leave the turret while in the air, he has to point the guns straight down toward the ground. In this position he has a small trap door above his head that opens up into the waist gunner's compartment. After he climbs up from the turret the normal procedure would be to close the door, rotate the ball until the guns point aft and parallel to the fuselage, and then lock the turret in this position. This decreases drag and is the normal landing position. A landing made with the guns pointing down could inflict serious damage to the aircraft and personnel.

In this instance—thinking he would later re-enter the ball—Mac left it in the guns-down position and went to the radio room where he could visit with the other gunners who had gathered there. Now this was also where the gunners were positioned during landing. They sat on the floor, facing toward the tail, with their backs to the forward bulkhead. This was the safest position for them in the event of trouble on landing.

In a matter of thirty minutes or so the mission was completed and we started home. I called the tower and received permission to land— "use runway 26, wind 10 mph with gusts, altimeter setting 28.92" and so on. We would be number one to land as there was no other air traffic in sight.

The copilot called for the crew landing check on the interphone. Every man on the ship had to acknowledge that his position was ready for landing. The bombardier reported that his guns were stowed, bomb-bay doors closed, and so on. The engineer reported the top turret stowed for landing, and he took his station between the pilot and the copilot to help monitor the gauges and do whatever was needed. The radio operator confirmed that his trailing wire antennae was retracted and the top window in the radio room was closed. The ball turret gunner was expected to report from the radio room that the ball turret was stowed, locked, and ready for landing. After everyone had checked his position the copilot notified me the aircraft was ready for landing and proceeded with the cockpit check.

I returned to tower frequency for any other instructions they might have, as well as reporting my position, turning final, gear down and locked, aircraft secured for landing. The tower acknowledged, "Roger, Able Fox 246, have you in sight, number one on final approach, clear to land." Good, we won't waste any time in the pattern today.

At 200 feet above the runway the tower called, "Able Fox 246, permission to land denied. Pull up and go around. Please acknowledge." Oh well, they probably had some trouble on the ground that I couldn't see. We wouldn't have to leave the pattern, just pour on the power—the props are already at high rpm—get the gear up, and come around again.

On the downwind leg of the pattern we completed the landing

check again and the copilot notified me that all positions were checked and the aircraft was ready for landing. I called the tower again, reporting on the downwind leg, "Landing check complete. Request permission to land." They answer, "Roger, Able Fox 246, number one in the pattern cleared to land. Give call on final approach." Again at 200 feet over the runway the tower called. "Able Fox 246 permission denied. Pull up and go around."

"Roger, Tower. Able Fox 246 executing go-around procedure." Obviously they had more trouble than I thought, but they would get their problem solved eventually.

In the meantime we went through the landing check again and proceeded as before. The same thing happened on our third approach. Oh well, they would get their act together and we would get down. Besides, it is a beautiful day for flying, the crew needs practice on their go-around procedure, so we're all learning and logging more air time.

So we try for the fourth time. Again we followed the same procedures, but—pull up and go around. Well, you only need so much of this kind of experience, and I can take a hint. I began to suspect there was something wrong with the airplane. I asked the copilot to start the landing check again and again he reported that everything was secure and ready to land. Before starting our cockpit check I switched back to tower frequency and called, "Ardmore Tower, this is Able Fox 246 requesting landing instructions. I suspect there is something wrong with my airplane since we're not allowed to land. But my crew reports the aircraft is ready for landing. So if it is the aircraft just give me a clue and I can assure you that I will solve the problem." The Tower reported back, "Able Fox 246, when you stow your ball turret you will be allowed to land."

This is rather embarrassing to a first pilot because every ship within receiving range of Ardmore Tower now knows that we have committed a real goof. You could almost hear the laughter in the tower as we sheepishly flew away.

I switched back to the interphone and in a very quiet but firm voice stated, "Fellows, I don't mind flying in circles, but we are going to do so until somebody stows the ball turret instead of just *reporting* that it has been stowed." Believe me, there was some frantic activity on board that aircraft as every gunner checked his position before the next landing check.

When we re-entered the pattern we were real pros on landing procedure and there was no holdup this time. I also knew that the engineer, who was the ranking NCO and the crew leader, would do some chewing before the day was out. The pilot was fined $5 before the day was over too, to remind him that this was a mistake that could have been prevented. But these were small matters involving a potential disaster to an airplane and crew, or so one thinks at age twenty-two. These things wouldn't happen again.

April 24, 1944

Another day gone by and time grows shorter proportionately. We now have sixteen more days of flying left. Needless to say, we are still behind in our missions. The weather has been the main contributing factor. While we haven't been in the storm center of all the weather activity down this way, we have been on the edge of it and have been hampered by strong winds, low ceilings, thunderstorms, rain, hail, and blowing dust. Today was really the best day we've had here—blue sky, no winds, and a real warm spring day.

As far as any news from here there really isn't any. Things are just the same as usual. My bombardier and navigator have been quite concerned with me lately because they say I live like a hermit. Since my copilot has moved into town no one is in my room with me so I'm quite content to be alone to read and sleep any time we might have off. They have tried numerous times to get me to go to the show with them here on the post. Up until last night I've always refused. First, because I feel that I can't waste the time and secondly, I felt that if I wasn't working I should be sleeping.

Last night I finally gave in and went with them as we had a couple of extra hours off. Today they felt as if they had really done a good job. Don't get me wrong, I haven't really developed any habits or manners of a hermit. I have just been busy devising schemes and methods to make the crew function better, and brooding over a few responsibilities which have been placed on me which they do not fully realize. You see, they are concerned only with the worries and responsibilities which affect their own position. In my case I'm concerned with the worries and have the responsibility of all ten positions. I can't quite explain how it works, but here the pilot is held responsible for everything that affects his crew. He answers to the Squadron Commander and the crew answers to him. It's just the old Army chain-of-command. The Big Boys bite me so I bite the little ones.

Incidentally we have had a slight change in set-up. Four more crews were added to my Flight so now we're a Squadron and the official title is Squadron Leader.

April 25, 1944

. . . Life here is as usual. We're still flying lots of high altitude formation and high altitude camera bombing in formation. It's kind of fun but there's a lot of work and strain to it. My copilot is getting to the point where he

can fly pretty good formation so that gives me a chance to rest occasionally and eases lots of the worry. I hope they don't take him away from me and send him to Transition because I've really worked with him to get him in shape. But if he gets the chance I won't stand in his way because he has lots of ability and is just an all-around good pilot. Besides, I like him well enough to want to do all I can for him. The rest of the fellows are doing all right in their positions and I still feel that I have the best crew on the field.

Incidentally, I have a new tail gunner as of day before yesterday. Larson is still in the hospital so he was taken off the crew. The new fellow seems like a very good fellow, maybe even better than Larson. His name is Martin J. Smith—a Buck Sergeant. I haven't had time yet to find out where he's from or anything else, but will find out all that tomorrow. . . .

I haven't any idea of what will happen when we leave here. I am sure of one thing, though, and that is that we won't get any leave while stationed here. I rather doubt if we get any after leaving either because I think we will go right to a staging area for overseas replacement. But that is only my opinion based on rumors, and you know Army rumors! I wish I could tell you one way or another about it, but I can't. All I can do is hope and pray that I will get to see you before then.

I would like to have you get me a small book of poems—one containing some of those that we like best. Also when you send it put in Elbert Hubbard's Scrapbook. *I would kind of like to read some of them in my spare moments.*

I am going to close for now. I have a few minutes left but Work and I have been working on letters to send to my crew's folks, so we want to write a couple of them tonight. I should have written them long ago, but you know me and my letter writing. Work makes a good Executive Officer!

April 28, 1944

Yesterday I was through in time to go down and pick up my package at the post office. The knife is swell—just what I wanted and the sheath will fit on my belt. It is recommended that we carry it in case of a bail-out or other situation. Thanks a lot. I really like it.

We had quite a busy day yesterday. We flew from 4 a.m. till noon, or rather, we were on the line that long. We flew only five hours and forty minutes. My engineer wanted to get married last night so I got him out of flying and retreat so he had the whole day off. The rest of the enlisted men and myself stood retreat at five. Then we all got dressed for the big wedding. I even splurged for a haircut and barber shave! I went in and saw the Squadron Commander and got the whole crew off today. I knew that if we got him married it would be late and we wouldn't feel like getting up at four and flying. He didn't much want to give us today off because today is the big

"Cap" and "Sis"—Leonard and
Leora Patton

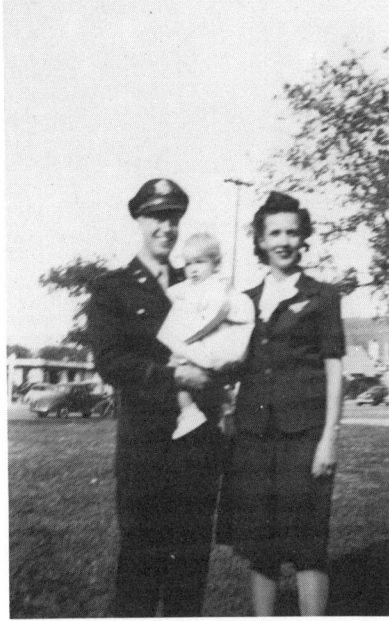

Myron, Margaret, and Kim Doxon

George and Mary Hinman

Ed and Mary Brown on their
wedding day

group formation with the other fields participating. I argued pretty strong, and he kind of likes our crew so he finally gave in.

Anyway, to proceed: The wedding was to be at eight so we went in town for dinner and were all ready, but then it was put off until nine-thirty. We finally got them married in the presence of the whole crew at the Baptist Church. Poor Brownie was so nervous I didn't think he was going to make it. Good thing the service was short. After the wedding we went over to a lady's house where my radio operator lives and had a gab fest. We broke up the party at eleven-thirty—left the newlyweds to themselves and we came home.

Brown is having his wedding pictures taken at one today so we're all going in and have a crew picture made. Just as soon as they are finished I'll send you one so you can see the fellows I'm working with.

April 29, 1944

Today I received two letters from you and also a box of cookies. I hope you realize how attached I'm becoming to your cooking. What a lucky guy I am! Dimit and Work agree with me and they watch my mail like a hawk so they won't miss out on any of the goodies. . . .

Incidentally, we have had a slight change of schedule—we are supposed to be all through flying by the 2nd of May. That means we have only three days of flying left. I am pretty sure we are going back to ground school. We can't possibly finish all of the flying we were supposed to have here, but, at least, we have done most of the important missions. So I guess we won't miss out on too much. Doggone, they sure keep us guessing. We don't know from one day to the next what is going on. There is only one thing fairly certain and that is that we will be leaving here by the 18th of May.

May 1, 1944

Here it is the first of May and another month gone by—just one more day of flying left. The last two days the weather has been so bad we haven't been able to get in the air. Consequently we can't possibly finish even our required missions in one more day. In my case I would have to have at least three good days. We still haven't been to Galveston. It's definite that we will quit flying, though, for a while. We are going back to ground school for a week, then those who still need more flying will go back to the line for a week or until they do complete their flying. That takes care of our last two weeks here at Ardmore.

Our proofs came back yesterday and the pictures were exceptionally good for a group. Of course I had a silly grin on my face in all of them, but the pictures of the rest of the fellows were really good. . . . They're not regular portrait pictures—they're like those squadron pictures I had when I was in Cadets. We should get the regular pictures in a couple of days and I'll send them right on to you. . . .

Guess what?! Today I found a billfold containing over three hundred dollars, but there would have to be an identification card in it! I didn't know the fellow but he was a navigator on one of my buddy's crew. Boy, he sure was a happy guy when I gave it to him—so happy, in fact, he tried to give me a twenty dollar bill for returning it. I refused, though, because he was a married man and I figured he could probably use it just as well as myself.

Oh yes, while we are on the subject of money, you can wire or send me fifty dollars anytime before the 18th of this month. I'll probably need it to move out of here. Later in Staging Area I'll probably need more but you can send that to me later when I see how much I need depending on where we're going.

I'm now going to tell you something about the more personal side of Army life. The reason I think to tell you now is that today I received your letter telling about our friend who is having trouble accepting Army life and facing a combat tour overseas. I've seen this start since I've been here and watched it grow. It's commonly called "combatitis" or "third phaseitis." The instructors say it happens in every class when they are about to finish up. As you know, we're the next class to leave here—don't know where we're going or why—but one thing is certain and that is combat. Outside of the pilots, I don't believe the rest of the men have thought much about it up until now. The pilots have been trained for this and told to watch for it from the beginning, and have looked forward—rather I should say, expected—this. But, for the rest of the crew, it has just now dawned upon them what they have gotten into. For the gunners, bombardiers, and navigators the Air Corps has suddenly lost a lot of glamor. Life has suddenly lost a lot of glamor. Life has suddenly become very dear, combat very close, and their imagination playing tricks on them. It leaves them tight-lipped and very much engrossed in thought, or rather, in idle dreaming, without which they would be better off.

Surrounding us is an atmosphere of nervousness and, in some cases, even making us antagonistic toward those who have relatively easy jobs, or who at least have security. In cases where their job is not done properly they assume an attitude of "who cares, it's me that's going overseas, not you." They give the Permanent Personnel a little trouble and no end of worry. Some would like to quit right now and would if a court martial didn't stare them in the face.

It's quite an odd thing. You can hardly describe it—in some cases you can't see it, but it's a feeling you know that's there. It's nothing to worry about because they are all good men. They can and will do their jobs. It's just something you have to put up with now until they get their minds in condition for what's coming ahead. These are all generalities and do not necessarily apply to any one crew even though I write in first person.

P.S. I forgot to tell you that Work and I have all the letters written to my crew's folks.

May 4, 1944

Doggone, I sure have a time with my cookies! Fontana came over to get his one but wouldn't leave until he'd had about six or maybe more. Then Dimit, Work, and Doxon wanted a sample. I'd have been better off to have given them the box and kept the sample myself! . . .

As you have probably guessed we have quit flying and are in ground school, today being the second day of it. We are now scheduled for six days of ground school, then return to the flight line to pick up the rest of our missions. I still have to have at least three days of good weather to finish. Still have some high altitude bombs to drop and some high altitude formation plus the Galveston trip. Oh well, I refuse to worry about it now. If the weather holds I'll finish. If not, it probably won't make any difference anyway.

May 5, 1944

Nothing of interest here today—a routine schedule with hour after hour of lectures. Only three more days of it left. . . .

May 10, 1944

After so long a time here I am again. Same old story so I'll not bother you with it again. Instead I'll tell you what I did on my letter writing night. The evening that I had free I went to town to the picture show, The Memphis Belle. *I enjoyed it very much. It is a picture of actual combat, no Hollywood in it. That we know for sure because we have four of the first pilots who were on that raid here as instructors. Also the fellow who filmed most of the picture is our Group C.O. Well, it was very interesting to us to know these fellows, talk with them, work with them, then go to a show and see just exactly what they went through and what they did. So much for that.*

We are now back to flying. I didn't finish ground school—the weather looked as if we might be able to fly so we were pulled out of ground school only to sit on the line and watch the clouds go by. The last two days have been reasonably good, though, and we did get a lot done. All I need now is just one more good day. I'm still sweating out the Galveston mission—sure hope they have good weather there tomorrow.

Oh yes, I forgot to tell you how our big formation bombing contest came out with the other fields. We came out on top! No competition, they said, but I'm convinced we worked for it. . . .

I'm going to close for now as I have a thousand and one things to do and hardly enough time to get them done. With only eight more days left here we'll really have to hustle to get everything done. I'm pretty sure when we leave here we'll go to some place in Nebraska—Camp Kearney, Grand Island, or some such place. If we don't get a leave at our next station I would say that within four weeks from now we'll be in one of the theaters of operation. If that's the case I'll promise you I'll be home by Christmas. But I'll tell you more about that when the time comes.

May 14, 1944

We finally flew our big Galveston mission and it was a long, hard, grueling flight. But it was also very rewarding as far as experience and accomplishments went. All members of the crew had a good workout and I was very pleased with their performance. It far exceeded my expectations. I can truthfully say we now look and act like a real "bomber crew." We certainly pulled some real boners in the beginning, but the rough edges are now gone. I only hope they have the same trust in me as I have in them.

Our very last flight here was a dog-leg cross-country and we were allowed to choose our own route. I called Roco (rhymes with cocoa) [Work] in and told him to plan a route that would take us over the homes of as many crew members as he could work in with the amount of flying time we had. I wanted to give as many of our boys as I could one last look at home. Work plotted a good course and there were some happy boys on that airplane. We didn't break any flying regulations but we sure bent some in our let-downs and pull-ups over the homes!

Two "boners" come to mind at once. One involved us and the second involved another crew. Ours first:

When Doc first came aboard the aircraft he felt that it was an awfully big airplane, not too maneuverable, and not all that much fun to fly. He had his eye set, the same as every other pilot, on a nice

single-engine fighter that you could loop and roll and do all kinds
of aerobatic maneuvers. Or if not that, at least a B-25 or an A-20—
something that was hot and highly maneuverable.

I tried to explain to him that while the B-17 was big you could still
make some pretty sharp turns with it. You could stall the aircraft,
do wing-overs, and other unusual positions that would produce some
real flying sensations. I told him if he wanted to get familiar with it
he could stall the plane and get the feel of what a stall was like in
this big airplane. He could have the thrill of going over the top when
she breaks away, but not to be too violent as the crew didn't have
any safety belts, or if they had safety belts they wouldn't be fastened
as they were working around the airplane. We did tell the crew we
were going to stall the airplane and to be prepared for some unusual
positions.

I assumed we would ease the power off gently, pull the nose up
until the airplane stalled, then as it started to break over, catch it
with full power on the engines. But Doc's idea was a little different.
He wanted it to break clear away—which he did—but not on the
first one. We made three or four stalls with each one progressively
a little steeper and a little rougher than the one before. Of course
when you are in the stall phase just as she breaks away you experience what the pilots of today and the space shuttle people feel with
their weightlessness.

Although we didn't become completely gravity-free, things in the
airplane had a tendency to float around. On the first or second one
the flight manuals started floating around the cockpit. We had some
extra fluorescent light bulbs that would be used in night flying to
illuminate the instrument panel. These hadn't been installed but were
lying on the console. They were floating around too. We were having a good time laughing about that.

The boys back in the radio room noticed that their things were
also floating around. They had the top hatch open and we had a
camera on board. Our mission did not require a camera so it was
still in the radio room in its storage box. Evidently it had not been
turned in by the preceding crew. I don't know, but I imagine that
box weighed close to twenty or thirty pounds. On the last stall Hinman called me and said, "Do you know the camera that was in the
box is gone?" "What do you mean it's gone?" I answered. He said,
"On that last maneuver it just floated up and out the top hatch." Of
course my next thought was, "Did it hit the tail plane?" We hadn't
felt anything. Hinman assured me it hadn't hit anything. It was just
plain gone!

This sobered us up a little bit, and we decided we had done enough steep turns and stalls. By this time Doc had found out the airplane was much more maneuverable than he ever thought it would be. These were the most violent maneuvers we ever made in the B-17 until we reached combat. Then we did some really violent maneuvers!

Anyway we were all wondering how much one of those cameras costs, and if we would have to pay for it. All kinds of scenarios went through our minds.

When we landed at Ardmore a jeep pulled up to the aircraft and we were asked if we had a camera on board. We said we didn't, which wasn't an actual untruth. We might have had one when we left, but we sure didn't have one on landing! So the jeep proceeded on to the next aircraft and so on down the line. We didn't run into any problems over that because no one on the crew had signed for a camera.

But it also brings back to mind that on our way back from Galveston we had one B-17 in our unit return without the top gun turret. How that thing got out of the aircraft I'll never know. But Doc is of the opinion—and I suspect he's probably right—that after the formation had broken up this crew decided to loop the aircraft, and as Doc says, it was probably an awfully poor loop. They stayed on their back too long, and this was how they lost the turret. Our losing the camera looked pretty pale in comparison. Now there was a crew that was going to have to give a lot of answers!

May 18, 1944

Leaving immediately for Kearney Army Air Base, Nebraska. Will wire if possible from there.

Incidentally, there were no first pilot promotions. We are all leaving as 2nd lieutenants with the exception of Fontana, who has been a 1st lieutenant ever since we met back in flying school.

May 20, 1944

After another one of those enjoyable train rides we arrived here late yesterday afternoon. The ride wasn't nearly as bad as lots we have taken, but even at its best it was far from comfortable.

Before leaving Ardmore I sent you a note plus a letter from one of the fellows' sister. I thought perhaps you might enjoy reading it. I also had a letter from Brown's father and one from his mother. I want you to keep these letters for me. I had occasion just prior to leaving to meet some more of the fellows' parents. It was rather a touching time but, nevertheless, the duty of a pilot. They have all expressed trust and faith in my ability to bring their boys home. I can readily assure anyone that I too have the same confidence and that it's only a matter of time before we'll be home.

Now about the leave situation—it's very bad and it's definitely decided that there will be none except in cases of emergency, verified by the Red Cross.

You are probably wondering how, when, and what goes on here and in the future. Well, so am I. I'm sure you are thoroughly disgusted with the brevity and vagueness of my letters. I don't blame you, but I think you understand the restrictions we're under. The regulations don't mean so much in themselves, but our necks do. So you can see we have a good reason for squelching any rumors before they get started. At this point of the game there's not much to say. I promise I'll write you at every opportunity. I'll try to call you this evening if it's at all possible.

May 22, 1944

. . . Right at the present things are kind of screwed up. We don't know as yet whether we'll fly or go by boat. Some of our fellows have already received new airplanes and they know for sure what the deal is. The rest of us are still hanging in the fire waiting for somebody to make up their minds. They can take just as long as they want as far as I'm concerned.

I won't be able to wire or call you when I leave here, but will write so you'll know when I leave. You are the only one I'm writing to while I'm here so you'll have to let my folks know. I tried to wire them my new address like I did to you, but was refused by the telegraph office. They're kind of tough with us, but you know why. Incidentally, I received the money okay. Thanks a lot. I also received the last letter you sent to Ardmore today. The number of missions is now thirty, but I'll have them and be with you Christmas.

Above all, don't worry about me—I know you will, but don't let it get you down. You know me, I'll look out for myself, for I haven't spent all this time training without an eye to that. Besides, I know what I have to come home to so I just won't be taking any unnecessary chances. That's a promise!

May 23, 1944

I'm rather surprised at the fact that I'm still here. But as yet things are still all messed up and it seems as if nobody can get any orders on us. They manage to keep us busy, though, with a few classes and training films the whole day. The war of nerves is well underway. We are a little used to it, so in another day or so it should wear off—that is, if finger nails and shoe leather hold out. None of us are any too anxious to leave, but then in another way we'd like to get started so we can get it over. Boy, I sure want to get it over so I can get home to my wife and little one—that's paramount with me.

If we should get an airplane it wouldn't take us very long, probably a couple of days to get over. But if we go by boat it will probably slow us down, maybe two or three weeks. It makes little difference to me since I don't have any choice anyway. They say everything happens for the best so one way or the other will be okay.

That's just about all the news from here. There are no rumors. This is one time when everyone is content to keep his mouth shut and wait for orders.

May 28, 1944

Surprised to find out that I'm still at Kearney? Well, I am too! Our stay of over a week here has set a record at this field. They were beginning to refer to us as part of the Permanent Post Personnel. But I can safely say now that our stay has just about come to an end. I presume that you have already received my temporary APO number, but to be on the safe side I will include it at the end of the letter.

The orders have been received on us, but as yet we do not know their content, only the APO address. But this much is sure—we will not fly away from Kearney. We could possibly fly away from the POE [Port of Embarkation] which will be our next stop. If we did fly we would not receive our own plane. It would be via ATC [Air Transport Command.] There's a very strong chance that we might be ferried across that way because we are shipping out of here four crews at a time. I think I prefer that way to going by boat. After all, we are supposed to be fliers. Don't know what difference it would make except for probably a week's difference in travel time. In any event it looks as if we'll probably be on hand for D-Day.

Now to relate what I've been doing the past three or four days and why you haven't heard from me sooner. Let's start with Wednesday as that was the first day with nothing scheduled. Wednesday I slept the clock around for twenty-four straight hours and, believe me, it was wonderful. I got out of bed only long enough to eat two meals.

That brings us to Thursday. The setup here is that you're restricted to the post all day, but can go to town in the evenings. Of course now we are restricted all the time. To continue—Thursday my crew challenged another to a game of baseball, which, by the way, was Foster's crew. Needless to say, we beat them easily. That took care of all morning and the early part of the afternoon. At five o'clock we were able to get off the post so we all went to a riding academy, rented some horses, and had fun chasing jackrabbits all over the countryside. We rode until about 9 p.m. Then, as we were in the mood for more fun, we went to a roller-skating rink and stayed there long enough for everyone to have a good spill which, incidentally, didn't take long. After that we called it a day and went home to bed.

Next comes Friday in which we just about repeated the events of Thursday except that we played ball early in the morning with Flores' crew and chalked up another win. My boys haven't lost a game of baseball, volleyball, or basketball since we've been together. While none are exceptional players they just work together and we always come out on top.

Friday afternoon we spent washing all our dirty clothes, and believe me, we had enough of them. There's no laundry service here and we didn't care to carry any dirty ones with us so it left us just one choice. I sure miss you at times like that, but you know I miss you all the time, anyway. After putting out the laundry we went over to the stables and those of us who weren't too stiff from the day before went for another long ride. When that was finished we put in another hour on roller skates, then bowled for a while. Work says to tell you that I may lead the league in horseback riding but when it comes to bowling I'm not much competition. By the time we had bowled three games we were tired enough to start a "back to the sack movement."

Now for Saturday. All good things have to come to an end sometime so we had to quit playing and settle down to business. We went through a complete clothing process. We were issued lots of new equipment and turned in most of the old stuff. I even turned in my heavy leather pants. The new things they gave us are wonderful—I like them far better than the others. We also got a lot of junk which we'll probably never use, but regulations say we must have it so we have it! The rest of Saturday was spent trying to pack. Boy, what a job! You can take just so much and it has to be in the right bag in the right place. They have a baggage inspection just to make sure you have everything in the right place and also to see if you are taking all the required equipment. . . .

This morning was Sunday so we got up just in time to go to breakfast and then to church. First Sunday we've had a chance to go to church in quite some time. . . .

There are lots of things I'd like to tell you but it is almost impossible to put them on paper.

P.S. I can't promise how soon you'll hear from me again but will make it just as soon as possible. You can start writing any time to my new APO. . . .

Don't worry about me, I'll be okay, and don't forget we have a date for Christmas and I'll keep it. In the meantime keep your chin up.

May 30, 1944

This is it! If you don't hear from me for a while don't worry as it is all a part of the game. . . .
Feiss, Fletcher, Flores, and Fontana all say "so long" for now.

The day we left Kearney, Nebraska, for New York City the honor of being the Officer In Charge Of The Troops was conferred upon me. What this meant was I would be in charge of the troop movement and I would carry all official papers and the sealed orders for the crews. These papers were to be delivered to the Commander of the Station we were reporting to in New York City.

As I read my orders as troop commander, I saw that we were to change trains and train stations in Chicago, but there was no mention of what we were to use for transportation. Well, Army Air Corps crews should travel in good style. After all, we were the glamorous and the elite who would fly and die, if necessary, for our country.

With this thought in mind I asked the major who had presented me with the honor if buses would meet us at the train station. I would have four crews to transport—sixteen officers and twenty-four enlisted men. The major said, "No." So I scaled down my expectations somewhat and inquired, "Trucks?" At this the major looked at me and said, "Lieutenant, didn't they teach you how to march in Cadet School?" "Yes, Sir," I answered.

"And did they teach you how to give commands?"

"Yes, Sir."

"Then you will have no problem placing your troops in formation and marching them to the other station."

"Then, Sir, will there be a '6 by 6' to carry the baggage?"

"Lieutenant, you know eighty pounds is all the weight you are allowed to have with you. A good field pack for a soldier would weigh far more than that. You shouldn't have any problems."

After a very weak "Yes, Sir," I was stupid enough to ask if they had included a map with the directions on how to reach the other station. His reply was, "You're a commissioned officer. Surely you can figure out some way to perform your mission." I was very happy to say "Yes, Sir," and disappear. He didn't even wish me well.

Seven years earlier, at the tender age of fifteen, I had arrived in Chicago at the same station at which we would be arriving. I had spent one night in Chicago and left the next day. I had no idea where the other station was located. During the train ride it came to me in a flash that our waist gunner, Joe Firszt, was from Chicago. He was very familiar with the area and I had him write down the street names and directions we should go to change stations. I had him put this in writing just in case he decided to go AWOL when we reached his home town.

In reality the distance between stations was probably a good country mile. But there we were in formation at route step—all thirty-eight of us—the officers dragging their B-4 bags and the enlisted men with their barracks bags over their shoulders, bent double from the weight. The people on the streets at that early hour were indeed treated to a look at thirty-eight real sad sacks, the pride of the U.S. Army Air Corps, staggering down the streets of Chicago enroute to battle.

Since there should have been *forty* men staggering along those Chicago streets, the reader may wonder where the missing two had gone. Brownie and Joe Firszt believed in improvisation. They took a taxi and were waiting for us at the other station.

The Main Event

"Aye, 'tis a great contest going on over there. 'Tis a great contest."

European Theater of Operations

Eighth Air Force

Third Air Division

Thirteenth Combat Wing

Ninety-fifth Bombardment Group (H)

412th Squadron

June 18, 1944

Here is the letter you've been waiting for. It has been some time since you've heard from me. I only hope you received the cablegram and the last V-Mail change of address. My last address is for my permanent station.

I doubt very much if I'll receive the letters sent to my first APO. There was a mix-up some place and we are not where we thought we were going to be. Outside of the mail situation, though, it worked greatly to my advantage so I guess I can't kick. Maybe I'll get the letters sometime, but it won't be for a while.

I know you're very interested in where I am and what I am doing. I would sure like to tell you but the censors say "no," and I know you understand. I will say one thing, though, and that is that I'm with the best outfit in the ETO and I'm not just kidding. I feel very fortunate to be a part of the 95th Bomb Group, and more so to be in Squadron 412. When I get home I'll be able to tell you why.

I don't want you to worry about me. Things aren't bad over here. In fact, I kind of enjoy it. The people I'm working with are swell guys and they give you credit for what you do and treat you accordingly. That's something new for me after Cadets and Training Schools. I have finally found out where most of the good men in the Air Corps are—they're overseas! . . .

We have a lot of fun over here and the food is exceptionally good—even better than Cadets. Only recently I have procured the best bed in the ETO. I got it on a midnight requisition and will tell you more about it later.

Since our identity was closely tied to our squadron and groups, let me introduce you to ours.

The 95th Bomb Group was one of the older groups in the Eighth

Pathfinder radar ship. Mickey radar unit mounted in ball turret position. *(Boeing Archives)*

Air Force. It was formed in September 1942 at Geiger Field, Spokane, Washington, where I enlisted.

The 95th was the sixth heavy bomber group to arrive in England. They flew their first mission May 13, 1943, with the 92nd Bomb Group, which was then located at Alconbury. After seven missions with the 92nd Bomb Group the 95th moved to a new base at Framlingham. Within a month they moved to their permanent home at Horham, Suffolk, and remained there until the end of the war in the European Theater.

During this time the group flew 321 combat missions, plus eight supply missions to the Continent at the cessation of hostilities, and became the only group in the Eighth Air Force to earn three Presidential Unit Citations. They led the raid on Münster on October 10, 1943. On March 4, 1944, nineteen aircraft from the 95th Bomb Group flew the Lead, with twelve aircraft from the 100th Bomb Group, to become the first U.S. heavy bombers to drop bombs on Berlin. The Eighth Air Force heavy bomber gunner who held the record for the most enemy aircraft shot down was from the 95th Bomb Group.

The 412th Squadron was commanded by a number of fine men and contributed its share to the success of the group, along with the 334th and 336th Squadrons.

The 335th Squadron of the 95th trained all PFF (Pathfinder) "Mickey Ship" lead crews for the Thirteenth Combat Wing. These were primitive radar ships with the capability of bombing through an undercast or a smoke screen, and were officially known as H2X aircraft. The 335th also supplied some lead crews for other groups outside the wing.

The 95th participated in three England-to-Russia-to-Italy shuttle raids. They also flew a shuttle from England to bomb Regensburg, landing in North Africa, and bombing in France on their return.

In the course of the war they lost over 1,700 men and 192 airplanes in action. The replacement crews did their best to uphold the motto "Justice With Victory," as well as to protect the group's reputation for honor and integrity, which had been established by the original crews.

June 21, 1944

Remember I told you I had procured the best bed in the ETO? Well, I don't have it any more. It seems that I had swiped the Colonel's bed! Needless to say, he was very unhappy about it so I had to give it back. Didn't even give me a chance to argue about it. Oh well, it was too soft to rest on anyway, I keep telling myself.

Another thing I almost forgot about telling you. I now have a bicycle. It cost me six pounds (i.e. 24 dollars and some odd cents). Boy, am I getting hot on it. If I don't get hurt on it there's nothing else to worry about. It really comes in handy, saves a lot of steps. Everyone has one and it's about the only mode of transportation available. . . .

Now something about this country. It isn't anything like home—all very different, kind of hard to explain—it is all so quaint and old. The villages are small and the people seem to be living in the eighteenth century, yet, at the same time, it's all very picturesque. The English countryside is about like I had pictured it from story books. Little cottages all over and very small grass and hay farms of an acre or two, sometimes less. Everything is green wherever you look and tiny black roads thread their way in among the cottages like a spider web. Everything is done on such a small scale. The farms are small, the houses small, the roads are very narrow, the cars are Austins, Fiats, and the like, and they all drive on the wrong side of the road!

London was somewhat of a disappointment to me, but only because I didn't understand their way of life when I was there. I might enjoy it now, but England is no substitute for Washington. I'm hoping I can remember all the little incidents that happen so you too can enjoy my experiences in the United Kingdom. Believe me, you'll laugh yourself sick at some of them.

*Today I signed up to go to a stag Miami Triad. Looks as if we might
rejuvenate memories of the good old days. One of my buddies here who lives
in our Nissen hut is a Sigma Chi from Northwestern. His tail gunner is
from Dayton [Washington] and his engineer and Brown are old pals. So we
now have quite a bond of friendship between the two crews.*

*I have run into a lot of Washingtonians here—some from Walla Walla,
Seattle, Kennewick, and all around. One of them is saving the* Walla Walla
Union Bulletin *for me. That reminds me that I must go pick them up shortly.*

We arrived in England—or rather, Valley, Wales—on D+1–Day via
ATC. The airport was just a runway in the Welsh farm country.
Upon deplaning, knowing the invasion was in progress and want-
ing some information about the war, I walked over to a Welsh farmer
not far from the runway, and asked if there was any news from the
Continent.

"Aye, 'tis a great contest going on over there. 'Tis a great contest." These were the first words to greet my ears in the ETO.

Our crew was assigned to the 412th Bomb Squadron on June 16,
1944. Major Don Pomeroy was our squadron commander.

As crew housing was very short at this time, two crews of officers
were assigned quarters in Squadron Operations. A bunch of wooden
foot lockers approximately three deep in width were stacked from
floor to ceiling. Squadron Operations thus had half of the Nissen
hut and we had the other half. This was not a very satisfactory ar-
rangement for the squadron or for us.

Lieutenant Gordon Braund's crew had reported in one day ahead
of us and were bunked in four single beds, with mattresses, no less.
His crew consisted of Lieutenant Paul Baird, copilot; Lieutenant El-
mer Murray, navigator; and Lieutenant Raymond Davis, bombardier. When we arrived there were two old angle-iron double bunks
for our crew of officers. These monstrosities were so dilapidated and
rickety that Frank Dimit was prompted to say that it was the only
bed he ever saw that could lean in three directions at the same time!

These bunks were complete with "English biscuits"—the straw-
filled pillows. It took three of these "biscuits" to make a single mattress. Needless to say, the ones in the top bunk would wake up in
the morning suffering from a form of motion sickness while those
in the bottom bunk were losing sleep because of the creaking of the
beds as the top man rolled over. As the biscuits would separate,
with the top and bottom ones disappearing, you would wake up
draped over the center one. This went on for several days. Luckily
there were no casualties.

One morning as we were passing a building near the officers' club

Front view of Operations 412th Bomb Squadron, bulletin board and bicycles, crew quarters in the rear

we saw some remodeling going on. We looked inside and here were four single beds complete with mattresses. Myron Doxon decided we could put those beds to better use, so he and Dimit worked all night carrying those beds down the hill to our crew quarters. The sorry-looking double bunks with the English biscuits were then carried up to the Club Area and set up in the room that was being renovated. What a sad sight it was, too—those old iron bunks leaning to the four winds in what was now a fairly attractive looking room. Little did we realize that this was Colonel Karl Truesdell's pet project, the beginning of a VIP quarters in anticipation of a visiting general!

It was said that when the good colonel looked in on his new project and was greeted with this sight, the smoke was blacker and heavier than usual from the perennial Truesdell cigar. An order was issued forthwith to all squadron adjutants that the beds must be found and returned within twenty-four hours, and that nothing would be said. However, if that deadline was not met some heads would roll and some hides would be nailed to the door of group headquarters.

There was quite a stir in all the squadrons as the search was launched. Captain Steve Stone was the adjutant for the 412th and no one will ever be able to describe the expression on his face when he looked in the back of squadron operations and saw the four beds that were missing. For a moment he was speechless—it was then that I realized that the Permanent Party people took these shenanigans much more seriously than flying personnel, who would fly for a while and then be gone, one way or another. Captain Stone, still suffering from apoplexy but partially regaining his composure, mumbled something about a court martial, and if it happened to him four officers would surely go with him.

Immediately three second lieutenants started dismantling and hauling the beds back to the VIP quarters in the squadron truck, which was readily made available. The fourth was busy administering first aid to Captain Stone and assuring him that everything would be okay because there were still three hours left on the twenty-four-hour deadline.

Thus it was that Fletch's crew became a well-known Nissen hut name throughout the group, and they had yet to fly their first combat mission!

This incident ended some time later when Colonel Truesdell, showing the "humanitarian" that he was, had four beds similar to the ones we had borrowed delivered to the rear of the 412th Squadron Operations. Later on at the club I received the admonition to the effect that enough was enough, and "I don't want to hear anything except good about you fellows again." He was heard to mutter as he walked away, "Hell, I wouldn't have slept in them either, but there should have been a better way!"

June 23, 1944

Our mail still hasn't arrived and no indication of when it will. We still have hopes of getting it—just takes time. I imagine there are things a lot more important which have to be done first. Because of censorship it really doesn't leave me much to write about, especially with no news from home.

June 26, 1944

Life is just the same here from one day to the next. Nothing unusual—nothing to write about—still no mail.

This is kind of personal and you don't have to answer it if you don't want to. The question: Am I a father yet? I've been pacing the floor every night and smoking cigarettes by the pack, but I can't tell whether I'm having any luck or not.

In spite of a low-key letter this was really a red-letter day for our crew. We flew our first full-scale practice mission in England. Gordon Braund, Paul Fiess, and Nelson Day, all first pilots of the new crews who arrived when we did, were in the formation for the first time also. All of us "Green Hands" were mixed in with the veterans. We were all a little nervous, but we knew we did a good job and were complimented on our formation flying by some of the veterans, along with the group commander at our pilot's interrogation. We were also given some good advice about how to react to certain life-threatening situations. We were really walking on air, but didn't dare write about it, still not knowing, because of censorship, what was permissible.

June 27, 1944

Had a hard day today—got up at eleven, had breakfast and dinner all at the same time. Spent a couple of hours in the library reading all the latest news reports. Then came home and read poetry to Doc and Dimit until supper time. Later we took a bike ride for exercise, after which we played ping pong until we were worn out. I must quit working so hard, that's all there is to it! Some day when my grandchildren ask me what I did in the last war I'll have to answer very meekly that I toured England on a bicycle!

Sure wish I had some news from home. It would make writing so much easier besides boosting morale. One of these days Uncle Sam will finally catch up with me and I'll probably have more mail than I'll know what to do with. Oh happy day!

June 28, 1944

Guess what! I just got beat two games in a row pitching horseshoes! Brown and Smith really worked Dimit and me over. But we'll show them tomorrow—the grudge fight is on.

Dimit challenged me to a ping pong game which we'll play pretty soon. I'll let you know how I make out before I finish this letter. Today has been a repetition of yesterday except that I got up at nine o'clock this morning. What a life—too bad I'm not in the States so we could enjoy it.

Sherry, I have a confession to make. I've been hoarding!! Yes, every week bit by bit I've been hoarding my tobacco rations until I now have a whole box of fifty cigars. I'm all set just waiting for you to send the Cablegram that will make me the happiest guy in the ETO. When that news gets here and we get all these cigars lit up the smoke will be so thick the Germans will think the whole of England is on fire!

Back again—the game is over. Dimit just won three to two. Oh well, you have to let them win to keep up the teamwork and friendship of the crew. Same old story—pilot sacrifices ability for goodwill!

June 30, 1944

Doxon broke the ice today by receiving the first letter. Maybe business is picking up. Perhaps tomorrow will be my day.

Received a couple of Walla Walla Bulletins *today and have just about caught up on the April and May news of the old home town. When I started reading news of dear old Whitman College it almost got me down. We have a lot of fond memories centered around that institution. But our real joys of life are yet to come when we settle down in our own little home and raise the family we now have started.*

July 1, 1944

Here it is the first of July. The weather is cool, damp, and rainy practically all the time. Occasionally we have wind which reminds one of March weather at home. Sometimes you can see the sun, but the occasion is rare and never for more than a half hour at a time. This would be a very poor country for romance because the hours of darkness are short. At eleven o'clock at night you can read a newspaper with as much ease as at noon. At twelve darkness prevails and lasts until about 3 a.m. Then comes the dawn and another day in the ETO has started.

I can't make up my mind whether I welcome or dread the coming of a new day. About the only thing I would welcome now would be a trip home to you. It seems that about the only way I can get home will be to sweat out the dawns for the duration. So, in that case, I guess I'll have to concede the point and usher in each new day with the consolation that it's just one more day closer to when I will be home.

Bath day was yesterday. Today I washed all my dirty clothes. Boy, what a laundry I put out! You know I'm getting pretty good with these domestic duties. You can't afford to let me get away 'cause I'll probably make you the best little wife when I return. But me thinkest that I shall be very glad to turn the little duties over to you. . . .

Just had a talky-talk session with the rest of the boys on the crew. We were reminiscing, talking about what we were going to do when we returned to the States, and, of course, a few other various and sundry subjects. In the end we decided the crew would turn out en masse for church in the morning, this being Saturday evening.

Received my first pay in the ETO yesterday—twenty-three pounds, nine shillings, and two pence. In good old American money that would be ninety-four dollars and sixty-five cents. Living expenses are very reasonable here. After adding up all expenses it comes to twenty-nine dollars a month. Maybe a shilling more or less either way, but I can't kick about it. This is one place where we really get our money's worth. Twenty-one dollars for mess bill, club dues four dollars with a free snack bar at the club. Things aren't as nice as in the States, but dollar for dollar this is the real deal.

We were just getting settled in our Nissen hut home in the 412th Bomb Squadron when a young man, a crewman on another flight crew, came by and stopped in for a social call. He was curious about where we had trained in the States and whether we had been on any of the bases where he had received his training. As it turned out, we had been at different fields and could not provide him with any information about the friends he had left behind.

Had we flown a combat mission yet? The answer was no, and we didn't have any idea what combat would be like. His crew had over twenty missions. They had had some rough ones and he would be happy to explain what combat was like and what would be in store for us. We were all eyes and ears as he proceeded to crawl up on the top of one of the rickety bunks and dangle his legs over the side. He was carrying a small air pump—the kind you would use to inflate bicycle tires—and it had a holder which could be used to fasten it onto the bike. He had just purchased it, and he was enroute to work on his bicycle when he decided to stop and visit with us.

As he started to tell his combat tales we noticed he was very hyper. As the stories continued his eyes took on a rather glazed look and the bicycle pump was getting quite a workout as he twisted it around in his hands. The longer he talked the more agitated he became. The bicycle pump by now was rendered useless—it had been twisted and bent, the plunger with the handle looked like a pretzel.

As the stories became more violent his speech was starting to slur and by now his eyes had a very faraway look. His body movements had become jerky and appeared to be uncontrollable. In this state he jumped down from the bed and took his leave, completely oblivious to the condition of the bicycle pump which he still clutched in his hands.

We were glad to see him go, and as he left the room we were in complete awe. We looked at one another and questioned whether this was a performance designed to impress the new recruits, or was this "combatitis" in full bloom. Or, as Doc would remark, "have we just witnessed the performance of a man who is one-quarter brick short of carrying a full load?" In my opinion it wasn't an act. The performance was too genuine to be faked. What had we gotten ourselves into? Maybe we should go home now. But only time would tell. We too reached the point where we were under great stress, but physically and mentally we may have carried and hid it much better. However, we never adjusted to it. We had reason that day to stand in awe and wonder, but we were not yet smart enough to realize it.

July 2, 1944

Just sweated out another mail call. Still having the usual luck—no letters. I hope you are having better luck with my letters than I am with yours. About another week of this and I'm going to volunteer to go back to the States and investigate this postal system. I'm quite sure they would authorize this visit too. As you can readily see I have been here too long already!

There's not much to write about today. We went to church as we had planned, and have spent the rest of the day reading and sleeping. . . .

July 3, 1944

Happy days are here again! Today I received fourteen letters—two from my mother, two from Cap and Sis, one from your sister, Mildred, and nine from you. They run pretty much in sequence but a few are missing. I'll probably receive the others before too long. . . .

July 4, 1944

I'm getting so lazy doing nothing that one of these days they're going to ask me to do something and then I'll feel insulted. All I can say is that if we don't get started pretty quick the war will be over and I'll still be riding my bicycle along with a lot of other ETO happy fellows.

Incidentally, no one has been injured seriously yet on our biking tours although Dimit wore a little skin off his hands and scraped some off his leg. As yet I've lost no hide but have had several good spills. (Boy, he sure missed a bridge completely one day. M.D.D.) (Hand is healed—barbed wire fence will never be the same. F.S.D.) Sometimes these bicycles get a little tipsy!

Now that the boys have put their two cents worth in I'll continue. How do you like my new stationery? We're just about destitute for something to write on. That is just to prepare you for the shock should you receive some letters on stationery with perforations about every four inches!

July 5, 1944

Received a very nice letter from Mildred and have answered it already. There isn't much I can write that's of interest, or, at least, what people are most interested in. I could refer to my work more closely than I do and it would probably get by. But I look at it this way, why take a chance? The rules were made for my safety and the least I can do is try to live up to them.

When you have time please send me stationery. Forget the envelopes, but send the paper—also a scarf and any kind of candy bars available, if there are any.

July 6, 1944

Now for the events of the day—no mail but perhaps I'll have better luck tomorrow. I hope so. Now then, remember I said if they ever asked me to work I'd probably be insulted? Well, let me tell you tonight I'm very highly insulted! Oh well, I must get into the routine of things sometime, so it was just as well to be now as later. I'm more firmly convinced than ever now that I shall be home with you by Christmas.

Mission #1, Abbeville, France, July 6

Frank Dimit, Bombardier

Left coast of England over Bixhill—between Hastings and Eastbourne. Hit France at Bayeux. Our target was pilotless bomb or rocket installation.

Didn't see target—too damn busy trying to get rid of bombs. Load was hung up, and was only able to salvo half my load. Had trouble with bomb-bay doors. Finally solenoid jammed and motor in bay caught on fire. Doc and I finally cut wire and put out fire. More fun. Learned one lesson—always have axe handy.

Flak was light but plenty accurate. High squadron caught it all. Picked up 23 holes—no casualties.

Head up and locked this a.m. When I checked chin turret, grabbed

Frank Dimit raising the red Mission Alert flag, occasionally referred to as "Maggie's Drawers"

triggers when I reached for dead-man switches. Fired three rounds from each gun. Scared hell out of me, crew, and ground personnel. Guns were in full down position. No damage except two big holes in hardstand.

We were a spare ship today but one of the boys aborted and we took his place. *[End of mission notes by Frank Dimit]*

Robert "Roco" Work, Navigator

It wasn't long until the crew grew accustomed to seeing "Maggie's Drawers" flying in the breeze before a mission. For several nights these highly keyed men slept all too lightly, wakening frequently when RAF planes returned from night raids to the Ruhr. Or perhaps it was their early morning sleep which was disturbed by the unbelievable roar of the Eighth Air Force heavies forming for an attack on some continental target.

Then came the seemingly interminable days of practice missions as Fletch learned to fly the 95th way and Roco pondered over problems of navigation in England. But the training flights finally ended and the night before the first mission arrived with far too little fanfare. For several days they'd all been scanning "The List" to see when it would be. When the time came there were parched throats, pounding hearts, and throbbing pulses! Tomorrow was to be the culmination of nearly two years of training in the methods of waging war! Tomorrow, perhaps, there would be empty bunks where these young men tossed fitfully tonight.

As is the Army custom, the officers and enlisted men lived in different barracks so we don't know what they did that night. But, anticipating an early arising, the officers prepared to rest before the big test. Just before turning out the lights Fletch took out his Bible, by request, and read a few chapters. Each man had his own private religious beliefs, but that night they jointly turned to God for guidance. Fletch has a nice reading voice (he used to be a radio announcer before the war) so it was fine to hear him as he read. Then, when the lights went out, each man held his own communion with his Maker and sought solace for his tortured mind. Prayers were said in that hut in England—not prayers for safekeeping, but pleas for guidance. These men didn't seek safety; they sought strength— and He came to them!

Sleep was slow in coming on the eve of that first mission, and when it came it didn't bring rest. All sorts of pictures passed through their minds as they lay there: Would it be a rough mission? Do you suppose our ship will be disabled? Will *I* be injured or killed? Why didn't I get in the Finance Department? Muddled, selfish thoughts— they were "sweating it out."

It was around 0130 when the CQ roused them from their dreams chanting a ritual that would soon plague every startled awakening. "Lieutenant Fletcher, Lieutenant Doxon, Lieutenant Work, and Lieutenant Dimit—it's one-thirty, breakfast at two-fifteen, briefing at three o'clock." With that he was gone to spread his cheerful dirge throughout the squadron area and we were left to stretch before actually getting up. Suddenly the thought came: "Will I sleep here tonight?" And then we shook off our fears, literally as well, for it's pretty cool in the early morning in England. But it wasn't the temperature that rattled the teeth. It was fear!

At the mess hall a bedlam greeted us as we entered the door. The smoke of burning grease assailed our nostrils and smarted in our eyes as we filed in for our "real fresh eggs." Perhaps a slice or two of salty bacon also on the plate and to a table for the first problem: Can I get them down? After a drink of grapefruit or tomato juice it usually became easier, but it didn't take much to satiate our appetites that morning! Each mouthful became an additional lump of lead in the pit of our stomachs and we were soon ready to board the truck that would take us to briefing.

Here we found another riot of noise and haze of smoke stirred up by those who'd preceded us. Few of the fellows were flying their first mission and they weren't quite as obviously frightened. But a discerning eye could spot the haunted look in their eyes and the sharpness of tempers that would flare up in a flash if something went wrong. Ever so meekly we sought four seats together and tried to relax until the briefing officer arrived from the other briefing where he was preparing the gunners.

When he arrived the door was closed and everyone tensed up for the bad news which would come as soon as the roll had been called. With a true sense of the dramatic characteristic of all briefing officers, he whisked back the curtain which had covered the map and route for the day's mission. Gasps of dismay greeted this act when it became evident that Bremen was to feel the weight of our bombs. For Bremen rated near the top of the list of "roughies."

"Gentlemen, your target for today is the Rosenheim Oil Plant at Bremen. In keeping with the current attack on oil, the Eighth Air Force is going out in force again today, sending over a thousand bombers against synthetic and natural oil targets in Germany. The First Division is sending five groups of B-17s to Magdeburg, the Second is going to Hamburg with six groups of B-24s, and we in the Third Division are putting up five groups to Bremen." Then follows the technical details of assembly and departure, zero hour, fighter rendezvous, etc. "There are 280 heavy guns in the target area, of which 135 can be brought to bear on you if you follow the briefed course. A sharp right turn after bombs away will get you out of the flak the quickest."

Through our heads echo these substantial figures—280 heavy guns—yipe! Soon afterward navigators and bombardiers are dismissed for their separate briefings while the pilots remain behind for instructions pertaining to their duties. For the next three hours everyone will be in a hurry to climb into their flying clothes and attend to all the minute details that are so essential for a round-trip. But wait, something just came in—this target is scrubbed and there will be a new one ready in just a few minutes. Whew! At least it can't be much rougher. Finally the route is put up, and to our surprise it's a short trip to the Pas de Calais area. That's right, a flying bomb site on the coast of France—why, we'll be back before lunch! Then we go through another and shorter briefing, for takeoff time is rapidly approaching. Only twelve guns at this spot. It should be a milk run, and we're due back at 1115. Golly, we thought, perhaps this isn't such a tough war after all!

Later, filled with vital information, we climb into our ship, *Government Issue,* named for a characteristic tan roll found in all latrines. Our first incident of note occurred before the 1st pilot and navigator even got to the ship. Dimit was loading his chin turret and checking the solenoids when everyone was startled by a loud *brrrt* emanating from his direction. Someone had left the gun switch turned on and Frank tore two holes in the concrete hardstand about four inches deep when his gun cut loose. There were only about five rounds from each gun, but they did make the gravel fly! After that our preparations were completed without incident and we taxied out for the takeoff.

Naturally we were delegated a place far back in the formation because of our newness to the game—number six in the high squadron. With the engines roaring in our ears as Fletch and Doc completed their check, the rest of us fiddled with this and that to make doubly sure that everything was as it should be. Eventually, it was our turn to take off so Fletch locked the brakes and ran up the engines to maximum power before releasing them. With a lurch of acceleration we gathered speed and those who could watched the airspeed meter, knowing we'd need at least 110 and preferably 130 or 135 mph before he could lift her off the runway. Flickering slightly as we zoomed down the runway the needle crept slowly upward past 60, 70, 80, 100, and we crossed the yellow line indicating one-third of the runway was left; 110, 120, and at long last 130 mph when Fletch eased back on the stick. The ship vibrated when Doc kicked the brakes to stop the spinning wheels before he flicked the retraction switch, and then climbed smoothly upward as our airspeed neared the normal.

That part of the day's drama was a success. Let's hope the rest goes off as well. We continued to climb and circle the field to join the formation leader who was already at assembly altitude and firing red-green flares. When things still went okay, so that we were sure we wouldn't be forced to abort because of mechanical trouble, Dimit went back to the bomb bays to remove the safety pins from the bombs. By the time he had returned to the nose we were in position and about ready to leave the field. The next thing we knew England was dropping away in the rear and we were over the Channel.

None of us will ever forget the first view of France, which was then still occupied territory. The sky was cloudless, the water was a deeper blue even than the heavens, and there were the rocky shores of Calais. Other groups ahead of us were opening their bomb-bay doors for the bomb run. But that was before those twelve guns began sending their death-dealing shells our way. I guess the flak is always closer on the first and last missions every crew flies (or so it seems) but that day we figured we were the only plane that those damned flak gunners could see in the sky. Twelve guns—there must be twelve hundred! Not yet convinced of the danger of flak, the navigator was standing up behind the bombardier trying to pick up the target when a near burst brought home the fact that he was being shot at, and damn it, he wasn't being missed by much. Then it was that terror set in. Stamping his foot to accent his words, Roco proclaimed long and loud that no one would ever get him to fly another mission any place under any circumstances whatsoever! "I won't, I won't, I won't," he kept crying out. "You can't get me to do this again!" Suddenly it dawned on him that he hadn't turned the mike switch on while he was screaming out his fears.

Every heart in the ship stopped momentarily when Smitty frantically called out, "Tail gunner to pilot, tail gunner to pilot, I'm hit, I'm hit!" Sending Lynch back to check on him, Fletch sweat blood for a few minutes until Lynch's easy drawl came over the interphone. "He's all right. A piece of flak just bounced off his chute harness!" That episode had hardly let us breathe a deep breath before Dimit called out, "Bombs away!" and Fletch swung into some evasive action on the way to the rally point. And before we knew it we were turning back toward England and starting to let down from altitude as we crossed the Channel. As soon as he could make himself heard over the sighs of relief, Fletch asked Mac to look under the wings for oil or gas leaks. Upon receiving a negative report he said something about, "That was close," and went back to the interplane frequency to learn landing instructions. Already we could see England below us and Roco ventured a guess at the Estimated Time of Return to the base.

After five hours and ten minutes that seemed more like five years and ten months we settled none too gently onto the runway and proceeded to our hardstand. Swiftly gathering up his equipment, the navigator barely waited for the props to stop turning before he jumped to the ground, where only a large oil spot prevented him from kissing the earth. Anyway he patted it very affectionately and climbed back in to remove his guns. By the time everyone had gotten his equipment in the truck the ground crew had counted the holes in various parts of the ship. Twenty-three was the sum and you can imagine our surprise upon returning to interrogation to find that we were the only crew of the day to suffer any battle damage at all. Just like we thought, every one of those twelve guns had been shooting at *us! [End of mission account by Roco Work]*

Our first combat mission was to Abbeville, France, a second-choice target. We were to attack sites which were launching areas for the V-1 buzz bomb which had plagued London and a lot of England. When the target was changed the "old timers" heaved a sigh of relief and let it be known that we were going on a milk run (a very easy mission), since most of the targets would have very few anti-aircraft guns.

It had been the practice up until then to break up a crew for the first mission so they could see what combat was like, and have a chance to gain some knowledge while flying with an experienced crew. Or if that wasn't possible, at least the pilot would be sent as copilot along with a crew who had already received their baptism of fire.

We did not want to start our tour that way and requested that we be allowed to begin our tour on our own as a complete crew. We had confidence in our abilities, and besides, we had survived all of our training mistakes. What could possibly be worse? Surely not the Germans. We were completely ignorant of the ways of combat, but we would learn. When we made this request our squadron commander, Major Don Pomeroy, was noncommittal. It was possible that he knew much more than we. But here we were, on our own, unsupervised, in a war-weary airplane headed for battle.

We had looked forward to this day for months. Now we would find out what all our training had been about. We were off the ground with only a few minor mishaps due to nervousness, with an embarrassed crew member and a rather nervous ground crew left behind. Only twelve flak guns were expected at our target, and this news had caused a round of cheers from the old hands at our briefing. We easily found our place in the formation. We would be the last ship in the high squadron.

Before long it appeared that all twelve guns were firing right at us. The glamor was rapidly disappearing—then the one message I never wanted to hear was coming over the interphone. In spite of the chill that went up my spine the sweat was pouring. "Tail gunner to pilot—I've just been hit." Why would anybody volunteer to do this? My next message was, "Hang on, Smitty. Lynch, check him out."

After what seemed to be an eternity, Lynch's Oklahoma drawl announced, "He's okay. He was hit in the chest and had the wind

knocked out of him. He'll have a bruise, but it didn't break the skin."
Thank God!

We were taking a beating. When Frank called, "Bombs away," we immediately started evasive action. The formation loosened up and everyone was on his own until we reached the Rally Point. We then formed a tight formation and headed for home.

"Gad, won't he ever close the bomb-bay doors?" The answer came immediately: "Bombardier to pilot, the bomb-bay doors won't close." Almost immediately the engineer reported the electric motor for the bomb-bay doors had shorted out and was smoking like crazy. The only way to stop a certain fire was to unhook the hot lead to the motor. The motor is located on the forward bulkhead in the bomb bay, approximately three feet down from the catwalk and close to the fuel transfer lines. A fire in this position could eventually burn through the fuel lines, setting the whole aircraft on fire or creating an explosion.

The copilot left his seat and joined the engineer, along with the bombardier. The gunners and radio operator left their positions and came through the open bomb bay on a very narrow catwalk, bringing with them the two ropes which formed the safety support in the bomb bay. I was notified that they had a plan to disconnect the hot line to the motor. I told them to go ahead as something had to be done quickly. There was no time for a conference—these were trained people and I was confident they would do their best. I would fly the aircraft in formation until they solved the problem, or until they felt it was necessary to abandon ship.

Unbeknownst to me their plan was to lower the copilot headfirst down into the open bomb bay. They intended to accomplish this by hooking the two ropes onto the D-rings of Doc's parachute harness. The waist gunners would snap the other end of the ropes into the rings on their parachute harness. The radio operator and the bombardier planned to grasp the gunners around the waist, thus anchoring them. The engineer planned to crouch down at the bulkhead opening into the bomb bay, taking Doc's legs under his armpits, locking his own arms around Doc's legs, with his fingers interlocked in an "Indian grip." As the waist gunners slowly inched forward with their anchormen, putting some slack in the safety ropes, Doc was lowered into the bomb bay with a fire axe in his hand. When he felt he was in position he swung the axe, and after several blows was able to sever the hot line, disconnecting the motor. Our fire hazard had now been averted. Dimit inched his way along the catwalk, 15,000 feet above the Channel, replacing the ropes, while the others returned to their positions. Doc had been given a view of the English Channel which he was in no hurry to repeat.

Our next problem was, "Can you land a B-17 with the bomb-bay doors open?" We knew the stalling speed would increase but we could solve that by coming in a little hotter than usual. We knew also that the open bomb-bay doors have plenty of clearance when the aircraft is at rest on the ground, but what will happen on the shock of landing? How much will our landing gear compress when it takes the full weight of the aircraft? Let's be on the safe side and put the crew in a crash landing procedure.

The aircraft touches down; this crew now knows that you can land a B-17 with the bomb-bay doors open with relative security. When we reached the hardstand and crawled out we found we had twenty-three holes in the aircraft—and this was a milk run? What would a toughie be like? At interrogation we learned that we were the only plane in the formation to have battle damage. The age of innocence was over. This was the last mission where we left the base in happy anticipation of a tangle with Jerry. We had learned that Jerry played for keeps and that this was a dangerous game.

We were so green that we did not realize that the actions of these men, who saved our ship and our lives, constituted "heroism," and it is sad to report that none of them received the Distinguished Flying Cross. This in a day and age when these medals were awarded for completing a combat tour. Rules could change, but heroism would not.

July 7, 1944

There was a wonderful letter from you awaiting me when I returned today. Today's letter was dated the twenty-third of June. So now I'll wait for the gap from the seventeenth to the twenty-second to fill in. In this letter there was no mention as to whether you had ever heard from me. I hope you have because I know my letters mean as much to you as yours to me.

I have written to everyone at least once, but now I'm back in my usual routine of writing only to you. Gosh it has only been a week since I was griping that I had more time than anything else. Time has changed things slightly, though, and I don't know when I'll get around to write them again.

In case you're worrying about me, don't. Things aren't bad. Not good, but I know it could be worse. Don't worry one bit, though, Sherry, because I know your prayers will be answered. In that much I'm confident. Our whole life is still to be lived and I know that the joy the future will bring will completely overshadow any sorrows that this separation has caused us to bear.

The fellows always ask about you and how you're getting along. Believe me you're a pretty popular gal with ten men. They all send their regards and hope you're getting along fine.

Mission #2, Merseburg, Germany, July 7

Frank Dimit, Bombardier

Briefed at 2:30 a.m. for a target in Germany. Synthetic oil refineries (Leuna Oil Refinery) at Merseburg, near Leipzig.

95th led the big show today. We flew a wing formation with the 390th and 100th. We were flying #3 in second element of low squadron—tail-end Charlie in purple heart corner.

Tail gunner's, radio, and left waist's oxygen system went out just after we hit the coast of Holland just west of Zuider Zee. So we aborted.

It was a rough mission. Gordy Braund's crew came back alone with #4 engine out. Maybe Someone upstairs is looking after us.

Saw no flak and no fighters except ours. Golly, those fighters of ours sure looked good.

Fingers getting worn out from putting pins back in bombs. Carried 20 250-pound G.P. [General Purpose bombs].

P.S. *July 9.* Sun is shining today—we received credit for the abortion. Chalk up #2 for us. We believe we received credit for this one because we brought back some "hot news" about some ships off coast of Holland. The next day we saw in the paper where Beauforts had sunk six merchant vessels in that vicinity. *[End of mission notes by Frank Dimit]*

Roco Work, Navigator

Without even having a day to think over what they had just been through, our heroes found themselves alerted anew on the evening of their first trip against the Hun. This time they were almost too tired to bother about worrying over where they might have to go. For even though the flight had been a short one, the strain on their nerves had been almost more than they could bear, so they went to bed early in the evening, within an hour of learning that they'd probably fly again on the next day.

Sure enough, 0300 found the CQ rattling at their door with a slightly different chant, the essence of which was the same. . . . Hurriedly donning their clothes and downing their breakfasts with little more zeal than they had displayed on the previous day, these four young worthies again presented themselves for briefing. Sacre bleu! Listen to the old timers moan this time. It was Merseburg, undeniably the roughest target that can be found on this earth! There were between 350 and 400 guns in the target area, 120 of which would be unable to bother those groups which followed the briefed route from the Initial Point of the bomb run (IP) to the target to the Rally Point (RP). Because undercast conditions were expected, the IP was quite a way from the target so the special instruments could be used to their best advantage in picking up the target. And the RP was picked with great care as well, to give the maximum possible time for the formations to regain their proper spacings.

Being as yet frank novices at the game, Fletcher's crew were not as frightened as might be expected because they didn't know enough to realize what was before them. This day they were assigned to a ship which was beginning to be known as a "battle weary" because of the large number of missions that had already been flown in it, and also because of the many patches covering former flak and bullet holes in the metal skin. The name of that notable craft was *Roaring Bill,* and no one quite recalls what inspired such a cognomen. Taking its idiosyncracies in their stride, the crew scrambled to their places when the time came and began the ritualistic last-minute check of oxygen regulators, gun belts, etc. So takeoff time found them, if not eager, at least resigned and ready to go.

As on the previous day our boys were delegated to be fill-ins in case some one had to leave the formation going across the Channel. And again they quickly found a spot: number six in the low squadron. So when the time came to depart from the shores of England they were all settled back for the long ride in. Mac began to crawl into his ball turret before they were out of sight of land, because, he said, "It's warmer in there." As they approached Holland at an altitude of 18,000 feet, Frank and Roco were engaged in the process of determining that they were on course. Everything seemed to check as they crossed the narrow strip of land that separates the Zuider Zee from the North Sea.

Suddenly George came on the interphone inquiring of Mac and Smitty how much oxygen pressure they had left. Roco was amazed to hear them answer that their needles pointed at 125 pounds and were falling rapidly, and he called Fletch so he would know of the situation. A short conversation with George, who'd gone back to look at the ball from inside the ship, led Fletch to realize that if he chose to continue with the formation it would necessitate three men going the remainder of the distance on walk-around bottles which would have to be constantly replenished from the main system. Therefore he signaled the group leader by giving the proper response for leaving the formation, which was lower the gear and rock the wings. This way we could maintain radio silence.

By this time Mac had come out of the ball and was nursing a walk-around bottle in the radio room, while George had switched to an oxygen line on the opposite side of the ship, as had Smitty. Since he didn't as yet know the cause of the abrupt drop in pressure, Fletch couldn't be sure how soon the oxygen for the entire ship might give out. So he made a diving turn to the left, losing altitude as rapidly as possible without gaining too much speed. During the conversation, Roco had realized that a course home would be in order and had one ready when they had reached a safe altitude to remove their masks. With Frank's aid he pinpointed their position on the map so they could tell how far in they had gone before turning back. Just after leaving the Dutch coast Smitty called Roco to report that there were about eight medium-sized boats in the Channel, but scurrying toward the safety of the coast. Their position also went into the navigator's log for the interrogation.

By this time Brownie had gone back through the bomb bays to determine the cause of the trouble. A short inspection showed that the oxygen filler hose to the ball turret had become unfastened from its normal position. As a result when Mac twirled his ball around, the hose caught on something and eventually pulled loose from its connection, thereby allowing the precious, life-giving oxygen to escape. Since there are four systems which carry oxygen throughout the plane, only the positions fed off that line were affected. Accidents happen even on the best of ships, and this *Roaring Bill* had long since lost any claim to such flattering terminology.

Roco's course for home was correct and not many minutes elapsed before they were on the ground again. Four hours and fifteen minutes they had been in the air, all to no purpose it seemed at that time. Rather disgruntled over their misfortune in going through all the preparations and nervous plannings only to be forced to return early, but nonetheless rather happy that they hadn't had to fly over Merseburg, they gathered their equipment and changed their clothes. Then Fletch and Roco reported to the intelligence officer in charge and told all about what had happened.

When they told him about the ships Smitty had seen he grew much more interested and copied all the details, after which he telephoned them to the proper place for such information—hot flash. It must have been a good tip, for the next day's papers claimed that Coastal Command aircraft had attacked and sunk six out of eight enemy ships in the neighborhood of the Frisian Islands, where the observation had been made. Who knows, perhaps that's why our boys were given credit for a mission. At any rate, George's alertness in noticing the loss of pressure prevented what might have been a very embarrassing situation for Mac in the ball alone, to say nothing of the others who might not have caught on in time to make the necessary changeover! *[End of mission account by Roco Work]*

July 8, 1944

In a few days I'm going to start sending some newspapers home. Read them if you like, then save them for me so we can go over them together. Along this same line—anything we do here you can read in the papers at home just a few hours after it happens. If you like you can save clippings and dates, then we can have some fun with them later on when I get home.

July 9, 1944

Today was nothing out of the ordinary. We got up just in time to go to church. Afterwards we partook of dinner and breakfast all at the same time. This afternoon and evening has been devoted to sack time and reading. I read a whole pocket book this afternoon, don't even remember the name. It was some murder mystery thriller, pulp stuff, but it was the only thing I could find in the trash can. Reading material is at a premium.

July 10, 1944

Here's a tidbit of news that may be of interest to you. We now have to sweat out thirty-five missions!

The cartoons you've been sending are a godsend. Keep them coming. We get a big kick out of them as they always manage to make us laugh and cheer us up when we're pretty low in spirit.

July 10

Doc Doxon, Copilot

At noon today we had a really rugged practice mission—sixty ships. What a wreck to fly to put on a good show for the colonel. We flew aircraft #8140, *The Pregnant Goose.*

Mission #3, Munich, Germany, July 11

Frank Dimit, Bombardier

This was our first pathfinder mission. We flew over an undercast the entire distance. Was damn glad they couldn't see us—heavy flak. Threw out window [aluminum strips] to deflect radar. Aiming point was center of town.

Climbed through 10,000 feet of overcast after takeoff to rendezvous. Sweating that out was worse than the mission. Plenty dangerous when several hundred other planes are circling through the soup to get to altitude.

Had to crank up bomb-bay doors. Helluva job at 24,000 feet. Learned two lessons: put up hand rails in bomb bay and have crank and extension in front end of plane. Had to walk catwalk with doors open again to get extension.

Crew performed perfectly. Great bunch of guys. With only three missions we all feel like veterans. *[End of mission notes by Frank Dimit]*

Roco Work, Navigator

Four days after their failure to get to Merseburg, Fletcher's crew was again routed into the predawn grayness. This day's briefing pleased them only because there were only thirty-two more missions to be flown—if they made it both ways! The briefing officer spoke fluently about what a favor we would be doing the Londoners if we creamed the target. The aiming point was an assembly building for robot motors used in the buzz bombs which had been causing some trouble in "southeastern England" the past month.

The target area was on the outskirts of Munich, with approximately three hundred guns guarding the city. The route as briefed led across some 150-odd heavy guns with a sharp break to left after bombs away in order for least exposure to flak. All the facts given, everyone scattered to see about his particular pre-mission duties.

Munich, which lies far south in Germany and less than fifty miles from the Swiss border, promised to be a plenty rough target. The route, while essentially flak-free, was a tortuous one because of the planners' attempts to do many things.

The problems are essentially as follows: First, the route must avoid, if possible, all known ground defenses with the exception of the target itself. Since nearly every city of any size had a vital industry to be protected, antiaircraft defenses made it mandatory that all large towns be skirted by at least six miles (normal range of flak at 20,000 feet). Second, it was hoped that the target wouldn't become obvious because the bomber stream was headed for Munich from the very start. So a few additional turns had to be inserted to keep enemy fighters from being gathered for a concerted attack. Last, and of primary importance for this mission, the route with all its twists and turns must be short enough to ensure that all the bombers would have sufficient fuel for the return trip.

As a result of all these problems for the planners, this route to Munich zigzagged with many turns through the flak areas of Holland, Belgium, and France before settling down to a more direct route to the target. That promised a particularly difficult day for the navigators since a solid undercast was expected over most of the distance.

When Frank got out to the ship he called the crew together and announced what he'd learned at his briefing: "Remember the 'Beer-Hall Putsch' that was in Munich? Well, HQ seems to think there are a lot more Nazi big-dogs there today. Regardless of the rules of civilized warfare we're out to kill Germans with these incendiary bombs! Our aiming point if it's blind bombing—which it probably will be— is the center of the city. We're going after arms, legs, and elbows!"

After the usual amount of sweating the boys finally discovered it was time to crawl into the ship and begin the day's work in earnest. All preparations completed they took off, climbed through about 10,000 feet of clouds and came out on top without event. Dimit didn't have any pins to pull this trip because those 500-pound incendiary clusters go off on general principles when they get to a preset altitude. That is, the cluster of fire bombs scatters and each individual bomb starts a separate fire, which is mighty hard to extinguish. Soon they'd gotten into position and the long haul across most of southern Germany had begun.

During the penetration Roco marveled anew at the navigation instruments which enabled this huge striking force to make good a narrow corridor between flak batteries even though a solid undercast prevented visual navigation. In a few minutes, however, he was too busy trying to keep track of where they were to worry about such fine points. As the target drew ever nearer on his map Roco decided to warn the crew about putting on their flak suits when they were ten minutes from the IP. At the start of the mission there was the normal chatter over the interphone that comes from youth setting out on a great adventure, but the nearer they got to the target, the less anyone had to say. After their fighter support had been identified no one said a word except for short answers to Dimit's checking to make sure everyone was all right.

At last the time came and Roco gave the warning that the IP was near. Fletch and Doc put on their flak helmets that Brownie handed to them. Both were sensitive to the fact that flak comes up from the ground. Therefore, they sat on their flak suits. At first thought this sounds silly, but they'd already found them too heavy and cumbersome to fly formation. Brownie, of course, had no suit to wear because the upper turret doesn't leave the room, but he did wear that helmet. George had discovered on the first mission that it was nearly impossible to toss out "chaff" with his suit on, so he spread his on the floor and knelt on it while he threw his bundles out the chute. Lynch was never very trusting, so he wore his parachute and flak suit both when they went down the bomb run. Powerful man, that Lynch lad. And Smitty in the tail somehow felt better dressed for the occasion so he wore his properly, too. Once the ship got on course Dimit was anchored in the nose. Only the strangest of circumstances could get him off his seat and the bomb run wasn't strange enough. Not half strange enough! Frank would twist around to fasten the shoulder straps for Roco, then Roco would stagger to his feet and make Frank's suit secure.

By the time these details had been attended to on the Munich trip it was time for Dimit to open the bomb bays. There was that rumble one could hear even above the roar of the engines—even on a practice mission the sound of the bomb-bay doors coming open sent chills up their spines. As they turned onto the bomb run a barrage of flak appeared in the sky ahead. Seen from this distance, the black smoke looked like a huge cloud; individual bursts were not distinguishable. "Remember we make a sharp left turn after bombs away, Fletch," Roco said, and then all was silence over the interphone.

Seconds ticked by and became minutes. Little by little the smoke pall broke up into small black smudges, and as the planes got nearer new bursts could be seen to appear over the target. Suddenly there was a mushrooming mass of flames in the middle of a preceding group of ships when some poor souls suffered a direct hit and the entire ship disappeared into thin air. All that remained was a larger smoke cloud and a few burning streamers floated earthward. At this distance the flak was fascinating to watch. They were close enough to be able to discern how each shell appeared as if by magic. Where there had been a clear space a second before there was a small puff of black smoke that rolled and spread before it eventually reached maximum size (about ten feet in diameter) and began to dissipate.

With each turn of the propellers the 95th sped nearer to what promised to be certain death, for it didn't seem possible that even one plane could penetrate the area, let alone thirty-six. And then they were under fire themselves. Sometimes near, sometimes far,

Flak and more flak

Plane shot down with tail trailing. Some stared death in the eye that day, but death blinked and chose another. *(95th B.G. Photo)*

the bursts appeared right among the ships. *Crump!* The plane lurched with the explosion as a shell burst somewhere near the left wing. In the space of a minute they flew through at least ten smoke clouds and the acrid odor of the powder became noticeable in the very oxygen they breathed. Lynch's eyes opened wide as he stared at a hole that appeared in the side of the waist. It missed him by at least two feet, but the suddenness of its appearance jerked him more vividly conscious of their danger.

Off to the left and slightly below them a plane wavered out from its position. Smitty watched with horrified eyes, expecting to see it blow up at any moment. But it returned to the formation almost immediately and he was somehow deliriously happy to see the recovery. As he watched the pilot feathered his left outboard engine, and Smitty could visualize him struggling to gain more power so the copilot who was flying could maintain position. Brownie had his turret facing forward so that he looked directly into the flak-filled skies before him. Even as he scanned the heavens for possible enemy fighters he saw a plane from another group begin to trail black smoke from a wing. Flames appeared, licking their way toward the fuselage, and Brownie could do nothing but watch as it became more and more evident that the crew of the plane above would have to bail out. And there they went, twisting and turning, one, two, three, four, five, before the ship slid out of formation and below his field of vision. Brownie closed his eyes to shut out the memory of what he'd seen, then murmured a prayer for them all.

"Bombs away!" That from Dimit when everyone had decided that the leader never would drop. George paused in his chaff throwing to make sure they'd all dropped out, then repeated, "Bombs away!" after which Frank started the doors closed. Already Fletch had pushed the throttles as far forward as they'd go and swerved to the left, following the leader who'd broken away toward the Rally Point. Everyone mentally got out and pushed to accelerate their progress toward the edge of the flak. And they were out of it in a few seconds, for the gunners below were more worried about the planes yet to bomb and let those who had already dropped proceed about their own business.

The Rally Point was reached and the 95th headed homeward. The air leader in the lead ship began calling the formation to tuck it in lest Jerry fighters continue the attack. None developed and soon the radio began to crackle out the bad news as men were heard telling about their troubles. Someone had a wounded navigator and two engines out. He needed fighter support to lead and protect him for he couldn't possibly keep up with his outfit. Another had a wing fire and the pilot was hoping to get over Switzerland before they had to bail out. At that precise moment Mac called Fletch to tell him there were several small holes in the bottom of the wing, and a little bit of gas seemed to be coming from one of them. "Okay, Mac, keep your eye on the leak and if it begins to look serious let me know," he answered. Then he gave the order that there would be no smoking on board the aircraft.

And so the long journey back to England had begun. The worst part of the trip was over (if fighters didn't attack, and it wasn't likely with the fine support those P-51s were giving) so the boys removed their flak suits and peered into out-of-the-way places for undiscovered holes. Roco announced that it would still be two hours before the Channel was reached and another forty-five minutes before they could get to their base. Even the long trip at altitude still to be undergone failed to dampen their spirits now, though, for they'd survived the flak and weren't much worried about anything for a while.

At short intervals more planes could be heard on the radio calling their formation leaders of their inability to keep up. One pilot reported that they had only fuel enough to reach the Channel so they'd have to jump. "This is Ozark P-Peter, will you attend to some personal items for us at the base?" "Go ahead, Ozark P-Peter, will do." "Ozark P-Peter. My navigator wishes you to destroy all letters and correspondence. Did you read?" "Roger, Ozark P-Peter, destroy all navigator's letters and correspondence." "Thank you. Ozark P-Peter, out!" And as coolly as that the pilot was telling everyone within range of his radio good-bye. If they were lucky they'd probably be German POWs; some might evade, but—

Finding his work pretty well caught up, Roco glanced out the window at the hundreds of airplanes around them. Suddenly struck by the size of the armada he started counting them. "Hey, you guys, I just counted better than 400 ships within sight right now. I'll bet Munich really took a clobbering today!" So it went. The time did pass by and finally he could tell them that the coast was only seven minutes away. Then across the Channel and back to their field and some chow. Wow, they'd been in the air nearly nine hours already! Time once again stood still in their minds, but eventually they could see their field ahead and preparations were made for the landing. In a few minutes they were on the ground. Interrogation, chow, read the *Stars and Stripes* and the new letters that had come during their absence, and then off to bed lest they be routed again in the morning.

Mission number three had been their first real toughie—lots of flak, with death on every side. The ship had over forty holes, but outside of a small leak in one tank, no damage worth worrying about had been done. Now the poor ground crew had a job to do, removing the wing and putting a new tank in the place of the punctured one. That ship wouldn't fly in the morning, but it would the day after! *[End of mission account by Roco Work]*

July 12, 1944

Life goes on around here the same as usual. Kinda in a rut, I guess. The sun comes up in the morning and sets late in the evening. The moon comes out for a couple of hours then gives way to the dawn—the endless cycle goes on. That's life in the ETO. Some days I work days and sleep nights and other times I work nights and sleep days. That, too, goes on in an endless cycle.

I'll give you a little tip. I'm not working for Uncle Sam any more. It's this way—I figure my training is paid for now. Any work they get from me from here on in they'll have to consider free gratis because no amount of money can compensate for what goes on.

Early July 12 we were briefed to go to Munich again, flying ship #7882, *Blues in the Reich*. The preflight went like clockwork, but at "start engine time" we couldn't get the #2 engine started. Both the ground crew and the flight crew became very frustrated. We tried everything possible, but it just wouldn't fire. In the end we watched the group take off without us. The one thing going through everyone's mind—was this a good or bad sign of things to come? But at least we had the whole day to reflect on this and the crew chief had a black mark on his record.

On every crew certain responsibilities were delegated to certain crew members. Not all crews used the same procedure we did, but as a result of our training experience and a couple of missions, I felt this to be the best for us. There would be some variation from time to time, but, basically, it followed this plan.

All crew members were considered to be observers. They were the eyes and ears of not only our airplane but also for the formation. If everyone was alert, collisions could be prevented and friendly and enemy fighters could be identified; in general, the whole welfare of the formation depended upon timely information from all observers.

The navigator, Robert ("Roco") Work, was the executive officer. His duties, in addition to his primary specialty of being responsible

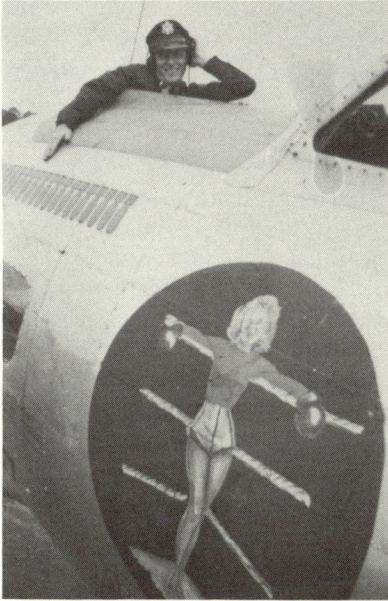

(Left) Robert Work, navigator. *(Right)* Frank Dimit, bombardier

for where the aircraft was and where it was going, included keeping the ship's log. He noted everything that took place on the mission, plus time and location. This was a very comprehensive report and was used to verify everything at interrogation. Some examples from the log might include where did we encounter fighters: how many; what were their maneuvers? Where and when would we encounter flak: how much; how accurate; tracking or barrage? What happened in our formation: did we see aircraft go down; where; what time; were any chutes seen? And what did we see on the ground and in the Channel? And on ad infinitum until the complete happening was recorded. Roco was assisted in this by the bombardier. He also checked out and returned all escape kits for the crew, and was responsible for his guns and their cleaning. It was a busy and thankless task, and he was rewarded only by the esteem in his own mind for a job well done.

The bombardier, Frank Dimit, was responsible for the bombs, their fusing and arming. He was assisted in this by the armorer gunner and other volunteer help. He was responsible for his guns and giving aid to the navigator. During the mission, at altitude, he initiated the crew check at fifteen-minute intervals, making sure everyone was physically okay, for a lack of oxygen could cause severe problems within minutes, while the victim would have a sense of well-being and euphoria. But of course his main job was what the mission was all about: to put the bombs on the target and do maximum damage to the enemy. He also performed other functions as needed—first aid and so on.

The copilot, Myron ("Doc") Doxon, and later, Billy Bob Layl, was second in command and also served as coordinator. He monitored the VHF radio and served as our voice link with the other aircraft in the formation, and with the base while we were still in range. He would summon fighters for people in trouble. Only the lead ships carried radio crystals tuned to the frequency used by our fighter escort, so we could communicate where help was needed. He took his turn at flying. We would alternate this duty, flying either fifteen-minute or half-hour shifts depending upon the stress of the type of flying we were doing and the condition of our airplane. He would also be available for any type of help that was needed in the cockpit or elsewhere in the aircraft.

The engineer, Ed ("Brownie") Brown, was really a jack-of-all-trades. He was our systems specialist, and gunner, and the ranking NCO of the crew. His was a job that could make or break a crew, and he carried his responsibility well. His knowledge of the aircraft saved our necks more than once. The things that he was called upon to do are far too numerous to mention, but he would troubleshoot every emergency on the plane. On takeoff and landings he sat on a belt seat between the copilot and pilot to help monitor the gauges and keep all systems within required limits. When he was not needed in the top turret, he was free to roam the aircraft aft of the forward compartment to check on the efficiency of the other crew members and to help with any special problems they might encounter.

The radio operator, George Hinman, whose primary duty was long-range communication, also had many secondary duties among which was manning guns, and from the Initial Point to the target and Rally Point it was he who dispensed "chaff" or "window" through a chute located in the radio room to the outside of the airplane. Chaff was aluminum foil cut in very thin strips and in varying lengths. It very much resembled the tinsel that is used to decorate Christmas trees. This would be dropped out of the airplane to sink toward the ground in hopes it would give false readings on the enemy radar, that was being used to track our progress and to aim the antiaircraft flak guns. The heavier the flak barrage the faster the radio operator would dispense the material. He had a good incentive! He was the second ranking NCO on the airplane and supervised the radio room and the waist of the ship, particularly the bomb bay at drop time. We

Myron "Doc" Doxon, copilot, seated on an aircraft towing tug

Billy Bob Layl, copilot for the last fifteen missions. Two good friends—the P-51, our little friend, and Layl

(Left) Edward Brown, aerial engineer and top turret gunner. *(Right)* George Hinman, radio operator, hanging on to antenna

needed to know if all bombs had dropped or whether we had a hung bomb or a no-drop. In either event, these bombs were dropped manually.

The left waist gunner, Robert Lynch, was also the armorer gunner. In addition to firing and maintaining his guns, he was responsible to the bombardier for the loading, fusing, and the eventual removal of the safety pins arming the bombs for the drop. He had a good working knowledge of the electrical bomb release system and he and the bombardier were the bomb and armorer specialists. All the people who were responsible for guns were required to be able to assemble them blindfolded.

The right waist gunner, Joe Firszt, was also a trained radio operator, and served as the assistant or back-up in case anything happened to Hinman. He was also trained as assistant engineer, so he found no trouble keeping busy on our crew since he could be assigned duties relating to three positions.

The ball turret gunner, Ken ("Mac") McQuitty, was our turret specialist. He was familiar with all turrets on the airplane, but his

(Left) Robert Lynch, armorer and left waist gunner. *(Right)* Joseph Firszt, right waist gunner

primary responsibility was to be found in his duties as gunner and observer. He had the only view directly under our aircraft to warn us of fighters or whether any other aircraft might drift under us on the bomb run. His was a lonely job as his only contact with other crew members came through the interphone system. In this respect he was like the tail gunner, the only other position that was isolated from the other crew members. In an emergency it would take time to get to either of these two men.

The primary concern of the tail gunner, Martin ("Smitty") Smith, was the tail turret and its two fifty-caliber machine guns. It was he who saw what was happening behind our aircraft, but he was too remote while we were in the air to have any additional duties. This isolated position had to be manned at all times.

I served as 1st pilot and aircraft commander. In this position I was responsible for everything that happened aboard this aircraft and its relationship to other aircraft in the formation. Only the 1st pilots attended four-engine specialized training in the B-17. It was up to the 1st pilot to teach the copilot all he knew about flying the aircraft

(*Left*) Kenneth McQuitty, ball turret gunner. (*Right*) Martin Smith, tail gunner

and its systems. He had to do the job well, for if the 1st pilot were incapacitated, the aircraft with all its responsibilities would then fall on the copilot's shoulders. All 1st pilots and copilots were given a certain amount of gunnery training—not as much as the gunners, but enough to understand their problems and to fire a gun if necessary. All pilots were given navigational training and were very adept at some forms of navigation, particularly radio navigation. But when it came to celestial, dead reckoning, and other forms, we knew only enough to understand what the navigator was doing. All pilots in Cadet School were taught code and had to receive and send at least twenty words a minute to be able to graduate. But this is one job we were happy to leave to a man who was much more proficient, the radio operator. The pilots also spent some time training on the bomb trainer, but this was only enough to make us understand the problems of the bombardier and to make sure we would provide him with a stable platform from which to do his job, which, after all, was the whole point of the mission.

Flying the airplane should be routine for the two pilots. This we

Eugene Fletcher, 1st pilot or
Aircraft Commander

should do by instinct and second nature from the countless hours of practice in flying and emergency procedures. This left our minds free to grasp the "big picture" and be concerned with all that was going on around us. Matters of judgment involving split-second decisions had to be made, and most of the time there would not be a second chance.

Thus it was that it took every one of us performing at our best to fly a successful mission. A bomber crew truly was the sum of its parts, and everyone strove to do his very best.

July 13

Doc Doxon, Copilot

We got stuck with a practice mission, drew ship #8140, *The Pregnant Goose,* definitely not our choice. The crew was highly POed. But Maggie's Drawers wave tonight. We have been assigned aircraft #7882 again—sure hope she starts in the morning. The weather was far from perfect today.

July 14, 1944

I will say we aren't recruits any longer in the true sense of the word. We know what the score is!! We got the real McCoy from the start. We all started together and we will all finish together.

Now I'll let you in on a few secrets of the crew. You know they've been sweating out the addition to my family. Well, as soon as they see me over the hump we have to start sweating Hinman whose wife is expecting in November or December, I forget which. Then after we pull him through we'll go to work on Brown who has only recently received the glad news that he too will be a papa. It looks like all the married men on the crew are destined to be family men. Everybody's 100 percent except poor Smitty. He did his best, but his wife had the same misfortune Sis once had. But it won't be long until we'll have him home and he can try again.

You asked me to have fun and see all of England that I can. There's really no place to go except London. Transportation is very poor and food is scarce. I've already seen London and the English countryside. Off the post there is no means of entertainment or amusement. Things over here are very austere—there are shortages of everything. It very definitely is not like the U.S. where, in spite of rationing, most things are still available. Whenever we eat away from the post or share tea and crumpets with the local people on the train we have the feeling we are taking something away from them, of which they have very little. Nevertheless, we do accept some of their offerings because we have no desire to insult their generosity, and they are doing their best to be good hosts in some very trying times. The ones we have met have to be very brave souls to carry on the way they do after all they've been through and still have a sharing nature. Maybe you can see now why we are content to remain on the post to see a show, eat, and log sack time.

I have a pass coming in a few days, I hope, then I'm going to some other posts and try to look up some friends. Don't worry, by now I've seen more than just England and somehow sightseeing just doesn't appeal to me— maybe it's the hostile reception.

Mission #4, *Maquis, France, July 14*

Frank Dimit, Bombardier

Very secret mission. 95th Group made up the entire wing today of three groups. We dropped enough supplies to equip 10,000 men. (Free French Force of 50,000 men.)

This is one mission we won't forget, doing a little good for a change.

Frenchmen seemed damn glad to get supplies the way they shouted and waved.

Saw no flak or enemy fighters. Fighter escort swell.

Hope we never have to take off at night again. Took off at 3:47 a.m. and it was pitch black. Climbing through that was worse than climbing to rendezvous through overcast. Really sweated it out, worst part of the mission. [*End of mission notes by Frank Dimit*]

Roco Work, Navigator

Our next trip out was the first one where we felt we'd really accomplished something. It was unique in that we were aroused earlier for the briefing than any other mission we ever flew—0030. At the briefing we learned what we'd hoped to be true, that our group had again been picked to drop supplies to the "maquis" by parachute. The canisters on the ships contained nearly everything up to the famous "jeep": pistols, rifles, bazookas, ammunition, medical supplies, etc. Our target was in far southern France, along the banks of the Dordogne River about sixty miles directly east of Bordeaux. It was planned that we'd cross into France, just skirting the bottleneck at Caen, at an altitude of 17,000 feet. Proceeding well beyond the advance units of our armies who were still struggling on the Cherbourg peninsula, we were to begin a descent in sufficient time that we'd be only a few hundred feet above the ground when we released the containers. This was so positive target identification could be managed and so the supplies would not be too badly scattered before the maquis got them collected.

Taking off at 0345 we chattered happily to one another over the interphone, overcome with delight that we could add another mission without undergoing dangerous flak. In a fairly short while all elements of the formation were in position and the time came for us to depart over the southern coast of England. As usual there was a pretty thick cloud layer over the Isles that day so we couldn't see a thing below us until we were well out over the Channel. Even then there were too many clouds for us to catch more than an occasional glimpse of what we had most wanted to see—the small portion of France that had been captured from the Germans.

But as the planes droned steadily onward the breaks below became more and more frequent until by the time we were two hours from the target it was CAVU [ceiling and visibility unlimited] from the ground up. The descent began as scheduled and every man stirred uncomfortably with the thought of what Jerry fighters could do to the outfit if they suddenly attacked at this lower altitude. Of course there were plenty of those "Little Friends" around, but it's always possible for a stray enemy fighter to sneak in when least expected. Down and down the formation went. Soon everyone had removed his oxygen mask and laid it aside for the time being. Soon the planes were so low that it became uncomfortably warm in our heavy flying suits, but there wasn't the time to change for the target was only twenty minutes away. At this altitude the war seemed far away and quite unreal. There were few military installations this far south in France and the weight of Allied bombs had not destroyed the beauty of the countryside.

Because of the nature of their underground work the maquis had to operate from out-of-the-way headquarters, as far from any German units as possible. Similarly, to avoid having the supplies fall into German hands they had to choose relatively inaccessible places for the drops. In case German spotters saw us flying at that low altitude it wouldn't take them long to decide that something of the sort was going on and they'd be sure to do everything in their power to intercept the canisters. Specific signals had been arranged and markers erected so we wouldn't have too much trouble finding the exact spot to drop.

In due time the IP was reached and we made a false run over the target area with bomb doors closed to make sure that the lead bombardiers had located where they were to drop. Sure enough, there were the bonfires and markers laid out on the plateau exactly where we'd been told they'd be. Circling to approach from the proper direction we opened the doors and tightened up the formations so the canisters wouldn't be too badly scattered. Frank hunched forward on his seat so he'd be sure to toggle our load at the same time as the leader. Everyone else scanned the skies at intervals to make sure no Jerries would catch us with our doors down. In between we eagerly scoured the countryside for glimpses of our secret allies below. French peasants ran from their homes as we roared overhead, cattle scattered, chickens ran this way and that, every living creature abruptly reacted to the unusual occasion.

On one farm we could see a farmer stop his plowing to shade his eyes from the sun and gaze at us. When we were near enough that he could see the insignia on our wings his arms went over his head in a wave. Soon we were so close we could actually recognize the fact that he was smiling and cheering us. Just as our plane passed over his head he removed his hat and the last glimpse I had of him brought tears to my eyes. This Frenchman, in far southern France, had crossed himself and stood with his hat over his heart as if he were saluting us, then his head bowed down, seemingly in prayer.

When Frank sang out his "Bombs away" over the interphone I jerked out of the reverie I'd slipped into when watching the farmer beneath us. The doors came closed and we circled once more to see where the canisters had fallen. Hundreds of men were running across the fields toward the dropping area and several trucks appeared from nowhere to move these supplies to a safer spot. By the time our formation had been regrouped for the return flight some of the trucks had already been filled and were driving off down the twisting trails to some hiding place even farther removed from prying Nazi eyes.

Nothing particularly eventful occurred on the climb to altitude, and even though we'd been flying for five hours already we weren't very tired. The interphone was buzzing with comments of the occasion just passed and time flew by as swiftly as the aircraft in which we were flying. Soon I realized how close we were to the invasion coast and prodded the boys to quiet down and get back on the job of watching for enemy action. There was always the possibility that there would be some activity near the lines. Our hopes of a clear view of the battle area were dampened considerably when clouds appeared ahead of and below us. Soon we were again over a solid cloud bank and started across the Channel to England.

As we neared our base there were a few breaks beneath so we didn't worry about having to let down through the clouds. Right over the field we flew and the peel-off began. In due time we were on the ground and back at our hardstand. Our spirits were high after this mission: no flak, no fighters, no trouble of any kind. The former missions were negative in our minds because we'd had to destroy something. On this particular trip we were lending aid to what later proved to be an extremely valuable band of allies. Every minute of sleep that had been lost the night before was gladly forgotten, and the fatigue from the long flight was as nothing. For on today's trip against the enemy we had done a real job and done it well. *[End of mission account by Roco Work]*

Mission #5, Paris, France, July 17

Frank Dimit, Bombardier

Briefed at 3:30 a.m. for target on Yonne River about 60 miles southeast of Paris. It was a three-track concrete railroad bridge. Takeoff was set back one hour to 7 a.m. because of light ground fog and our fighter escort could not leave ground.

Carried 2 2,000-pound bombs and flew #5 in the lead squadron of lead group. 95th put up an entire wing again. Target was creamed but good. Encountered moderate but inaccurate flak. Intelligence wasn't sure of flak gun emplacements, but we sure found them.

Saw no enemy fighters—had good escort.

Had rough time on letdown over England. Area covered by thick, low clouds. Ran into several traffic patterns of other fields getting back to our own base.

Swell day for intelligence observations. Boys picked up several interesting notes on marshalling yards, a truck convoy, and an airfield, besides flak gun emplacements.

Picked up some swing music on radio on way home. Listened to it over France and Belgium. Strange way to fight a war. *[End of mission notes by Frank Dimit]*

Roco Work, Navigator

Mission number 5 came up three days later in direct support of the ground troops, although this fact wasn't made clear until later in the summer when Patton's tanks made their drive across France. The target was a railroad bridge over the Yonne River about eighty miles southeast of Paris and forty miles southwest of Trayes. The nearest town of any size is Sens, France, a town of about 30,000 before the war.

Perhaps the outstanding feature of this mission as far as Fletcher's crew is concerned was the absence of any flak batteries in the target area. The usual prebriefing and postbriefing duties were performed with the same meticulous care that characterized the preparations for every mission. Guns were loaded, flak suits were counted, oxygen pressure verified, etc. All the innumerable small tasks were done.

Once aloft everyone kept an apprehensive lookout for other aircraft, for over England—America's largest aircraft carrier—there is an everpresent danger of collision. However rendezvous altitude was reached without any incident worse than an occasional jousting due to prop wash.

No one who hasn't spent many hours in the air can realize what a potent force this prop wash can be. It originates, of course, as a wind created by the rapidly turning propellers. The terrific thrust of the blades causes the air to swirl and twist in all directions, at a high velocity. If one tosses a matchstick upon surging water, he naturally expects it to be buffeted about by the changing currents on which it floats. That is precisely the same in the air. A plane's wings, which for all general purposes could be said to float on the air, are also tossed about by the unsettled air through which they pass. Severe downdrafts caused by whirling props will drop one wing of a B-17 like pulling the plug in a wash basin. This boiling, twisting air extends back of a propeller for a considerable distance until it eventually loses force. In the case of a B-17, the four propellers cause a terrific mass of turbulent air.

When flying into prop wash a wide-awake pilot can always prevent disaster. At the first brush with the wash, the wing tip trembles noticeably and gives a warning of what may come. The main lifting surface of the wing is in smooth air, but the tip has penetrated this surging air mass and flutters in response to the unsteady air. As soon as enough of the wing has gotten into the prop wash to cause instability in flight the pilot must make instantaneous corrections to return to level flight. Fletch was that sort of a pilot—it takes brains, not brawn, to fly a four-engine bomber. At the first hint of trouble Fletch and Doc coordinated beautifully to counteract the danger. No sooner would the left wing start to drop than they had full opposite aileron applied to lift it.

The greatest danger from prop wash lies in the possibility of midair collision while out of control. When flying close formation such as is used in the fight against Germany, a violent change of attitude caused by prop wash may put a bomber directly in the path of a nearby plane. Just split seconds could find two or more planes locked in collision.

To return to mission number 5—No troubles were experienced during rendezvous so Frank crawled back to remove the pins from the two 2,000-pound bombs we planned to drop on that bridge. Out over the Channel they proceeded, crossing the coast into Holland over an island at the mouth of the Rhine. South past Antwerp and Brussels they roared, drawing intermittent flak barrages from batteries just off course to either side.

On this mission our boys were flying *Full House,* so named because of the numbers 97797 on the tail. The route to the IP was short and quite soon that spine-chilling rumble caused by the open bomb-bay doors could be heard above the engines' thunder. The squadrons peeled off to make the run and George started tossing out his chaff in case some unexpected railroad guns were encountered.

Without a burst appearing in the sky the group made the run, Frank made his singing "Bombs away," and the squadron turned off to the Rally Point. From there the group swung back over the target to more accurately assess the damage. The bomb smoke had completely obscured the bridge from sight so they knew the bombing had been a success.

Skirting the heavily defended area around Paris, the group headed homeward and returned to its base without incident. Once again Fletcher's crew had flown against the Hun—this time for seven hours—and encountered no troubles. Now there were but thirty to go; the tour was 14 percent completed. *[End of mission account by Roco Work]*

July 17, 1944

You know the letter I promised you? Well, I'm really sorry but I'll have to beg off again this evening. I have a delivery to make in the morning so I should go to bed early. I hope you understand and will forgive me. When I got home from today's work there were two more wonderful letters waiting for me. They were dated June 3rd and June 5th.

Mission #6 Hemmingstedt, Germany, July 18

Frank Dimit, Bombardier

Briefed at 2:15 a.m. for target in Germany. Target was an oil refinery on eastern side of Denmark peninsula, about 40 miles southeast of Kiel (Hemmingstedt). Carried 10 500-pound demolition bombs.

Flew as a spare, but soon found a position in the formation—ended up at #3 position in first element of low squadron. Flight time was seven hours. . . .

Saw no enemy fighters and very little flak—not very accurate. Hinman threw out chaff. Had P-51 escort.

Listened to German symphony music on way back. Some war—take music appreciation course and give Germans hell, all at the same time. *[End of mission notes by Frank Dimit]*

Roco Work, Navigator

Next morning early we were routed out again and, after the usual egg breakfast, found our way to the briefing room. When the curtain was pulled back we greeted the target with sighs of satisfaction, for there was no flak evident during the entire mission. As the briefing officer began to give us the story of the day's attack, we grew slightly less elated, however. It seemed that the primary target to be hit by visual methods only was Hemmingstedt, a small town on the Danish peninsula. There we hoped our bombs would find some underground storage tanks for oil. And at that target there were no known flak guns.

The rub came on the secondary, which we were to attack in case the weather did not permit visual sightings. Instead of dropping on the primary target by PFF as we usually did, we were instructed to continue on to Kiel and bomb the dock area. The entire Kiel area contained about 150 heavy guns and we had no desire to test the accuracy of their radar. So naturally we all prayed for visual conditions over Hemmingstedt; the weather man, incidentally, forecast that there was a fifty-fifty chance of going in without cloud coverage.

After everyone had attended to his own particular postbriefing duties we gathered in the ground crew's tent to discuss our prospects for the day. Overhead there wasn't even a suggestion of a cloud and we hoped strongly that similar conditions would prevail on the Danish peninsula. Eventually takeoff time drew nearer and we piled into the ship for our last-minute checks. In a few minutes we taxied out on the perimeter in position. The usual gnawing in our stomachs caused by other reasons than hunger began to make itself known, and then everyone crossed his fingers as Fletch poured the coal on and we started down the runway.

As usual we were airborne without the slightest bit of difficulty and shortly found our place in the formation circling the field at 13,000 feet. Right on time we departed for wing and division assembly, and our coast out point, Great Yarmouth, was hit on the nose. Climbing over the North Sea we went to coordinates 5400-0500, 5415-0700, and proceeded toward the RP at 5420-0837. Suddenly Doc came on the interphone to tell us that our air leader, Colonel McKnight, had established contact with the weather ship and had been informed that the primary was completely cloud-covered. At this time all of us began sweating, for we certainly didn't fancy the thought of going on to Kiel. Within ten minutes, though, Fletch came on to inform us that the decision had been reached to attack the primary on PFF instead of going on to Kiel. The reason for the change of plans didn't matter in the least, so long as it was true.

By DR (dead reckoning) I could tell we were quite near the IP and I decided not to trust the information given to our briefing officer. Maybe HQ didn't think there were any guns at Hemmingstedt, but I, personally, wasn't going to place too much credence on it. So I announced over the interphone that I was putting on my flak suit and everyone seemed to think the suggestion worthwhile. When Frank opened the bomb-bay doors there wasn't a hint of flak ahead, and below there was nothing but a sea of white clouds. For all we could tell looking down we might have been over the North Sea yet.

At the turn on the bomb run we all tensed up as always and debated with ourselves our judgment in joining the Air Corps. Nothing happened to back up our momentary indecision, though, and Frank sang out that welcome "Bombs away!" without our even seeing a burst of flak off in the distance. We made the RP good and headed westward on the way home, congratulating ourselves on not being shot at for the third straight time when Smitty announced none too calmly that where we had just been there was now a large cloud of smoke in the sky. Flak had suddenly started coming up and we felt quite happy that we had been the first ones over the target and were not just now bombing. Sometimes a group is lucky that way; the gunners on the ground are a little slow in starting to fire and the run can be made without a bit of flak. Then, just as the turn off the bomb run is made, the bursts begin to appear.

Evidently we had caught the flak gunners napping this morning. At our tender altitude of 18,000 feet, we'd have been pretty easy marks, too.

Then Smitty came back on the interphone to tell us that dense clouds of black smoke were rising through the clouds where we had bombed. Evidently our PFF attack had been accurate, for there was little doubt that the smoke was caused by burning oil. Rising to approximately 10,000 feet, the heavy smoke made us even happier than before. Now we not only had credit for another mission in the bag without going through any dangerous flak, but also all indications pointed toward success in the bombing.

On toward England we flew and below us the clouds began to dissipate in direct contrast to the way they had acted a couple of days before. Instead of clear weather over the Continent and messy stuff hovering over the Isles, we were amazed to see better conditions over Great Britain than we had seen in the vicinity of northern Germany. There's no accounting for the oddities that occur in Europe!

And so we returned safely to the base with the knowledge that there was now one less mission to be flown. Upon finishing interrogation and having a bite to eat at the mess hall we wandered back to the squadron area where we learned that we had finally earned a pass. For the next forty-eight hours our time would be our own. Plans were formulated in a hurry; we would all go to London together and any deviations from the party would take place there. But this is a story of combat in the air. The battling with "Piccadilly Commandoes" is an entirely different story! *[End of mission notes by Roco Work]*

July 22, 1944

Here I am back again. As you've probably guessed I did get my pass. We took off for London and had quite a time. Met a lot of fellows whom I knew and had been wondering about. . . . We had lots of fun discussing our present situation and swapping bits of combat news—where and what we'd been doing. Each knew where some other buddy was and what had happened to him, although all the news wasn't good. It was good to find out what goes on some place besides your own. I will again say that I'm darned glad I'm with the outfit I am.

Now getting back to London—we saw the Changing of the Guard at Buckingham Palace and lots of points of interest including Piccadilly. We found a place where we could get a steak. It's called the Athens Cafe. We all suspect that it was horse meat but no one mentions it because, after all, a steak is a steak! I've never seen anything quite like this here and hope not to see it again—you have your life in your hands with Jerry overhead.

I think I've just made my last trip to London. No, I take it back. I'll have to go once more to pick up a battle jacket which I'm having made. What I started to say was that I'm too allergic to Doodle Bugs [buzz bombs] to spend much more time there. Now let me tell you about our battle jackets which the four of us are having made. First, we bought new blouses so we could have the material. . . . The tailor says we can get them in about three weeks. All four are the same. Boy, wait until you see them, they'll knock your eyes out! The cost is a little over ten pounds ten shillings, or about forty-two dollars American. This includes wings, patches, bars, and combat ribbons all embroidered on.

Last night when we got back there were eight letters waiting for me and today I received five more. Maybe you think I haven't been having a field day reading all my mail!

While we were in London we stayed at the Regents Palace Hotel, and during the night the top two floors were heavily damaged during a raid, giving us all a good scare. Consequently, London lost a lot of its glamor. Now about our Ike jackets—we had them lined with fiery red silk. This was not visible from the outside, but was flashy when the jackets were removed. Besides, we knew it was there when we wore them, and this was our way of expressing pride and loyalty to the 95th Bomb Group, whose radio call sign was "Fireball Red." That name always sent a tingle down our spines when we heard it used on the radio on our way home from the target. Absolute radio silence was maintained on the way to the target, but coming home emergency transmissions were permissible to summon fighter protection for those returning home alone, or to effect a rendezvous of cripples so they might travel home together for mutual protection. There was a time coming home on three engines when Doc and I put together a formation of ten cripples from different groups, complete with fighter protection and flying along at 130 mph with old "Fireball Red Leader" bringing them home.

Mission #7 St. Lo, France, July 24

Frank Dimit, Bombardier

Rather unusual mission all the way round. Briefed at 8:00 a.m. We were to bomb inside our own lines. Our troops had withdrawn 1,500 yards in order to give us a chance to blast an opening in the German lines. This direct support of ground forces by the heavies had worked around Caen and we were hoping it would work here. The group carried 100-pound demos and 20-pound frags. Our ship carried 38 clusters of 6 20-pound fragmentation bombs.

Had to climb through overcast again today. Target was clouded over so we didn't drop the bombs. We looked for target of opportunity, but no go. Had to bring bombs back. We flew #6 in lead squadron of the high group of the wing. Were supposed to fill in diamond of high squadron, but after an abort, we filled in this spot.

Had trouble with bomb-bay doors again.

Saw first ship go down in flames. First wing over caught hellish flak after dropping bombs. Plane evidently caught direct hit. Hard to explain feeling it gives you, but you wish to hell you were back at the base.

Work didn't fly with us. Lead ships were the only ones to carry navigators. *[End of mission notes by Frank Dimit]*

July 25, 1944

It has been a busy two days in the ETO. Some new deal—they're making me earn my money now. I don't think it's here to stay, though, should pass in a few days.

*I can't tell you what I did this morning, but this evening we were pre-
sented the Air Medal, which was recently earned by the crew. As soon as
time permits I will mail it on to you. . . .*

Mission #8, *St. Lo, France, July 25*

Frank Dimit, Bombardier

Same mission today as yesterday. Briefed at 5:00 a.m. Same target,
same load. We flew in #2 position of low squadron of the high group
of wing.

We went in at 12,000 feet—plenty of haze and fog. Tried to go in
at 16,000 feet but couldn't see the target. Don't know how much
damage we did, but we'll find out soon. No write-up about this
support in papers. Guess they want to keep it quiet.

Bob Work didn't fly again so I had to double in navigation.

Bomb-bay door motor burned out before we took off so had to
crank doors both ways.

Fiess flew on the left wing in #3 slot. They picked up a little flak
(25 holes). We didn't get a scratch. Flak was light and accurate.

Sgt. Wilson just came in and we are to receive our Air Medals
tonight at 6:30. So I guess we'd better clean up for the Colonel. *[End
of mission notes by Frank Dimit]*

On July 24 the Eighth Air Force was called upon to act as forward
artillery for the ground troops trying to break out at St. Lo. When
we reached the target area we had a solid undercast. Since we couldn't
see we didn't bomb. The bomb-bay doors were closed and we brought
our bombs home. The base was a beehive of activity—planes to be
serviced, repaired, refueled, and made ready—for we would try again
tomorrow.

On July 25 we were given the same briefing as the day before
which was essentially this: "Since you are bombing in close proximity to the front lines every precaution must be taken to protect
our own ground troops. Your bombs must not be released until you
are sure you have passed across our own troops. The distance will
be measured not in miles, but in yards."

With the equipment we had—and some common sense—we could
protect our own people and still inflict heavy damage on the enemy,
as well as demoralize those who would survive. This would be a
shining hour for the Eighth, and we would prove that heavy bombers
could be used in close support of ground troops.

On our base the briefing people were thorough and the law was laid down, "If you don't know where you are, don't bomb. Bring them back the same as yesterday. There will be no mistakes. Everything must be on the safe side or you will endanger the lives of our own troops. There is an absolute safeguard built in—this will involve your ILAS equipment in the aircraft."

The ILAS (Instrument Landing Approach System) is a radio beam which normally would be sent down the middle of a runway for the pilots to line up on for the final approach to a landing. This system is very accurate and can pinpoint the center of a runway. Today the narrow radio signal would be transmitted down no-man's-land between the opposing forces.

In the aircraft the pilot has a radio receiver connected to a round gauge with a needle in the center. The needle is hinged at the bottom. The gauge is divided in two—one half is yellow and one half is blue. When you are exactly on course to the runway the needle is centered between the two halves. If you stray only a few feet right or left the needle will move into the corresponding quadrant and you must make immediate correction to center the needle.

But this day instead of flying down the beam we would fly across it, which means that the needle would stay in one quadrant, gradually moving closer to the center. When the plane crossed the beam the needle would cross the center line and be in the opposite quadrant. You then would know positively that you had crossed the line, or the beam, that separates the two forces.

"There may be broken clouds over the front lines, so all bombing will be done by group lead aircraft using PFF, Mickey Radar ships," the briefing officers told us. "All other ships will toggle their bombs out when they see the lead ship bomb. The lead ship will follow the normal practice of dropping two smoke bombs. When you see the two smoke bombs and your ILAS needle is in the proper quadrant then drop. Don't guess. Drop only if all things check out. It is very simple, all you have to do is follow the directions.

"You will not take your navigators with you as this is a short run and all navigation will be done by the lead ships. Fly a tight formation so the bomb patterns will be precise. Bombing will be done at 16,000 feet. There will be very little if any enemy resistance. You will be over enemy territory no more than a half hour or so."

Our group was in the first third of the task force, so we were able to see whether we would encounter serious enemy opposition before we reached the target.

Everything went as scheduled—all rendezvous were made on time. There were breaks in the undercast just as we made landfall on the

Squadron flying through smoke trails from the lead ship and bombs exploding on target in center of photo *(95th B.G. photo)*

French coast. As we started on the bomb run, with the bomb-bay doors open, the task force's lead groups were already heading home. The opposition was very light.

We were beginning to fly past the smoke trails of the preceding lead groups—long plumes in groups of two starting from bombing altitude and arcing toward the ground for several thousand feet. This could give the false impression that you were past where someone else had already bombed, if you forgot about drift.

The bombardier called and asked which quadrant our ILAS needle was pointing to. We replied that we still showed over friendly troops, but it was gradually moving to center. He pointed out that we must have a slight head wind because some of the smoke trails were now rather far behind us. Within a couple of minutes the needle moved into the enemy quadrant and we notified our bombardier that everything was "go" as soon as he got the signal from the lead ship. In less than a minute the lead ship, with two smoke bombs arching out, dropped its bomb load. Our bombardier dropped on the smoke signal, closed the bomb-bay doors, and the group headed for home.

We could now see the following groups coming in as we were going out. It was a tremendous sight—both the incoming and the outgoing groups stretching for miles. The heavens roared with 3,000 aircraft: bombers, medium and heavy, fighters, reconnaissance, and ships of every description. For the people on the ground, with the engine noise from the constant bomber stream overhead and the bombs exploding in close proximity of the lines, the shock of the noise alone had to be terrific and terrifying.

We had to feel good because everything had gone perfectly. Jerry was catching hell. We had achieved the purpose of our mission. When we landed everyone was tired but happy.

Toward evening we learned that a tragedy of mind-boggling proportions had occurred. Some errant group of a later task force of the Eighth or Ninth Air Force had dropped their bombs while still over the forward lines of the assaulting American troops. A general was killed along with many other American troops. An Associated Press cameraman from Detroit also became a casualty. The picture from his camera later was published in *Yank* showing this "Hell on Earth" in action. Ernie Pyle, the famous war correspondent, wrote a very touching story of the agony on the ground and the probable feelings of the air crews in England that night as they learned of the tragedy that had been left in their wake. Since what he wrote in conjecture was, in essence, the true feelings of the air crews, I only hope he learned the truth of his writing before his own demise.

We were sick. Everyone shared in the anguish along with those who were derelict. We had never seen a malfunction where a lead ship would drop early. A malfunction occasionally caused a "no drop." It was very hard to imagine any case where equipment failure could do this without human error present. But in battle nothing is impossible.

I do not know the official version of what happened, but I do know that a rumor immediately surfaced in which a lead bombardier was supposedly influenced while flying through the drifting smoke trails from other lead ships to conclude that he was now over enemy territory, and dropped his bombs in spite of the fierce opposition from his fellow crew members. When the bombs from this lead ship dropped, the others in the unit did likewise.

This was a rumor, but it was plausible. Equipment malfunction, human error, guilt or innocence, rumor or fact—these were out of our province and in the hands of those in the higher echelons.

For us it was saddening that it had to happen, and we would not know how or why. But such is war. Not all things are reasonable or even explainable. But, grief aside, viewed in the light of expendability which applied to all of us, the casualties were far less than if air power—even though fallible—hadn't been used.

July 27, 1944

Life here the last two days has been no different than usual—very peaceful, very quiet, and definitely no excitement to speak of. Back in the same old rut with plenty of sack time. I'm getting to the point where I can sleep for fifteen hours straight without once being interrupted. Not bad, huh! . . .

July 27

Doc Doxon, Copilot

Alerted again. This time we had the engines started before the mission was scrubbed. Must have been weather. Lightning struck the outhouse with Baird in it.

Mission #9, Merseburg, Germany (Leuna Oil Refinery), July 28

Frank Dimit, Bombardier

Fiess's crew flew in the formation with us today. Overcast all the way in and out. Navigating damn difficult. Thank goodness weather information was right on the money.

Hit intense and very accurate flak at Kassel, Germany. Damn near got us. Someone had to be looking after us. Flak bursts were so close to nose I thought it would blow it off. Bob Work did wonderful job of navigating. Entire crew was great.

Fighters looked damn good on way out. Had three P-51s escorting us. I'd like to spend my next pass buying drinks for our little friends. Great bunch.

Skies of Germany are a mighty lonesome place for one B-17. Have never been so lonesome and scared before. Nine men against the Third Reich isn't good.

Group came back from target shot to hell and with several wounded on board. Some never got back. It was a rough mission. Hope they creamed target and we don't have to go back again. Needless to say, our crew is very happy to get back. *[End of mission notes by Frank Dimit]*

July 28

Doc Doxon, Copilot

We almost made it to Stalag Luft today—three hours out of Germany alone. Boy what a lonesome sky. Those 51s are sure pretty when you are alone.

Roco Work, Navigator

Upon our return to operations ten days later we felt pretty good about this business of fighting a war. Shucks, hadn't we just completed six comparatively easy missions? What is there to worry about? At briefing we found out. Merseburg was the order for the day. By now we had a healthy respect for the place even though we had never reached the target. Enough of our friends had returned from that devastating flak and told us about it so that we shivered in our boots at the mere thought. Nevertheless, that's how things stood and the regular preliminaries done with we found ourselves at 20,000 feet over Cromer, departing England on course and on time.

Flying number five in the high squadron of the high group made us feel no better than if we were "tail-end Charlie." When Merseburg is the target one might as well be sick in the hospital! At any rate, with many uncomfortable thoughts running through our heads we proceeded on into Germany and gave thanks for the solid undercast beneath. It's true the navigation would be more difficult, but everyone knew the Jerry flak gunners weren't nearly as accurate, either, and that seemed more important. One hundred ninety guns were all we were briefed on, but past battle damage suffered at Merseburg led us to strongly doubt the correctness of the report.

Suddenly, when still about fifteen minutes from the IP, Dimit tapped me on the shoulder to arouse me from trying to figure our ground speed and pointed at a formation which was fast disappearing in the distance. Grumpily I asked him, "So what?" His reply shocked me considerably, "So that's our group!" Looking out the right window I could see the reason. Number four engine was feathered and then I knew Fletch couldn't keep up on the three engines remaining. Group after group passed us in short order and finally Fletch was forced to give up his efforts to stay even faintly near our outfit or to join another. Doc was already calling for fighter protection over VHF when Fletch told Dimit to salvo the bombs. His answer will be always remembered as one of the most bloodthirsty utterances ever to pass through the lips of our noble bombardier: "But, Fletch, can't I toggle them out one at a time? They'll do more damage that way!"

So saying, Frank opened the bomb bays and sent ten 500-pounders—one at a time—screaming down into the undercast. Doc cut in to tell us three P-51s had been dispatched from the escorting force to give support on the way home. I couldn't be sure of our position because of the clouds below, but approximated it to be 5111-1010 and planned my course accordingly. "Better make a 180 to the right, Fletch," I said, and was startled to see that we were already in a turn to the left. Pilots seem to be reluctant to turn into a dead engine.

"The chances are that we'll come out of this turn right over Kassel, old boy," I warned him, but our course had already been committed. "The fighters asked me to turn to the left," he said, and I muttered a disparaging remark about our being the ones who'd have to tool through the flak and not them. However, everything seemed all right for a couple of minutes until Frank suddenly yelled out that we were approaching a large town and would pass right over it. At that precise moment all hell broke loose!

Huge puffs of smoke gave evidence to our nearness to several flak bursts. We went into violent evasive action as Fletch attempted to throw the plane clear of the danger by sheer strength. Heeding my plea to end up on a 180 degree heading he continued to wrench the controls until our B-17 groaned in protest. That flak was really close, and the flame of the explosions could be seen easily. Our "little friends" had scattered at the first indication of what was to come and they were now riding comfortably out of range on our left. Finally we got out of range, but our nerves were a wreck. No one had been hurt, miraculously enough, but we could see several holes in the wings and fuselage.

The flak served one good purpose, however. Now there was no doubt in my mind where we were. So I immediately set to work from that point while Doc, who'd taken over the controls, flew the heading I'd given before our "incident." Feverishly I figured and plotted, interspersing my efforts with longing glances out of the window hoping to see the ground long enough to get a visual checkpoint to verify my work. None appeared, though, and we kept on at a slow 130 mph due to the feathered prop. After checking and rechecking my work I told Doc that we should turn northwest to go through the flak corridor between Liège and Brussels in about five minutes.

Just afterwards Frank informed me that there were some sizable openings in the clouds up ahead and I immediately began scouring the ground for some recognizable point. Right when I had about given up in despair the clouds opened wider and I could see a junction of a railroad and a highway near a small town with a stream running off to the south. I asked Frank if he thought it was the same place I'd previously marked on my map as our turning point. After considerable scrutiny of the map and countryside below he nodded his assent and I glanced at my watch as I was calling Doc to take up the new heading. Not bad, I thought, only a minute and a half off my calculations. The credit wasn't too much on my work, though. If the winds we were given at briefing hadn't been accurate, even the best of navigation couldn't have gotten us there on the money.

Warning Fletch, who had taken over again, to be ready for immediate evasive action if we were fired upon going through that narrow space between the ground defenses at Liège and Brussels, I again set to work and started working out an ETA for the Dutch coast and our base. Suddenly Frank called out flak off to the right. I noted that it was considerably out of range and went back to my work, only to be interrupted again by Brownie, who had spotted a strange fighter on the horizon up ahead. If it was a Jerry he didn't feel like tangling with our escort, though, and he disappeared in the same direction we were going. About then those P-51 pilots amazed me once anew by asking if we knew where we were. In answer to Doc's relaying what I thought to be our position they allowed as how that was about right, and no more was said. To this day I haven't found out how they could tell so accurately. Maybe they had obtained their location through radio contact with England. I don't know, but it was a good trick at any rate.

At last I was able to tell Fletch to head west, and we saw the ground drop away to the rear through some more openings in the clouds. As we started to descend he wisely cut back on the throttles, saying that he didn't want to exceed 130 mph because too much air speed would cause the feathered prop to windmill. He then left the pilot's seat to check the damage to the aircraft. Doc allowed the airspeed to build up to 150 mph and the vibration caused the prop to unfeather and start to windmill. Waiting only long enough for the rotation to pump up sufficient oil pressure, Doc refeathered it. Fletch returned to his seat with the admonition "Do not exceed 130 mph," and all went well once again.

To our immense relief the shores of England appeared in view and we crossed the coast just as Fletch was calling the tower for landing instructions. These received in good order, he nosed the ship down again and we entered the pattern. In no time we were on the ground and each of us heaved a big sigh of relief. Mission number seven [#7 for Work, but #9 for the crew] had proved to be the toughest one yet and the strain on our nerves was terrific! After we were out of the ship a crew chief showed us where a chunk of flak from Kassel had cut one of the main engine mounts and left it fastened only by the slightest of connections. Then the thought struck home about what might have taken place during that violent twisting and dodging we'd gone through, to say nothing of the vibration caused by the prop's windmilling as we started back across the Channel. It was truly a miracle that the whole engine hadn't fallen off from the strain.

Thinking that my navigation was one of the big factors in our safe return, and seemingly forgetful of the fact that that was what I'd been trained for the same as they had been trained to man their guns, the boys shook my hand and mumbled their thanks to me for guiding them home. I felt proud that I hadn't let them down, of course, but after all, I only did my job the same as they would do theirs when the time came. *[End of mission account by Roco Work]*

July 29, 1944

Yesterday was a busy one, one I probably won't forget for a long time. Some day I'll be able to tell you all about it. Guess I forgot to tell you this, but I've been keeping a little day-by-day report of what goes on so we can read it together. It'll bring back all these instances to mind so I'll be able to tell you all about it. Also I've been keeping all important dates—like when I got here and when I leave—in my little green book. This way you'll know where your wandering husband has been spending all his time since he left you.

You asked once if the letterhead on the stationery pertained to my outfit. Yes, it does. I might add that there isn't a better Air Force in existence than the Eighth. Of course, the fact that I'm in it doesn't sway my judgment a bit. But when you see it in action it makes you feel plenty proud to be a part of it.

This series of events had its origin in Roswell, New Mexico, where I underwent specialized four-engine training in the B-17. During the course of this instruction I had an instructor who had returned from combat in the ETO. His name was Captain Johnson and he knew his job well.

One day he said, "I want to show you a maneuver for evasive action. It will not be usable in a formation, but sometime when you're returning from a mission alone and on your own—and you will be at some point in your career—this maneuver could possibly save your life by outsmarting the German flak gunners and their radar. For the flak gunners' tracking-radar to be accurate some things have to be constant—a steady airspeed, a consistent heading, and a stable altitude. With these conditions you are a sitting duck. Now what I want to show you is how to keep all these things variable and yet make good the heading you have chosen.

"At the first sign of hostilities, which will be indicated by some-one shooting at you, immediately lower the nose, ease back a little on the throttle, and start a turn to the left. Hold the turn until 90 degrees from your chosen heading. Let the air speed keep acceler-ating and lose approximately 500 feet of altitude, or whatever it takes to complete the turn. Then immediately pull the nose up and start a turn to the right. Increase the throttle setting and continue to climb until you've reached a point slightly above stalling speed—hopefully your turn has brought you back 180 degrees from the last heading. Each time you are overshooting your original heading by 90 degrees. The number of degrees does not have to be exact. In fact, if it varies some, all the better. The main object is to keep everything variable and to keep the radar shooting at where you were, rather than where you are going. By keeping your turns somewhere within the 180 degree frame you will eventually work your way out of the danger area, although you will be exposed longer to enemy action. But the advantage is that your direction of flight is always changing, your airspeed is either increasing or decreasing, and the altitude never remains the same. This can be a very violent series of maneuvers, but it is effective."

When I saw the first burst of four shells off the right wing tip and felt the concussion I automatically jammed the nose down and started a left turn. Obviously the instruction I had received was still lurking somewhere in the back of my head. My first thought was, "Jerry, you missed, but just barely, when we were straight and level and a sitting duck. But if you get us now you're going to have to work for it."

Then it dawned on me that I had been so taken by surprise that I had forgotten my original heading. I called the navigator and said, "Give me a heading to get us out of here." His reply was, "The one you had was fine." I then had to say that I'm sure it was, but I had no idea what it was. Scared? No, just absentminded would have to be my excuse. Immediately I was given the original heading.

At least I now knew where we were going, and the show we were going to give was nothing short of fantastic as we dove and turned and climbed and turned with the aircraft first gaining and then losing airspeed. The burst of shells, in clusters of four, were first to the right and above us, then to the left and below us. They were bracketing us, but they couldn't hit us. The system was working and eventually we were out of range.

In the meantime, the crew was taking a real beating. There was no chance to warn them. All they could do was grab something and hang on. There was one exception. The ball turret gunner, snug in the ball with his safety belt fastened, was obviously enjoying himself because I heard him sing out, "Ride 'em cowboy!" How I wished I had his confidence!

About eight months later when we were eventually returned to the States and stationed at Hobbs, New Mexico, I called the Base Personnel Locator in Roswell—this base had now been converted to a B-29 Transition School. My purpose was to locate Captain Johnson. I wanted to fly up and thank him personally for showing me the maneuver that had been used to save the lives of our crew. I was informed that he had perished in the explosion of a B-29.

Oh, the ironies of war and fate! This man had taken all the enemy could dish out in a combat theater, only to give his life in a training situation, still trying to impart his knowledge into the minds of his students. It was a sad commentary, but in the Army Air Force there would be no havens of security.

July 30, 1944

Here it is the end of another Sunday in the ETO. Today was spent the same as the others—church, dinner, this afternoon in the Link trainer and the show house. The show was Once Upon A Time, *starring Cary Grant. It was a four-reeler affair with no sense at all to it. It brought on a few good laughs, though, so it wasn't entirely a waste of time.*

You would get a kick out of the shows here. They just tossed a bunch of benches and boxes into an empty Nissen hut and we have a picture house. The projector is an antiquated job suspended in a box from the ceiling and the loudspeakers are tossed around any place where somebody is apt to sit. Now for the show—the lights are put out and the machine is started. The next five minutes are spent trying to focus on the screen. Finally the job is accomplished and you've missed the introduction of the movie. Things run along pretty smooth now for three or four minutes, then the picture doesn't appear on the screen but the talk goes on anyway. The operator immediately remedies this. The picture comes back and the sound track quits. So the operator makes a few more adjustments. Everything is all set now. Then what happens? The first reel is finished and now we have to rewind and set up the second reel. Then the whole process is continued until the last reel has been shown. By that time you are completely worn out mentally and physically for the benches are very hard and your neck is so stiff from bobbing your head around to see that you welcome the chance to get up and go home. Each time I swear it's my last but I always wind up going back. Ah! Such is the weakness of human nature!

July 31, 1944

Happy Birthday—and many happy returns of the day. Did you have a cake with candles? I should think that would have been in order, and I would have to be over here where I couldn't have any!

What did I do today? The same as usual, absolutely nothing. No, I take it back as I spent an hour and a half in the barber shop trying to get a five-minute clip. Finally got it too.

This morning was also payday. Wound up with twenty-two pounds, six shillings, and four pence. In good old U.S. currency that amounts to ninety dollars and five cents. Here's the low down: My base pay is $165.00, flying pay $82.50, subsistence for this month $43.40, rental $60.00, which makes a total of $350.90. Now for the deductions: Bond $18.75, Allotment $225.00, Insurance $6.60, Rations $10.50. That totals $260.85. By the mathematical process of subtraction I wind up with $90.05. Not bad! I can get along very easily on that and have all kinds of fun while still affording the necessities of life. Next month I may take out another bond for the little one. I think it would be a good idea, don't you? That way we could start a little schooling fund and keep adding to it from time to time. Then when college time comes around the money will be there and we'll never have missed it. Along about then I should have a raise in pay. If so, that's what I intend to do. Let me know what you think about this.

The mail situation was not much improved today. There is no reason or regularity in the way the letters come. Some seem to come by boat and some by airplane. Right now your letters mean everything to me as I'm anxiously waiting to hear how you are and what the latest developments are. This surely can't go on much longer. I've just decided that after this one you're not to have any more until after I get home! Right now I'd give almost anything to know that everything is okay and that you're feeling fine. Then I'll be happy again with no worries in the world.

You asked how the people here find time for romancing with only three hours of darkness. I'll give you a little tip—they do it in broad daylight with no questions asked, and no one thinks anything about it. Piccadilly is a mess. The "commandos" carry a card which exempts them from war work and they also carry a health card, which they are very happy to show while making their pitch. They don't want to be confused with "amateurs." Don't worry, we wouldn't fit in over here so we'll just stay up in the good old Northwest.

Mission #10, Mont Blanc, France, August 1

Frank Dimit, Bombardier

Mission was similar to #4. Dropped supplies to Free French. Briefed at 7:30 a.m. Target area was about three miles north of Annecy. Our course took us within a few miles of Geneva, Switzerland.

We carried 12 para-packs of supplies which included machine guns, medical supplies, and bazookas.

We flew #3 in the lead squadron of low group of our wing. 95th led the task force. No flak or fighters, except our own friends. Good mission, but long—flew 9 hours and 40 minutes.

Our division dropped enough supplies to equip 5,500 men today. Free French are doing a helluva lot of good. Have two panzer divisions tied up. Have been blowing up trains and bridges.

Saw some of the invasion coast on way back. Fiess and crew flew in the wing with us. *[End of mission notes by Frank Dimit]*

Roco Work, Navigator

Veterans of several missions by this time, some easy and some rough, we listened avidly to rumors that yet another maquis mission was due to come off soon. Some pointed questions put to individuals in the bomb dump brought the answers we wanted. Yes, there are supplies on the field—when they're to be dropped is still another question along with the chance that Fletcher's crew might not be scheduled to fly.

Late one evening the list was posted and we were delighted in two discoveries. The first one, was that several people who flew only on milk runs were up to fly next day—that was a good indication of the type of mission coming up. The other interesting discovery was Fletcher's name. We felt positive that we were to fly on another "supply mission."

Going to bed we discussed the possibilities and decided we were strongly in favor of a repeat, remembering our previous joy over having no flak nor fighters to bother us. When we awakened next morning the same thoughts ran through our minds and we continued to hope through breakfast and on to briefing. The presence of more brass than usual made us certain that something unusual was scheduled.

Then the briefing officer drew back the curtain and received a lusty cheer from the crews. Sure enough, the route made it plain even before he began his speech.

"Due in large part to the overwhelming success of your past trips to aid the French Underground, the 95th is to lead the Air Force today on another relief mission. The supplies are to be dropped in the foothills of the Alps southeast of Lake Geneva."

He went on to say that messages of appreciation for past aid were being received from the French by SHAEF [Supreme Headquarters, Allied Expeditionary Force] constantly, along with urgent pleas for even more supplies. Most of his eloquence was lost on our ears, however, for we were practically glowing over the near certainty that there would be no enemy opposition. The greatest danger would be in flying formation at a low altitude in this mountainous area.

Climbing in our plane we were still extremely happy over the prospect for the day. Therefore the drudgery of the preflight checks on equipment seemed almost a pleasure. After takeoff there was considerably more than the usual amount of chatter on the interphone, due in the main to our shining outlook on life. Even as we climbed to rendezvous altitude (12,000 feet) where we had to plug in our heated suits and don our oxygen masks, joy was obvious in everyone.

When we headed south across the Channel the altimeter finally settled on 18,000 feet, the thermometer on −15 degrees C. At this height we were safe from any possible light ground fire when we crossed the enemy lines, yet we weren't high enough to be very uncomfortable. From the coast southward everything went according to plan. Exactly as briefed the lead ship started a descent in plenty of time so that we'd be near enough to easily identify the target area. As we went southeastward Lake D'Annecy appeared ahead and on our right soon after Lake Geneva came into view on the left. [End of mission account by Roco Work]

This is the end of Roco's narrative, which was written in January 1945. The pressures of living interrupted its completion and denied us the vivid description of the final twenty-five missions. We do appreciate that which was recorded as it reveals the sterling, warm character of a dedicated navigator.

Lake d'Annecy, Switzerland *(95th B.G. photo)*

Paradrop in the Alps. Picture taken from low squadron. *(Paul Fiess photo)*

While it has been forty-two years since we flew this mission, I still remember it like yesterday. We were in the French Alps, as Work said, in the vicinity of Mont Blanc. This area is bordered by both Switzerland and Italy. The country was very rugged and by now we had descended to the level of the mountain top. We were busy looking for the valley that would lead to the drop area. Evidently the leaders were having some trouble identifying the right valley because we made several large circles, but that was understandable as this was a very isolated, rough country and every valley looked alike. But if we didn't find the right area the mission would be for naught.

Finally contact was made and we descended into a very narrow canyon. My first impression was that this canyon was too narrow and rough for a formation of B-17s—that was also my last impression as we continued deeper. This mission, from a piloting standpoint, was one of the roughest and most dangerous, from physical hazard, that we were to fly. It was the tightest formation we ever experienced. We wanted to live, and the canyon became even more confining. We knew the lead was sweating because he had to be responsible for all of us, and that the "tail enders" were really playing crack the whip. The canyon had several sharp turns and very steep side walls. Only a pilot could appreciate the real danger of this situation with no room to maneuver—tuck in real tight, and pray!

Around another sharp bend a larger opening appeared with several bonfires. The bomb-bay doors popped open and in a matter of minutes the valley was filled with parachutes, each lowering a canister of much needed food, ammunition, guns, and medical supplies. I was told it was the most beautiful sight anyone would ever see—the panorama of beautiful green mountains, a small stream, the partisans, and the gaily colored parachutes. But my eyes, for the most part, saw only the silver wing of the aircraft I was trying to fly formation with. I heaved a big sigh of relief when the bomb-bay doors started to close so I could call for high rpm and open the throttles for the climb on up the canyon and out over the top.

We were just starting to breathe easy as we gained altitude and could see Lake Geneva way off in the distance when Doc called and asked me to switch over to VHF on the command frequency. As I made the switch we could hear a pilot who insisted that he was low on fuel and was going to Switzerland. The commander demanded that he read off the amounts that registered as he flipped from tank to tank. Doc was doing the same thing on our ship. When the readings were complete, the commander requested that the ship remain in formation and try for home, but the pilot had made his decision and he left the formation. With good luck we might see him when the war was over.

Lake Geneva was a jewel in the distance. *(95th B.G. photo)*

We switched back to interphone and Doc informed me that we had far less fuel than the pilot who had deserted. All of a sudden the countryside looked beautiful. Lake Geneva was a jewel far off in the distance and the sun was shimmering off the snow on the mountain peaks. Switzerland could be a very tranquil and beautiful place to spend the rest of the war. Who said it wouldn't be tempting!

I looked at Doc and said, "Let's try for home." His reply was, "England's not that bad. I'll lean out the engines, cut down on the rpms, lower the manifold pressure and you can coast her home." It would have been a lonesome year because we didn't know anyone in Switzerland!

August 2, 1944

Sure would like to see Cap now—bet he's really in his prime! Eight-pound baby boy! I didn't know Cap was that good a man! Don't mind me, I'm just in unusually good spirits. Just call me Uncle Gene. Believe me, he had

*better send me at least a twenty-five-cent cigar! Be sure and let me know
what they name the baby. Michael Ray is good if they like those names. . . .*

August 3, 1944

No, I haven't received any of the Reader's Digest *yet, and very few people
here receive a* life subscription *to a magazine! But that's okay since up to
now we have been able to get them at the P.X., something that is very
unusual. I haven't received the* Chronicle Dispatch *either. That stuff all
comes fourth-class mail and it usually is a month or two behind when it
gets here. . . .*

*Now then, where have I been in my travels? I can't tell you any exact
places, but I can tell you the countries I've been over, so hang on, here we
go: England, Ireland, Wales, Scotland, France, Belgium, The Netherlands,
Germany, Italy, Denmark, and Luxembourg. Switzerland and Italy I wasn't
over but have seen them. Who knows, someday I may add more to that
group. I'll say one thing, the European countryside is really beautiful, but
it will never take the place of the good old USA.*

*I can't tell you how many missions I have in, but when I first arrived I
figured out a schedule and how many a month I would have to fly in order
to keep my date with you. I have even moved the date up a little. So now
just let me say that I'm running ahead of schedule. Looks as if everything
will work out okay, but I shan't make any rash promises because you never
know what's going to happen now with the war news as it is.*

We had now flown ten missions, and had experienced everything
that could happen to a combat crew. Experience has a way of giving
you confidence. But the unexpected also has a way of destroying
this same confidence when accompanied by an element of surprise.

This was to be one of those days. Formal briefing for the mission
was completed and everyone was at the aircraft making the final
ground checks, installing the guns, and performing all necessary
preflight duties in preparation for the upcoming mission, number
11.

I was in the pilot's seat making some minor adjustments and the
crew was scattered throughout the airplane pursuing their duties in
the usual fashion. The low-key background sounds of their preparation were suddenly shattered by the staccato firing of a 50 caliber
machine gun. Were we being attacked on the ground?

Glancing out the window I saw the right waist gun of the aircraft parked directly across from us swinging around and spewing fire, much like a loose fire hose under pressure.

With the scream of 50 caliber bullets whistling by, I hollered at the crew to hit the deck and lay flat on the floor, hoping to present as small a target as possible. In a matter of seconds, which to us seemed an eternity, the firing ceased.

Upon ascertaining that none of our crew was hit we jumped out of the airplane and could see several holes in the tail section, and a couple in the fuselage. The crew chief came running up to survey the damage.

In the meantime our gunners cautiously approached the B-17 with the runaway gun. In a few minutes they returned saying that the waist gunner had armed his gun and decided to stow it. The gun was stowed by a leather strap hanging from the ceiling which passed through the trigger guard, then was hooked to the fuselage and allowed to hang in this position. He was following a normal procedure, but had forgotten to shut off the power to the gun when he put the strap through the trigger guard and fastened it. As soon as he let go of the gun the weight pulled the strap against the trigger and wild firing commenced.

By the time the gunner could catch up with the gun and kill the power, we had become the recipient of some extra unwanted lead. The young gunner was not only embarrassed but was suffering shock because he thought he might have hit someone. Gunners have a way of understanding how these things can happen and they tried to console him with statements like, "Hey, this can happen to anybody. Forget it—no one's hurt. You just scared the hell out of us and shot down an airplane. Congratulations, but only the Germans will give you credit for it!" I'm sure they provided a lot of psychological help!

The crew chief said that he would need a couple of hours to inspect the damage, and then additional time for repairs and patching. I told him not to hurry—we only had forty minutes till start-engine time and we had already signaled for a truck to transport us to the spare aircraft. We were sorry to leave him with a battle-damaged aircraft without even starting the engines.

With a lot of hurrying we managed to get off the ground in our briefed position in the spare aircraft. What normally would have been a rather exciting and scary mission turned out to be rather uneventful, an anticlimax compared to what had happened on the ground. After all, the Germans were firing from over five miles away!

We concluded that we had not yet seen everything. This was the first and last time we were to be shot down before takeoff. War can be hell, but sometimes the preparation can be just as bad.

Mission #11, Hamburg, Germany, August 4

Frank Dimit, Bombardier

Briefed at 6:00 a.m. for target between Hamburg and Harburg. Target was one of the largest oil refineries in Germany.

It was a long over-water hop. Saw no flak until we hit the target area and then it hit us. Believe they have stopped throwing up flak in shells—it comes up in a blanket. 388th Group carried some new anti-radar equipment, and it seemed to work fine. But our group didn't get any benefit from it.

Number 3 engine gave us a bad time over target, but Fletch and Doc got it straightened out and we came back with the formation.

We flew #3 in lead squadron of lead group of wing. We led the entire 8th Air Force into Germany. Carried 20 250-pound General Purpose bombs. Didn't see the results of the bombing. Target was clouded over when we arrived.

Some of the planes didn't get back. It was definitely a rough mission. The old man himself, Col. Truesdell, flew command pilot. Logged 7 hours and 15 minutes form time.

There were some enemy fighters in the area but plenty of good fighter escort.

"Frantic Five," the shuttle raid (*95th B.G. photo*)

Glad to be back. Twenty-four more to go. Everybody OK. *[End of mission notes by Frank Dimit]*

The results were good—all twenty aircraft bombed, but we lost one aircraft and nine men. They ditched in the Channel. Fiess flew in the group with us.

August 5, 1944

I don't know when I'll be able to write again. So don't think anything about it if you don't hear from me for a couple of weeks. Everything will be okay so don't worry a bit. In all probability you should hear from me before that long, but I'm saying this just in case it should be that way. Anyway, I know you understand.

On July 28 we flew the mission to Merseburg. The aircraft that we flew was *Knock Out Baby*, #7257. We lost an engine and had a pretty rough trip that day, but she brought us home and we became quite attached to her. Since the aircraft sustained major battle damage it was not available for flying on our next two missions.

August 1 and 4 we flew two different aircraft while *Knock Out Baby* was being repaired. On August 5 I was called to the flight line to test fly her, a procedure that was required after an engine change or major repairs.

That morning on takeoff the airplane exhibited a tendency to settle back to the runway immediately after becoming airborne. This was not a dangerous condition but just something to know and be prepared to cope with. Her flying characteristics had changed since our last flight. This was not unusual, for no two airplanes fly alike. At the end of the flight I pronounced her combat ready, and the ground crew called her back into service.

August 6 we were briefed to go on a shuttle raid called "Frantic Five." First phase of this journey was over the Danish peninsula where we hit a Focke-Wulf 190 plant. Others hit a "heavy water" plant in the vicinity and some highly secret engine plants for V-2 rockets. We were assigned to fly *Knock Out Baby*.

Doc and I had a little pact. In order for him to become a good pilot I had agreed to let him make every other takeoff and landing. This was his day to make the takeoff. While we were at general briefing I tried to talk him out of it. He kept saying that we had made the agreement and he wanted to take his turn. I told him, "We have a particular problem today. When I flew this aircraft yesterday it had a tendency to settle back to the ground. Now the takeoff that you like to make is that the instant we are airborne you want to pull up the gear. I want this aircraft to be well airborne and have at least fifty feet of altitude before the wheels come up." Doc said, "Okay, I'll follow that procedure."

Later at specialized briefing I found out we had a rather unusual load. We had only half the usual complement of bombs plus two extra men and extra fuel in the Tokyo Tanks. The waist part of the ship was completely filled with all types of recreational equipment which was to be given to the Americans stationed at Poltava, Russia. They were the ground support people. I don't know how long they had been there, but apparently they were going to be there quite a while longer. I was briefed that I had an aircraft that, as far as weights and balances go, was within its normal weight configuration but probably out of trim in regard to where the weight was located. Having been forewarned I felt I would have no problem getting the aircraft off the ground. Caution with me had now become a virtue.

When I reached the airplane the bombardier was fit to be tied. He was really carrying on so I asked what was wrong. He came out the rear door of the fuselage carrying a baseball bat and said, "Where are my bombs? What the hell do they expect me to do, go down and club the enemy over the head with these damn bats?"

"I understand how you feel. I know you have only half a bomb load, but actually all the recreational equipment is for our people in Russia. Apparently the brass feels they need this equipment and it's our job to take it."

"Well, I'd much rather be carrying bombs—something you can do damage with."

"I'm sure you would, but there's a reason for everything, so we just go along."

I cornered Doc again and told him, "Doc, I'm going to renege on this deal we've made. I'm going to make the takeoff today, then I'll let you make two more later on to make up for it." "No," he said. "I'll do just exactly what you tell me." Doc has a way of being a good salesman so I finally agreed, but only under one condition— the gear was not to come up until I was ready, and I would operate the gear switch. Normally that's the copilot's job—brake the wheels to a stop and pull the gear up on signal from the pilot.

When we completed our ground checks and taxi time came, we taxied out, and lined up on the runway in our takeoff position. We were pretty well forward in the formation because we were going to fly in the lead squadron of the 95th Bomb Group, which was being led by Colonel Karl Truesdell.

We started roaring down the runway and as the aircraft finally reached 130 mph Doc eased back on the yoke and she lifted off the ground. At this same instant he hollered "Gear up," but I did not respond. At the same time his feet went up on the brakes to stop the wheels from rolling. At that moment the aircraft settled back onto the runway with the brakes locked, the gear still down. When she hit there was a cloud of smoke and screeching of tires. He immediately got off the brakes. She bounced back into the air and started to fly.

After we were about fifty feet in the air I pulled the gear up and was sure we had some tires that were ready to blow out. When it became safe enough to put McQuitty in the ball turret I requested that he spin around and look at the wheels to see if he could detect any damage. He said, "I can see long strings of rubber that have been pulled off the tires. It looks to me as if I can see the cord in some places. The tread seems to be gone."

At this point we had to make a decision. Do we want to go to Russia and land with two tires that are apt to blow out? Or do we want to abort the mission, go out over the Channel, drop the bombs, burn up some of the gas load, and then come back and land? We still don't know the full extent of the damage. But we're in the air; the most dangerous part of this mission is past. We might as well go on as we have to burn the gas and drop the bombs anyway, and if the recreational equipment will help the morale of the group in Russia we had better go.

We went on to Russia and at this point I told Doc, "There is no way you're going to get your landing this time. I have no idea what kind of runways we will have when we get there, but *I'll make the landing.* We're in an emergency condition. We have tires that could possibly blow out, and since I'm the one who will be held responsible, I'll do it. Now prepare the crew and the ship for a crash landing." This time Doc readily agreed.

When we reached Poltava there wasn't a runway in the sense of blacktop or concrete. There was a bunch of perforated steel mats hooked together. So actually we were landing right on the ground with these steel mats placed on top of it—no foundation, just mats laid on the native grass. The mats were full of round holes to make them light enough to carry. It also helped to hold them in place. The holes were approximately four to six inches in diameter—the mats looked like a giant sieve spread out flat on the ground.

The landing at Poltava was one of my better ones. We set her

Lt. Florian, official interpreter and cameraman for the 95th Bomb Group, with Russian soldiers *(95th B.G. photo)*

down just as gently as we possibly could. When we reached the place where we were to park we commenced to wonder, "What do we do now?" Here we were thousands of miles from home. Both tires would have to be replaced and we suspected the service station probably wouldn't have too many spare tires on hand.

We were carrying some of our ground crew with us, but there was also the ground support crew stationed in Poltava who would help in servicing the aircraft. These were the people who were going to get the recreational equipment. In talking with some of them we found out that on the preceding raid forty-seven aircraft had been destroyed on the ground, so they had a good-sized bone yard to pick through. By now they had already spotted our ruined tires and said there was no problem as they had lots of wheels and tires. They all expressed amazement that the tires had not blown out. Some-times you are lucky and it makes up for the bad times.

They then asked us if several Russians who were present could go aboard our airplane. We said okay. We still had a large supply of 50 caliber ammunition on board and they wondered why we still had ammunition left after crossing enemy territory. We tried to explain that we had the mission coming to Russia and we would have several more missions before we would have a chance to replenish our ammo. It was necessary not to expend our ammunition but to use it only to protect ourselves. The Russians didn't quite buy this theory. They felt any time you passed over enemy territory you should fire everything you had. We thought this was interesting because on our raids our bombs were our offense, the 50 caliber ammunition was strictly for our own protection. It was fired only at enemy aircraft and not used to shoot up targets on the ground.

That evening the ground crew busied themselves replacing the wheels and tires on our aircraft. By the next morning it was repaired. They thought it a fair exchange—tires for baseball bats. But Frank still wasn't happy—he wanted bombs. Some days you just can't please anybody—copilots, bombardiers, or Russians.

Mission #12, Rahmel (Gydnia), Germany, August 6

Frank Dimit, Bombardier

Briefed this morning for target in Poland, near Gydnia, which is close to the city of Danzig. Target was a FW-190 factory. We were to hit this target and then go on to a base in Russia.

We flew #3 in high squadron of lead group. Major General Kissner and Colonel Truesdell flew in the lead ships. We carried 6 500-pound general purpose bombs. Think we gave target a good pasting.

We are all excited about this trip. It's the second shuttle run from the U.K.

Shortly after hitting target, we were hit by FW-190s. Didn't get in a shot. Only saw one, but his yellow spinner and cowling looked as big as a barn. I've seen the Luftwaffe. P-51 escort took pretty good care of us. No ships down.

We brought a crew chief for our plane and a crew chief for a P-51 fighter with us. They liked the ride, and it was a long one—10 hours and 25 minutes.

Saw light and very inaccurate barrage flak over target. Was a good target to hit, but it's too far from home. That sack will really feel good tonight. *[End of mission notes by Frank Dimit]*

The 95th and the 390th made up the entire task force of seventy-eight aircraft. Two fighter groups escorted us to the target where we ran into a group of Focke Wulf-190s. They were the famed Goering yellow-noses. The 190s made a frontal assault on our group, but instead of breaking off the attack and going over or under us, they came right through our formation. This was a very unusual maneuver, but each one had a P-51 on his tail. It was impossible to fire on them. All we could do was hold our position and watch them fly through, praying that there wouldn't be a collision. It was a very hair-raising experience. The encounter was all over in a flash, and the fighter escort headed back to the U.K. with nine enemy aircraft destroyed. We then made rendezvous with the 357th fighter group, who had sixty-four P-51s. This group escorted us on into Poltava. Twenty-three of our B-17s were damaged. One plane ran out of gas and landed short.

A rather humorous mixup occurred while we were in Poltava. General August W. Kissner, Chief of Staff of the Third Air Division, was the Division Lead for the mission. Also in our formation that day was Lieutenant Paul Fiess of the 336th Squadron.

Just a few days before this raid word had come down from Headquarters that the pilots would now be referred to as aircraft commanders and the copilots would be referred to as pilots. This order partly contributed to the subsequent confusion.

All of the 95th aircraft were B-17Gs and were aluminum in color with one exception. Paul Fiess was flying an olive-drab camouflaged plane since his regular aircraft was out of commission. He flew a war-weary B-17, #1410, named *I Dood It*, one of the older aircraft still in use on the base. She was almost covered with mission bombs and with several Bs painted on the bombs to denote missions to Berlin. In other words, she stood out like a sore thumb.

When we landed on the steel mats at Poltava we were directed where to park. Fiess pulled in right beside us and it was then that I noticed several Russian jeeps following him. As soon as the engines were cut and the props came to a standstill the Russians surrounded his airplane. When the crew emerged from the aircraft there was a lot of handshaking and frivolity going on. A Russian gal in uniform appeared to act as an interpreter. They pointed to the Bs on the bombs and I heard Fiess say, "Berlin . . . Boom," with appropriate gestures. The Russians were delighted and they all had to hug him and kiss his cheek. I am sure they assumed he had flown all of the missions painted on *I Dood It*. They loaded his crew into the jeeps and away they went. I remember thinking it was nice to see him receive such a cordial welcome since it couldn't have been that much fun flying that old airplane. I had flown her a couple of times before, on practice missions, and she wallowed rather than flew. It was hard work.

Paul Fiess with Russian dignitaries; *I Dood It*, also known as *Berlin Bessie*, in the background *(Paul Fiess photo)*

Wheat field, Poltava. Standing, left to right: Dwight Stevens; Russian commander (with wings on cap); commander's executive assistant; Russian woman interpreter; Paul Fiess, wearing the cap he had exchanged for Fletch's at the evening festivities. Kneeling, left to right: Russian woman; Russell Williams *(Paul Fiess photo)*

Briefing room and theater, Poltava, Russia; housing and mess tents in background. Poltava was totally destroyed during the course of the war. *(95th B.G. photo)*

A government building in Poltava. All that was standing was this front wall; the rest of the building had been completely destroyed by bombs. *(95th B.G. photo)*

After about fifteen or twenty minutes a "6 by 6" came by and our crew was loaded in with several others. We headed for the housing and mess tents where we were informed that after chow we should change our flying suits and be in dress uniform because entertainment would be provided in a bombed-out building nearby.

That evening as we sat in chairs under the sky I noticed General Kissner and all of our ranking people seated in a line on the back of the stage along with the ranking Russians. The Russians were on the audience's left and the Americans on the right. There was a vacant chair between the Russian Commander and General Kissner.

Fiess and I were visiting back and forth, waiting for the entertainment to begin. A young Russian girl in uniform came by and she appeared to be somewhat agitated. In perfect English she said to him, "Oh, there you are. We have been waiting for you."

Fiess was a tall, good-looking young man but quite bashful and at this instant he was as red as a beet. He turned to me and said, "Give me your cap." I was wearing a Service cap, and Fiess was wearing his Garrison or Overseas cap with a lieutenant bar on it. I could have sworn that bar was also blushing. I said to him, "What for? My cap won't make you look any better." He roughly whispered, "They think I'm the Commander. Just trade me your cap." I said, "That's okay. I thought I was Napoleon once but I got over it. You'll be all right. Just ask her if she has a girlfriend and I'll go with you."

In the meantime the girl was gently tugging at his elbow. Fiess grabbed my cap, tossed his in my lap and said, "Shut up, this is no joking matter." I was astonished as I watched the girl lead him to the stage corner on the audience's right. As he mounted the stairs leading to the stage all of the dignitaries rose to attention. The Russian general greeted him heartily and signaled for him to sit in the vacant chair. All were seated and the entertainment commenced. The folk dancing was all performed by men and it was a spectacular display. The singing and dancing went on for over an hour, and the enthusiasm and exuberance was almost unbelievable. We were given a command performance.

When the festivities were over and we were back in our tent I said to Paul, "What happened? I know you were whisked away from your airplane in grand style but there must be more to it than that." He said that when the Russians pulled up to his airplane they asked one of the gunners, "Where is the Commander?" They meant General Kissner. The gunner, trying to become familiar with the order to use the term Aircraft Commander, said, "The Commander will be down in just a minute." Fiess unwittingly became a task force commander and was embarrassed no end. He didn't really realize what was going on until he got to that evening's entertainment and

Mess and housing tents, Poltava *(95th B.G. photo)*

the show was being held up. He said they had invited him to participate in some activities after landing but he begged off, saying he was tired and since we were going to fly in the morning he would have to be up early. But he told them he would attend the evening performance and that seemed to satisfy them.

The next morning as we went through the chow line a young lady in uniform motioned to Fiess. It was apparent she did not speak English. We were then escorted into a special mess tent with two tables. One was already occupied by several dignitaries from our Force. We took the empty table.

While we were eating the young lady appeared with a coffee pot and refilled our cups. Then she left the coffee pot on our table, ignoring the other table as she left the tent. One of the group came over to our table; it could have been General Kissner, I'm not sure because we were not acquainted. But whoever it was had sufficient rank to make some lieutenants quake even though we all were in flying gear with no rank showing. His statement, while not verbatim, carried this meaning: "Regardless of what these people think we still serve by rank and not good looks in this man's army," whereupon he took the coffee pot and started back to the other table.

As he turned with the coffee pot I said, "Fiess, won't this make one helluva good story when we get back to our base!" Before Fiess could answer this gentleman turned back to us and said, "This story stops right now. There has been a mistake here that could be very embarrassing to these people if they find out what happened. Since they are our allies it goes no further. Now we have played along with it, but the play-acting is over. Only a few people really know what happened and you are among them. If word of this ever leaks out we will know it came from you, and I will have your hides nailed to the wall as an example for all to see. Do you understand me?" There was a second of stunned silence and then a chorus of "Yes, Sirs!" "Good," he said. "Now that we understand one another, let's go fly."

But this did not end the incident for Paul Fiess. When he reached his airplane the Russian commander was waiting and ready to fly with him. Through the interpreter he let Paul know that he would like to ride in the copilot's seat on the raid to Trzebinia. Paul refused, saying that he needed the help of his copilot, Dwight Stevens—it would be a long mission with over ten hours in the air. But the Russian commander, who was a rated pilot, was determined to go, so he stood between the two pilots with his arms draped over their shoulders, enjoying every minute of the ride. He did express displeasure that, after hitting the target with the bombs, Paul would not descend and allow the gunners to shoot up the ground targets. These Americans were crazy—bringing ammo home while there were still Germans to be killed and targets to shoot up!

Lieutenant Fiess was a division commander for two days, and true to his word, it was never mentioned again where anyone could hear. We valued our hides and had no wish to risk a court martial or cause trouble.

Mission #13, Trzebinia, Poland, August 7

Frank Dimit, Bombardier

Briefed at 5:00 a.m. for target in Poland about 10–15 miles west of Cracow. Target was large oil refinery at Trzebinia.

Carried 16 250-pound General Purpose bombs. Flew #4 in lead squadron of low group.

We were part of a first today. This was first mission to take off and return to a Russian base.

Creamed the target. Smoke up to 8,000 feet and flames up to 2,000 feet.

Light flak over target. Not very accurate. These boys don't get the practice that they do in Germany.

Logged 10 hours and 10 minutes form time. Only in enemy territory about an hour and a half. Poltava is long way behind lines now. Saw Russian front today. Saw several towns in flames. This country has had the hell kicked out of it.

Saw dogfight today. Had ringside seat. One FW-190 went down. Pilot jumped out. Enemy fighters made no passes at us. P-51s took care of them. [End of mission notes by Frank Dimit]

Our bombing results were good. Fifty-five aircraft out of our task force of seventy-eight were capable of flying. We received minor damage. Spooked by a wing fire, Lieutenant Dancisin's bombardier and navigator bailed out near Zhitomir, Russia. The next day we left for Italy.

Mission #14, *Buzau, Romania, August 8*

Frank Dimit, Bombardier

Briefed at 4:00 a.m. for our third leg of the shuttle run. Target was airfield at Buzau, 30 to 35 miles east of Ploesti, Romania.

Carried 16 250-pound G.P. bombs. Flew #3 in high squadron of lead group. Creamed target.

Flak—pathetic. Expected terrific fighter opposition, but P-51s took damn good care of us. Our group hit one airfield and the other group hit another. When a picture was taken of these two fields last month there were 230 aircraft on them. That's why we expected so much opposition. But the P-51 pilots reported that when the airborne Germans saw us coming they took off like scared rabbits. They saw about 60 ME-109s. If they had hit us we would have been pretty well beaten up.

Landed at Foggia Air Base—base of 463rd Bomb Group of the 15th Air Force. [End of mission notes by Frank Dimit]

By the following day our twenty-three damaged airplanes had been repaired and our B-17s were back in the air headed for Foggia, Italy. We were again flying in the formation led by Colonel Truesdell.

When we were a few minutes from the Initial Point the gunners spotted a large formation of airplanes along with a few stragglers. These planes were at 10 o'clock and about level with our formation, but they were so far in the distance they could not be identified. But we all knew they had to be the enemy because this was a very remote area, far removed from everyday battle. If they were fighters we would have our hands full.

Almost immediately these planes changed their course and flew away from us. We judged this force to be over sixty planes. Obviously they didn't want to fight. It appeared that they were running away from us. That would suit us fine. It was always better to see Jerry's tail than his nose.

All of a sudden we were making the turn at the IP and starting the bombing run on the Airdrome. Our bombardier had a little free time today. He set his bomb-sight on the target, but he would drop our bombs manually on a signal from the colonel's ship. Since we were in formation we flew the plane manually. About half way down the bomb run the bombardier called and said that there was something unusual on the runways. I suggested that maybe they were aircraft ready to take off—at 28,000 feet they would be hard to identify. But he said, "No, I am looking with field glasses and they aren't airplanes. It's something very unusual, almost like men in formation, but I really can't tell just what it is."

At this point our conversation ended because we were now receiving some light, inaccurate tracking flak. It is always inaccurate if it doesn't hit you. That's the criterion. We continued the bomb run and soon the bombardier called "Bombs away." It was a report that was always good to hear, even though it was not necessary because the plane would literally jump about fifty feet in the air simultaneously with the release of the bomb load.

We immediately headed for the Rally Point and soon realized that the colonel's plane was on fire. We were flying in a position where we could observe the colonel's ship. We kept reporting to him what we could see of the fire, which was under the left wing. His situation was not improving and soon it appeared that he had made a decision to abort the formation. He wiggled his wings and lowered his gear, which was the signal he was leaving. His two wingmen, not understanding, left with him. We immediately notified them to get back up because if the ship blew up we would lose three ships instead of one. They then returned to the formation, and we soon lost track of the colonel's airplane.

After we landed at Foggia we kept scanning the skies looking for our leader. Our search was rewarded as the colonel's airplane ap-

Main Street, Foggia, Italy, 1944 *(95th B.G. photo)*

The shell-pocked buildings of Foggia show the ravages of war.
(95th B.G. photo)

peared in the distance. The fire had gone out and with the crew intact they settled down on the runway with memories of some very harrowing moments.

We later learned that for some special occasion there had, indeed, been several formations of men on the runway. The aircraft we had seen were to be used in a massive flyover. Since this was a special occasion they either were not armed or did not want to fight. Anyway, the flyover they received was not only larger than planned, but carried a big bang which was not expected or even appreciated. The bombing results were termed excellent, but we would not know how well the personnel had fared.

Italy, August 10, 1944

Surprise! I have a chance to write a little sooner than I thought. Have really been having a time of late—picking up a little suntan too in this sun. Yesterday we went swimming in the Adriatic Sea, then rented a boat and sailed around for a while. Boy, what a time! . . .

I won't get to see Hallie—haven't the time, but I sure wanted to. They

Bargaining for melons with Italian boys in Foggia (*95th B.G. photo*)

built the airfield here—but I guess I can't do everything—after all, I'm still in the Army.

August 10

Doc Doxon, Copilot

Swimming and sailing at Manfredonia again. Ate cantaloupes and watermelon. Went into Foggia at night—no black-out. The town is filthy, has been bombed to small bits.

August 11

Doc Doxon, Copilot

We laid around camp and rested. Traded for some whiskey, cognac, and cantaloupes. Supposed to leave for England tomorrow.

Just before leaving for Russia I received the following letter from Hallie:

Corsica, July 25, 1944

Hello Gene,

Got your letter last night. Sure wish I could tell you something about your wife but you probably know by now. Wish you the best of luck in the world and hope it is a boy. Several of the boys here have had to sweat out the same thing—all would like to have been with their wives, but couldn't. All babies were born ok—so take it for granted yours will be too—I hope so with all my heart. We have been over eighteen months now so when one's wife just has a baby we suspect a rat in the woodpile.

Hope you like your group—I am quite sure that it is an old and experienced outfit—but be darn careful, Gene—don't ever get careless, but you are not of the careless nature.

Don't think Jerry will last long now. Just wrote to Blake Knox—he was wounded in or near Rome the day it fell. I've just returned from the Rome rest camp—had the finest time since I've been in the Army—sure lots of things to see.

We might meet up some day some place, but think this part will end soon. . . . The last time I saw you was at Geiger Field. How about dumping a load on Jerry for me! . . .

Bomb damage, Foggia *(95th B.G. photo)*

The enemy didn't fare too well either. Junkers 88 (Ju-88) destroyed on the ground at Foggia, Italy *(Paul Fiess photo)*

Wilma is fine. . . . It has been 19 months since I've seen her—that is a long, long time. Sure would like to go home and see her. A good wife to back a man up goes a long ways over here. Some of the boys have not had as good luck with their wives, but time heals all wounds. . . .

How are the women in England? They are really beautiful in Rome—but maybe they just look that way after 18 months. Rome is just like the States—so clean and nice.

Write soon. . . .

All the luck in the world to you,

Hallie

Hallie Fletcher is my first cousin, although our relationship is more like brothers. He was drafted into military service, and saw service with the Aviation Engineers. His unit was stationed at Geiger Field, Spokane, Washington, when, on June 22, 1942, I traveled to Geiger to enlist in the Aviation Cadet Corps. This was our last visit together until the end of the war.

Hallie's unit later shipped out to Africa where they built airfields, following the battle lines up through Italy, Corsica, and into France.

When we were at Foggia Main I was hoping for a surprise reunion, but the distance proved to be too great. Hallie was on Corsica building an airfield which we flew across on August 12 on our way to bomb France in support of the southern invasion. Unknown to me, Hallie saw the large formation pass overhead and later learned that this was our group, and that *Knock Out Baby* was carrying a bomb load which was dropped on the enemy airfield at Toulouse. Inscribed on one bomb in chalk was the message, "From Hallie via the Flying 95th." This was in response to the request to "someday drop a load on Jerry for me."

In France, at the war's end, he had the opportunity of returning to the USA in a war-weary B-17 whose days of reliability had long since passed—a fact that was proven when they made a three-engine landing in Brazil.

Mission #15, *Toulouse, France, August 12*

Frank Dimit, Bombardier

Briefed in Italy this morning at 4:00 a.m. for our last leg of the shuttle run. Our target was an airfield at Toulouse in southern France near the Spanish border.

We carried 10 500-pound G.P. bombs and flew the same position as usual, #3 in high squadron of lead group. Target was creamed but good. Was one of the best bomb patterns I've seen.

Flak was pathetic, but the low group caught a little. Think the gunners must have been asleep when we went over. Didn't see any enemy fighters, but expected to. Our own escort was fine.

Saw the Anzio beachhead and it's in pretty bad shape. Would like to have had a closer look at the Russian battle front to compare them. Don't see how it could have been any worse.

Logged 10 more hours today. That's a total of 39 hours and 45 minutes for the last four missions. That's a lot of time.

Fletch found out today he is a papa—9-pound baby boy. A big celebration is now in progress.

Was damned glad to get back. England looks better at the end of each mission. [*End of mission notes by Frank Dimit*]

August 13, 1944

Tonight you've made me the happiest fellow in the world! Nine-pound baby boy!! Honey, that was really worth waiting for. I've been running around on clouds ever since I got the news, which was late yesterday. I had just returned from a little sightseeing tour of Europe, Russia, Italy, and then back here to eleven letters and a package from you and the news that I was a proud papa. We were all dead tired but the news was what I'd been waiting for. Great clouds of cigar smoke rolled up as the celebration got under way with the uncorking of the sparkling vino we picked up in Italy! I wanted to write you last night but that was impossible as the fellows wouldn't leave me alone long enough. Just call me "Pop"! The boys are bound and determined the name will stick. The joys the baby will bring us will far exceed anything we've ever imagined. This was all we needed to make our life complete.

Now to answer a few of your questions which have accumulated in my absence. First, about the missions and when I'll be home. I have good reason to believe that I can come home after thirty-five missions. It's not a promise, but the deal supposedly works that after thirty-five we go home for a thirty-day furlough, then do another tour in another theater. That last part doesn't exactly appeal to me, for when I come home I intend to stay in the States. By the time I'm finished that can probably be arranged. Things are running smooth and I'm still ahead of schedule—the sum total is now fifteen. I'll feel like I've done something when the eighteenth rolls around and I'm over the hump!

Now for another list of countries that I've seen—hang on 'cause here we go again—I'm sort of like a traveling salesman: Sweden, Poland, East Prus-

sia, Russia, Romania, Bulgaria, Yugoslavia, Albania, Czechoslovakia, Corsica, Italy, and Spain. Want some bodies of water? Okay: Atlantic Ocean, English Channel, North Sea, Baltic Sea, Black Sea, Adriatic Sea, Tyrrhenian Sea, and the Mediterranean. If you add this list to the other you'll have all of them. . . .

August 14, 1944

I've been wondering if you ever received my Air Medal. It says here on a little piece of paper: "Awards and Decorations—an Oak Leaf Cluster is awarded for wear with the Air Medal previously awarded to the following named Officer, Organization as indicated, Army Air Forces, United States Army. Eugene R. Fletcher 2nd Lt." The citation was the same as with the Air Medal. You know, meritorious achievement, courage, coolness, skill, and all that malarkey which makes good propaganda. Of course, they forget to tell how many MPs it takes to get me aboard my ship before takeoff time. It isn't bad, though, so don't worry about me. The crew really makes a good team and we're always looking out for one another.

Had a V-Mail from Mother today and she said you and the baby are getting along fine, just exactly what I wanted to hear. . . . The fellows are looking for a pair of boxing gloves now. Hope he doesn't meet the crew 'cause they'll make a roughneck out of him in no time. No man ever had more to come home to and look forward to than I have. We'll finish this job over here before too long and before you know it we'll all be home. . . .

The fellows are getting a kick out of me because I don't even know my son's name for sure. By the way, which name did you choose?

August 15, 1944

You say I haven't said too much about Mac and Lynch. Let me tell you they are two real good, likable guys. Lynch is the armorer gunner—helps Dimit with loading the eggs, arming, and all the stuff that goes with that job. He is very quiet but he is thinking all of the time—stability is probably his middle name. He has a great smile and is a good old farm boy, the kind I'm used to. Whether I'm slopping the hogs or on a mission I'm glad he's with us.

Mac has an engaging grin on his face all the time and a twinkle in his eye. He is also quiet but comes up with a jewel now and then. He has his teaching certificate if I remember right. You'd think with this much education he would have more sense than to ride in the ball turret. I guess he's a braver man than I am. I wouldn't crawl into that thing on the ground, let alone in the air. Good thing somebody is willing.

Brownie is in charge of the enlisted men and with his experience and personality they have a real leader. Sometimes I don't think they even realize that he is leading—such is his way.

August 18, 1944

The past couple of days were spent in London. We were fortunate enough to land another pass so we went to the big city to pick up our battle jackets.

When we came home this evening there were eight letters waiting for me. Your letters were all written before little David arrived. Thank your mother for all the letters she has sent me. I'll try to write to her tomorrow. Things happened so fast I'm still running around in a daze. Gosh, it'll probably be weeks before I settle down to a normal way of life. But that's okay 'cause it's a great feeling being a father!

You wanted to know if we had ever got our own plane. No, we haven't been assigned one as yet. We've just about given up hope for one—it really doesn't make any difference, though. Some day I'll be able to tell you lots of things and you will be able to understand how things work over here. How often do we fly? There's no regular order. You never know from one day to the next what's going on. You just wait until someone comes in and wakes you up—then you know you're going out. But don't worry, we get plenty of rest. Uncle Sam does a good job of looking out for his men.

Many of the officers visiting in London or passing through would be assigned messing privileges at Grosvenor House at 44 Grosvenor Square. Grosvenor House was a "mess" operated by the military for Americans stationed in London. It was the only place where you could receive a decent meal, but we would rather take pot-luck at the local English eateries at that time of shortages and rationing—it was the challenge.

We liked to stay at the Regents Palace Hotel where you could have white sheets and breakfast in bed, albeit the breakfast consisted only of coffee, dry toast, and orange marmalade.

The management there loved to put the Americans on the top floors, and in the buzz bomb season you could spend the night jumping up, pulling on your pants on the run while descending several floors for safety. When the danger had passed we would trudge back up the stairs to the uppermost floors and sack out again.

This was a bare bones hotel that tolerated Americans, and the price was right. Besides, it was close to Piccadilly, which was the entertainment section of London, and would be the most obvious place to meet a buddy from another group.

Piccadilly Circus, London, with the statue of Eros encased in a concrete shelter for protection against bombing. *(95th B.G. photo)*

A strange phenomenon developed as we moved along in our flying career. We remained close friends with our roommates and the crews who joined the 95th with us. We visited with others and worked with them, but we did not come to know them or to associate with them socially. They were names on whose wings we flew, and later on names who flew on our wings. Unconsciously they were blocked out. If they did not return the hurt would be less.

I thought this might be just a peculiarity of our crew, but I later learned that this was widespread throughout the combat Air Force. On our trips to London much of our time was spent trying to find out what was happening to the people we had trained with and who were our close friends in another life far removed from here. They were our family—we had to know.

August 19, 1944

Received a letter from you today. It came through in record time—only 32 days!

Yesterday I received a few pictures which were taken on our most recent escapade. They were censored at the Base Photo Office but they asked us not to send them home by mail. It would be okay, though, to take them with us when we leave. Some of them are quite good and I know you'll enjoy them.

We took a bunch of pictures today of the crew. We might get the film developed but won't be able to get pictures reproduced. There's quite a shortage here of anything to do with pictures. The reason we took these is because Joe is being transferred to another outfit and we wanted to get the pictures while the whole crew was still together. . . .

August 19

Doc Doxon, Copilot

Wandered around today trying to get some pictures of our Russia-Italy trip. Weather is very bad—top of clouds above 30,000 feet as reported by the weather ship. The bombardier and navigator that bailed out in Russia returned today. Saw buzz bombs hitting tonight.

August 20, 1944

Today I registered David's birth with the proper authorities so that's all taken care of. . . . I'll increase your allotment and you can buy a bond a month for him.

Here are a few figures you might want. Base pay and overseas pay $183.33, Flying pay $91.67, Subsistence $43.40, Rental $75.00. Those statistics are for a married flying 1st lieutenant with one son. Hey, come to think of it that's me! The silver bars have been in vogue since the fifteenth. I found out this morning. Totaling the figures up makes a tidy sum of $393.40.

Brown and Hinman both made tech sergeant and the rest of the boys made staff sergeant. They're probably making more than I am now. I was sure glad their ratings came through because I've had quite a time trying to get them. The adjutant just heaved a sigh of relief and says he hopes I'll quit bothering him for a while now. But he's due for a surprise because I have a copilot, a navigator, and a bombardier who ought to be 1st lieutenants. And they will be in due time or the adjutant and I will go at it again.

We have been having some typical English weather lately—fog and rain almost every day. I guess winter time isn't far off. Hope I can finish before it gets too bad. The war news is quite encouraging so maybe it won't be too much longer.

Smitty modeling the dangerous 45-caliber pistol. From
left to right: Smith, Lynch,
Brown; kneeling, Hinman

Upon arrival at our permanent home in England we were all issued
a weapon—a bright, shiny, blue-black 45 caliber automatic with several clips of ammunition. We were ordered to wear this weapon at
all times because we were now considered to be in a Theater of War.
Who knows—maybe the Germans would invade England.

But the guns saw their first use as a means of putting out the light
on a night when someone was slightly inebriated, lazy, or unhappy
with a response upon asking for "lights out." Our crew was not
involved in these shenanigans, but we were present to see or hear
some of them.

Frankly, the gun scared me to death. I had grown up in the West
with real cowboys and Indians, and they had long since lost the
need for a revolver. It would continue to be alien to my way of life.
We were to carry this gun on our missions. In the event we went
down this weapon could be used offensively or defensively. I could
picture myself on the ground surrounded by a bunch of German
farmers with pitch forks in their hands and me standing in the middle of a circle with my "45" drawn, requesting them to surrender in
the name of our Fearless Leader!

But, in reality, I carried it on board the plane and strapped it to
the pilot's seat. At least I wouldn't blow my own leg off or injure

someone else if it went off accidentally. It was the last thing I wanted on my person in the event I was forced down in enemy territory. That gun made a lot of noise and I knew I could never fight my way out of enemy territory with it. In all likelihood it would get you killed. I was quite content to carry only my hunting knife. This would be my offensive weapon. It would not intimidate or scare some person whose home or city had just been bombed into seeking retaliation by shooting an American armed with a "45."

The order to carry this weapon at all times was changed, but not until it had created a situation that could have had some very dire consequences.

In the dark of night a captain left the Officers Club and was heading down the foot trail to his quarters when a shot rang out and the captain fell to the ground. A lusty, happy voice cried out, "I got one of the Sons of B———!" A young enlisted man suffering from delusions and alcohol was taken to the guard house and the captain was taken to the base hospital, where it was determined that he had only a leg wound.

Everyone knew flight crews were expendable—losses and wounded were to be expected. But this was a non-rated staff officer. They were not considered expendable. Therefore, all guns were turned in. From then on they were issued to each crew member after briefing and turned in after each mission. Thank goodness somebody got the message before a real tragedy occurred!

August 22, 1944

Today was another lazy day but the chance to rest was quite welcome. This morning was spent in bed, the afternoon in classes, and the evening at the movie. The show was The Sensations of 1944. *We got quite a kick out of it, namely the jive. It sure has been a long time since we've heard any music. At the present we have a deal on to get a radio—hope we swing it. They certainly are hard to get ahold of. It would be nice to listen to newscasts and radio programs again. . . . Right now our only contact with the outside world is through the* Stars and Stripes. . . .

August 23, 1944

Another quiet day. This is getting monotonous. We've been lying around so long that everybody is getting nervous and jumpy. One rough day, though, will sure put a stop to that. . . .

I spent all morning censoring mail. I read so many letters that I was getting "letter happy" when I quit. This afternoon was spent at the barber shop trying to get a three-minute clip job. While I was there the boys found some tin foil and a bottle of paste. When I returned I found I had silver bars on everything, including my underwear! Now I'm trying to think up some good counter measures for retaliation. I'll get even if I have to lie awake nights dreaming up something.

Work just returned with the news that we get a chance to earn our board again tomorrow. That's good. We'll get this over and get back home where we belong.

Mission #16, *Ruhland, Germany, August 24*

Frank Dimit, Bombardier

Briefed at 5:00 a.m. for target at Ruhland, a small town 65 miles east of Leipzig. Target was an oil refinery.

We flew the diamond in high squadron of high group. Carried 10 500-pound G.P. bombs. They contained a new explosive (B-2), supposed to be an improvement over RDX.

Saw Berlin for first time today. Had a good look at it—flew just out of range of their flak. That's as close as I want to get.

Flak was terrific at target area—most intense barrage I have ever seen. We were lucky—didn't pick up any holes until after we left target. Lead ship goofed up and took us into another flak area and they nailed us there. Picked up several holes.

Expected to be hit by the Jerries' new jet propulsion planes in Holland, going and coming, but never saw an enemy plane. Lucky us. Damn good escort—P-51s. Our wing was the last into Germany and last out, that's why we expected trouble.

Logged 9 hours and 10 minutes. Too damn long. One of the new crews didn't get back.

Most of the oil targets in Germany were hit today, judging from the fires we saw on the way back. [*End of mission notes by Frank Dimit*]

August 25, 1944

Happy Anniversary!! Today marks two years of happily married life—the two happiest years of my life. The little trials we've had to face are only temporary and will all be solved when we're together again.

Surely hope the pictures of David turned out okay for I'm anxiously awaiting a look at our little man. . . .

Things have been moving pretty fast over here lately. Maybe the end is in sight. They can't end this thing too soon to suit all of us over here. But it doesn't pay to be optimistic and then disappointed, so we just let things go and not make any predictions. We are beginning to wonder what they'll do with us if this should end over here before we finish.

August 27, 1944

Guess what? They made me work for a living today. Some new deal after this long rest. I thought they had forgotten I was over here—that was my mistake, though!

Mission #17, *Berlin, Germany, August 27*

Frank Dimit, Bombardier

Briefed at 6:30 a.m. for our target—in Berlin. Our target was a tank depot at Spandau, just 5 miles northwest of the center of Berlin. 500 flak guns in target area.

But we didn't get there. We hit weather just as we tried to cross the Danish peninsula between Flensburg and Kiel. The weather ship reported clouds up to 30,000 feet. We hit the first clouds and our group scattered like birds. We got through that bank and had begun to form again when we hit the next bank. We never did get out of that stuff until after we had turned around.

This was the Group's 200th mission and Lt. Col. McKnight really wanted to go in but we had to turn back. We hit a little flak over Flensburg on the way out. We came back alone—the same as everybody else. We really got split up when we hit the clouds.

We flew #2 in the high squadron of the low group of the wing. The 95th led the 8th Air Force today. It was to be our show all the way, but it didn't pan out. We carried 10 500-pound aimable cluster incendiaries. Our fighter escort was its usual superb quality going in.

It was some mission—we hope to get credit for it. *[End of mission notes by Frank Dimit]*

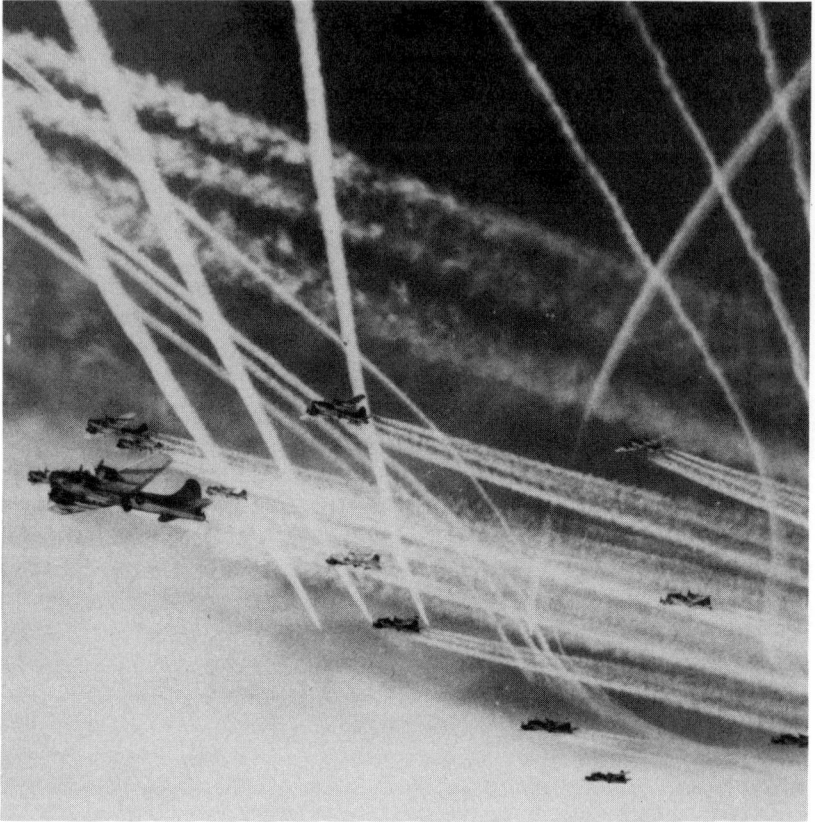

95th Bomb Group trying to reach Berlin for the group's 200th mission, but stopped by the cloud bank *(95th B.G. photo)*

The 95th, along with twelve aircraft from the 100th Bomb Group, had led the first successful raid on Berlin March 4, 1944, becoming the first U.S. Heavy Bombers to bomb the city. So what better way to let them celebrate their 200th mission than to return again to the capital of the Third Reich leading the Eighth Air Force. This was the reason for the "go for broke, derring do" attitude on the part of our leaders. Nine of our aircraft aborted and bombed a target of opportunity at Husum. For those of us, including Paul Fiess, who stayed with the leaders until we were completely immersed in the second cloud bank, it was one heck of a nightmare.

It was only after a high-flying Mosquito weather ship informed us that we would not break out of the overcast until after we had passed the target that the mission was aborted. Following a standardized

200th mission of the 95th Bomb Group; Aircraft assigned to Paul Fiess on the right; "200" formed with 100-pound bombs *(95th B.G. photo)*

procedure we made our 180 degree turn around in the soup. We were very fortunate that we didn't have a midair collision as we were not too well organized at this point. We all returned home alone without fighter escort. But it wasn't necessary because even the German fighters were too smart to fly in this weather. . . .

While we were on the mission the ground and flight crews, who were still at the base, posed for a picture to celebrate this event. They posed around and on aircraft #8283. One week later this aircraft was assigned to Fiess, and was the one in which he completed his tour on November 21.

Upon our return we were too tired to participate in that day's activities, but we were told that the next time the group received a "stand down" (a phrase that meant the group would not have to supply combat crews and aircraft for a specified period of time— usually twenty-four, thirty-six, or forty-eight hours) there would be a big party for everyone.

August 28, 1944

. . . That was really some newspaper clipping you sent. I don't object to my middle initial being "J," and I don't think Dad cares how they spell his

name, but I'm quite sure Major General Partridge would object if he knew he was referred to as just plain "Major." I take it the clipping came from the new Tekoa Gazette.

I got up at eleven forty-five this morning. If that hadn't been the time they serve dinner I wouldn't have been up that early. A couple of hours this afternoon were spent in class—then the rest of the time up to now has been spent reading age-old magazines and some short stories by Kipling. This rough life is beginning to tell on me—I'm getting so lazy that I even hate to walk up to the shower to take a bath.

An instructor I had in Ardmore just came in. He's a Captain now, a West Point grad. He just got over here and is still full of hot news about Ardmore and the friends we had. We've talked about two hours and finally have things under control—really enjoyed talking to him. Of course I told him so many tales about combat that I think he's just about ready to book passage back. Oh well, he'll find out in due time that I was merely kidding and he'll probably have a good laugh out of it. By the way, his name is [James] Frankosky.

September 1, 1944

Had six letters from you today—not in sequence—but that's due to the fact that some come by boat and some by plane. . . . Also received a letter from Mrs. Doxon congratulating us on our son, and one from a cousin of mine you've never met, Virgil [Winnett]. . . . He has been in Italy, or rather I should say overseas, for twenty-seven months. Hallie gave him my address so he wrote to find out all about my little family and wondered if I had an extra snapshot of my lovely wife—or, as he puts it, "the poor unfortunate girl that got stuck with me." I hate to disappoint him so send along a snapshot that I can send to him. He was pretty happy—two years ago he was a buck private, finally worked up to staff sergeant and then a few weeks ago received a battlefield promotion to 2nd lieutenant. He's with a tough outfit and I know that he really worked to get that. Good deal, says I. . . .

You asked about the food situation. That's a touchy subject around here. It's definitely bad—it's nourishing enough but always looks and tastes the same. No one is losing weight so it can't be too bad, I guess, but the poor mess officer is about as popular as a German flak gunner!

Virgil Winnett is a distant cousin of the author, but they retained a close relationship. Virgil had won a football scholarship to the University of Idaho where he played tackle. He was a towering man compared to the author, who was 5 feet 6 inches, weighed 125 pounds, and required a waiver of physical standards to enlist in the Army Air Corps.

When the draft was instituted, in the very beginning, local communities had a lottery drawing of all people classified 1-A. Those whose names were drawn were the first to be drafted. Virgil won the lottery and was one of, if not the first, to enter compulsory military service from the community of Dayton, Washington. He saw service with a tank division in North Africa and Italy, where, after a very tough battle with many casualties, he received a battlefield commission. He fought a long, tough war.

September 2, 1944

Today was not out of the ordinary. We spent the afternoon flying all over England just for practice. Today was Work's day. First it is formation so Doc and I won't get rusty. Then it's Dimit's day to practice dropping a few bombs just to keep in shape. Finally a navigational mission to keep Work on the ball. When the cycle has been completed we start all over again. It is getting somewhat monotonous. Not long ago we were enjoying sack time days on end. Those were the happy days when we were wingman with not a care in the world. Sure tough when they make you start working for a living.

We have seventeen missions in now so you can see we've slowed down. As yet we're not behind schedule, but have lost all that we were ahead. We should get our own ship sometime next week. They'll probably give us the one we've been flying lately. We're sure attached to it and all of us hope we'll get it. It has already been named, though. Someone christened it Knock Out Baby. *Its nose is graced by a lovely little blonde in boxing shorts and sweater, wearing gloves and standing in the corner of a boxing ring. We all wanted to name our own plane, but it's like I say, we just have a deep feeling for this one and I think we'll get it. . . .*

We were scheduled to fly a solo practice mission. This was to ensure that lead crews had plenty of experience, and was primarily a navigation mission. The navigator would have a chance to sharpen his skills—he would do work with his Gee Box as well as flying over and identifying the different "bunchers" and "splashers," which were radio aids used in forming the formation and joining the task forces. This would be a relatively low-level mission, around 10,000 feet or below, and for the rest of the crew just a fun trip. This mission could have been performed in our ordinary clothes—A-2 jackets, 100 mission caps, and maybe long johns.

After we had completed our briefing and Roco had outlined his course, which was only over land and about four hours in duration, I changed my mind about our flight clothes. The English weather is never to be trusted, so I informed the crew to bring their mission clothes—heated suits and oxygen masks. Probably won't need them, but just in case of an emergency have them with you.

By the time Roco and I finished our errands and reached the plane the crew reported that all preflight checks had been made. All we had to do was pull the props through by hand to check for liquid locks in the lower cylinders. If you could pull them through by hand you knew there wasn't any problem, so you could board the aircraft and start the engines. This we did. Everything went like clockwork—we were soon airborne and on our first heading, which we had received from Roco. Doc set up the autopilot. This would be a fun day for us. Let the autopilot fly and do the physical work, and we would enjoy the countryside while fiddling with the knobs.

We were making good progress and were about halfway through the mission when we saw a large cloud bank moving in. The base of the clouds appeared to be between 4,000 and 5,000 feet. We were flying at 8,000. I called Roco and he concluded we would have a better mission if we climbed over the clouds rather than going through underneath. We set up a climb condition and let the autopilot function, breaking out about 14,000 feet. It was beautiful above the clouds. The navigation was all by instruments anyway, so let Roco work.

It was starting to get a little chilly so I plugged in my heated suit and turned up the rheostat. I was glad I had changed the order and requested heated suits because this was the emergency that was always present while flying in England.

Doc suggested that while we weren't busy and everything was going smooth maybe he would go back through the aircraft and check on everyone. This would be a good chance to stretch his legs. I readily agreed but requested that Brownie occupy his seat and be my eyes on that side of the ship. This was fine with Brownie because the pilots' seats were the most comfortable place on the airplane and afforded a very good view.

Doc was gone about ten minutes when he called on the interphone and wanted to know if they could open the emergency bag, which was in the radio room. Each aircraft was equipped with an emergency kit. This was an olive-drab, heavy canvas bag about three feet long, eighteen inches high, and about the same width. It was closed with a heavy zipper running down the top, and the zipper end was sealed with a light metal seal. The bag contained all sorts of things that could be used in an emergency—extra oxygen masks, heated suits, medical kits, anything a crew might need if any of their personal equipment failed, and a lot of other things. The reason for the seal was to tell if the bag had been opened and anything had been removed. Since everything in the bag was inventoried it would have to be repacked any time the seal was broken. This would insure that the bag was complete, and was for our own protection. No one would want a bag with something missing—it might be the very thing you would need. In other words, you didn't open the bag frivolously.

When I asked what they needed, the answer was, "We need a heated suit and maybe an oxygen mask." "Okay, whose suit has burned out, and who has oxygen problems?" "Well, no one's suit has malfunctioned. We have an extra passenger on board and he's getting cold. If we get the suit we might just as well play it safe and put an oxygen mask on him in case we have to go higher."

There was something obviously amiss here as I hadn't authorized any extra personnel and had not been informed that operations had either. Somebody better fill me in on what's going on. "Well, we've got a cook on board." *"We've what?!"* "The cook from the combat mess hall is with us. We promised him a ride and this seemed like a good time for it—a low-level overland sightseeing mission without any danger attached."

The last thing we would want or need would be a casualty on board—and especially a cook—a cook whose presence would be missed one way or another come supper time.

"Break open the kit and make your passenger comfortable. We'll discuss this when we land." This was a "no-no" of major proportions, something that just was not done. How would I explain a cook on board a combat aircraft, even though it was only a practice mission?

A thousand scenarios went through my head. The best seemed to be "keep it quiet." Don't say anything—plead the Fifth, or drink it. Apparently the only ones who knew were the members of the ground crew and my flight crew. The ground crew wouldn't say anything, and with good luck no one would meet the ship except a truck driver to provide transportation back to the Ready Room.

The only problem was to explain logically the opening of the emergency kit. I let it be known that by the time we landed someone on board that aircraft better have a malfunctioning flight suit, and be prepared to justify the use of the emergency equipment. Doc readily agreed to do this, which seemed no more than right since he had been the perpetrator of the whole affair and had sworn the others to silence.

I then dropped the matter and let the cook enjoy the ride. It was my policy never to discipline people in the presence of others, or when I was mad. This clearly called for a "woodshed" tactic hidden from the view of others. But this would take place only after my blood pressure went down and my temper had cooled.

When this time arrived, the cook had been smuggled off, but not before he shook my hand and thanked me for the wonderful ride and for the highlight that broke up a monotonous life of eighteen months overseas. It would have served no purpose to put a damper on such enthusiasm.

For my crew it would be a different story. During the course of our little discussion it came out that the cook was a paying passenger. A wheel of cheese, two loaves of bread, and a gallon of strawberry jam—all of which would be generously shared with the 1st pilot if he could overlook the slight indiscretions of his fellow man. These people knew that a man could be tempted—maybe we knew one another too well!

September 3, 1944

. . . Just had some good news a few minutes ago. We are authorized to go on pass tomorrow. The fellows are now eagerly getting off their last-minute letters, shining shoes, and all that goes with a pass. We will undoubtedly go to London again and see if we can find some of the old buddies. There isn't much you can do on a pass, but the idea is just to get away from the post awhile and enjoy a change of scenery. It also relieves the anxiety of the mind for a while. But then again, when the pass is over you hate to go back to it all. . . .

September 7, 1944

Here I am back with my nose to the grindstone again. The pass went entirely too fast and we really had fun. Can you imagine breakfast in bed at eleven-thirty? Believe me we really caught up on our sack time—as if we were behind. . . .

Riding on the English trains is really an experience—a rather pleasant one I might add. The trains are smaller than ours and they look rather antiquated, but they are cleaner and much more comfortable to ride. They have two shock absorbers on each end of the cars. This keeps the slack out of the connecting links between the cars—consequently, they don't jerk and bang on starting and stopping like American trains. They are actually very smooth riding. I have never seen anything like a Pullman car here. Maybe the country is small enough that they are not needed. . . .

Our closest contact with the civilian and military population comes on these train rides. I find it very difficult to understand their speech, but we do communicate. Since these rides to London take some time we are generally offered tea by the other occupants of the compartment. Now the English like sugar and cream in their tea and it is already mixed in their thermos so there is no choice of "with or without." A time or two I have tried to refuse because I knew they did not have very much—everything being rationed or nonexistent. But you also have the feeling that if you refuse you will hurt their feelings, so, in the end, you compromise and accept on the second firm generous offer. . . .

September 8, 1944

Today was quite a day. Received three letters from you including the one which contained the pictures of David. I don't think I need to tell you how happy I was to get them—really have some little man, haven't we? Be sure to take more pictures with you holding him 'cause I like to see my two loved ones together. . . .

Now about the papers I sent—yes, those are the ones which describe what we have been doing. They're pretty sketchy and you won't get much out of them until I get home to explain them. Yes, the candy came through okay and was devoured almost immediately. No, there's nothing special I want or need. Don't ever send over anything of value because things get lost too easily. Should be home by Christmas so don't go out of the way to send anything.

September 11, 1944

Back again after a three day layoff from letter writing. We had a day and a half off for a big celebration. There were USO troops, several guest orchestras, both G.I. and top English—even Glenn Miller and his band. It was quite a show—all took place on the post and a good time seemed to be had by all. I would like to tell you the reason for the big time but it'll have to wait. Also flew a couple more practice missions over the English countryside, just for the heck of it.

On September 9 and 10 the 95th Group was "stood down" and the 200th Mission Party commenced. On the evening of the ninth I was ordered to report to Group Operations, with a skeleton crew, at 6:30 Sunday morning. When we reported in we were told that we were flying up to Birmingham to pick up some VIPs who would participate in our big party. We were to fly aircraft #0235, *The Zoot Suiter.* This had been Bill ("Catfish") Lindley's airplane, the one in which he flew as lead pilot on the Münster raid, a mission which brought the group a Presidential Unit Citation. Lindley had at one time also been squadron commander of the 412th Bomb Squadron. Both the airplane and Lindley were already legends in our group, and we felt honored.

When we took off that morning the weather was poor, a very low ceiling with visibility about one mile. Work gave me a heading, but to follow it meant going on instruments, then having to let down over Birmingham and not knowing but what the ceiling could be zero. This could be very dangerous, so I decided to remain in visual contact with the ground and fly around the low clouds when it appeared they were too low to fly under.

After a while Work came on the interphone and said that I had made so many turns in such a short period of time that he had not been able to keep track of all of them. By now we had him thoroughly confused as to where we were. All I knew was we could see the ground so we must still be over England. Well, to a navigator this is not much help. About this time Doc came on the interphone and asked if the "Gee Box" was working. This was a navigating device which was developed for use in the U.K. It was possible to get an instantaneous fix of position accurate enough to be able to line up on a runway, and it was possible to keep a running fix going. Work immediately responded, *"The Gee Box.* I had completely forgotten about it. I'll turn it on and get it warmed up." Within a few minutes he said that he had our position and we were only a few miles from Birmingham.

Soon we were on the ground and had our VIPs loaded. On the way back to the base at Horham I was told they were members of the Glenn Miller orchestra and they would be entertaining us in the afternoon at our big party. This would be the highlight of the social activities while we were a part of the group.

September 12, 1944

Hello again. Yesterday I received your letter of August 27 and today received one dated September 2. In a day or so the ones that fill the gap will

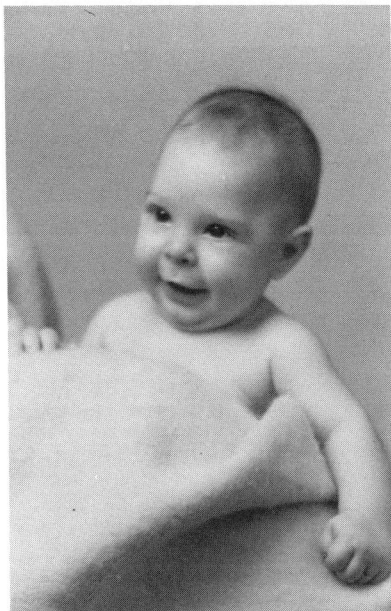

(*Left*) David Eugene Fletcher. (*Right*) Leora and Michael Patton, Sherry and David Fletcher

probably come in. I think that I get all of them, it just takes a little time. . . . So far I guess I'm about the only one in the barracks whose mail hasn't been spot checked by the Theatre Censor. Most of the other guys have had one or two censored. You don't have to worry about your letters as the Army doesn't touch civilian mail. So feel free to write anything you care to.

I get a kick out of the pictures of David. I'm always looking at them, admiring our little man. I've shown them to practically everyone on the Post. The guys think I'm worse now than when he was born—I don't brag any more than then, it's just that I have pictures now to back up my comments. They're all pretty envious that they don't have a son to go home and play with. Guess I'm just lucky! . . .

Incidentally, we are over the hump so now we're on the down grade. Chalk off number eighteen. Maybe we'll finish yet—never can tell.

Mission #18, *Ruhland, Germany, September 11*

Frank Dimit, Bombardier

Briefed at 5:30 a.m. for target at Ruhland. It was the same oil refinery we hit on our 16th mission, 65 miles east of Leipzig.

A perfect target for visual bombing but the joker closed the doors
(*95th B.G. photo*)

It was the most screwed up mess I have ever had the misfortune to encounter. Through good luck and the grace of God, the lead navigator had his head out. He was the only one in the lead ship that knew what was up.

We failed to hit our primary for some unknown reason, so we headed for the last resort target. I thought the lead bombardier was making for a small town with a fair-sized marshalling yard. He wasn't. About time for "bombs away," he closed the doors. The same thing happened at an average-sized town north of Frankfurt with a beautiful railroad yard, waiting to be creamed. But the joker closed the doors. We ended up bringing our 10 500-pound G.P. bombs back to the base. I never thought I would see the day when we would bring back a full load from the middle of Germany. There was positively no excuse for not dropping them someplace.

The lead bombardier passed up any number of targets of opportunity between the two bomb runs. Strictly a head up and locked affair. The command pilot and lead bombardier weren't worth a damn.

We started out leading the low squadron of lead group. Lost our wing men because of mechanical difficulties. Next position was #5 in lead squadron and after crossing the coast on the way back, we flew #2 in the lead. Next stop would have been lead. I know we couldn't have done a worse job.

Fighter support was good, but some enemy fighters got into our formation. Smitty and Brownie got in some shots at a fighter attacking from 6 o'clock. The fighter knocked down one of the boys from the 95th. He was in the low group of our wing.

The wing ahead of us was hit bad by fighters. Saw no flak today while we were monkeying around over greater Germany.

Damn glad to be back. *[End of mission notes by Frank Dimit]*

We were inbound to "somewhere" and were now flying the #5 spot in the lead squadron when someone called on the interphone and asked if anyone knew what the strange looking little bursts were about 2 o'clock level and about 100 feet out. The thought went through my mind that they looked like firecrackers exploding, but this wasn't the Fourth of July. Before anyone could answer, Brownie called out, "Bandits in the area 6 o'clock high and closing fast." At that moment the tail guns and the top turret started firing. We were being fired on and not being missed by very much.

The initial attack went right over us and the second wave went under us, hitting the low group. The battle for us was over in a matter of seconds. The enemy fighters descended on the low group of the wing ahead of us. This was a part of the 100th Bomb Group. Mac called on the interphone and in a quivering voice stated that the entire formation of twelve B-17s had completely disappeared. Horrified, I couldn't believe my ears and asked Mac to repeat. He stated again that the complete formation was gone. As the fighters went through, the B-17s were just wiped out—twelve aircraft and 108 men gone in just seconds. It was the first and only time we ever saw a complete unit wiped out. Our loss was pale in comparison.

At interrogation we reported the funny firecrackers and were told that the Germans were now experimenting with proximity exploding 20 millimeter shells, and we had just had a demonstration.

Eleven aircraft from our group hit the primary and their results were good. We should have been following them. As it turned out this was a day in which the Eighth Air Force fighters broke all previous single day records by shooting down 116 enemy planes. We later learned that the 100th lost only eleven aircraft instead of twelve.

September 14, 1944

It's now the end of another perfect day—received four letters from you. Also received a letter from Cap which I answered a while ago. I got quite a kick out of his student instructor problems. So to make him feel good I let him in on a few of my little problems. They aren't many, but doggone it, I can't quite seem to get used to having people shooting at me. Makes me nervous at times. . . .

What a life we lead! About the only fun we have is enjoying one another's company and for amusement kidding and playing jokes on one another. It's a good thing we all get along together so well. Instead of arguing and quarreling amongst ourselves like a lot of the crews we're always laughing and joking. Most people think we've been here too long. We thoroughly agree with them. We figure that maybe if we act crazy enough they'll send us home. So far no luck! . . .

I spoke to the C.O. of the squadron about a discharge so I could take that radio job in La Grande, but he told me if I didn't stop pestering him he was going to give me a job. I took him at his word for the only job he can give me is where people take pot shots at you. He thinks I'm crazy anyway—wanting to leave here and go back to the States where you have to eat steaks, drink milkshakes and cokes, live with your wife, go fishing, and wear civilian clothes. Me thinks he's been here too long too!

September 15, 1944

. . . *Dimit received a newspaper from home the other day and we ran across this article. Dimit knows the fellow well and we have been getting quite a kick out of it. After reading it you'll see why, so here we go: "Captain John W. Preble Jr., Stanton Blvd., has been highly commended by Lt. Col. T. Q. Graft, Air Corps Commander, Mediterranean Theatre of War, for the difficult task of preparing citations for proposed awards for various members of his organization. Attached to the Air Corps Intelligence Capt. Preble has served in the Mediterranean Theatre of Operation for fifteen months."*

We have just come to the conclusion that if our flying around and earning these awards is causing the ground personnel that much trouble and work perhaps we should quit. "For the difficult task"—I'll never get over that. It must have been rough typing those citations. Flak all over the sky, completely surrounded by enemy fighters, two engines out, part of the control cables gone, gas leaking out of the tanks, airplanes going down like flies— then the keys probably jammed on the typewriter. Some day when this is over some joker like that is going to try to tell me how he won the war and I'm going to blow my top. Yes sir, that poor fellow beating that typewriter must have had a rough time. Too bad he can't take time out and go for a ride with us. Gosh, I must be getting bitter so I'll get off the subject!

September 17, 1944

Not much to report from this side of the Atlantic today. It was a very quiet Sunday spent in the usual Sunday manner of church, sleeping, and reading. This afternoon, though, we got up enough ambition to build an aerial for the radio which was just recently fixed. We had the aerial all fixed and hooked up and music just poured out of the little box—so far so good—but then we decided to change a few things. After we did this the radio quit altogether and wouldn't even give out with static. We drew straws to see who was to tear the radio down and fix it. I lost. I tore it all to pieces and worked about two hours on it. Finally the fruits of my hard labor began to ripen as the static increased and finally dinner music became recognizable. Deciding to leave well enough alone, I quit monkeying with it. The fact that that was the only station we could tune in had nothing to do with it. Everything went fine until the program was over and the announcer came on. Doggone, if I didn't have a German station tuned in! The fellows became very violent and insisted that I work on it until I got an English station. I tried to argue that it would be much simpler if we would just study German—then we could understand the newscasts and programs. They didn't

Crew assembled in front of their first assigned aircraft, *Knock Out Baby*

quite see my point but, anyway, I refused to work on it any more. Someboay else fooled with it the rest of the afternoon and right now it isn't playing anything. The general consensus is that there isn't anything wrong with it that a new radio wouldn't help! . . .

We finally got an airplane—#257 Knock Out Baby. We were all very happy to be able to call it our own. We're pretty proud of it and we have some pictures which I'll send home in a few days. Someday I'll tell you just why we are so attached to that airplane. The ground crew that looks after it thinks we're pretty swell guys—don't know us very well, do they? They have fixed up lots of little extra things on it for us.

I don't know how you manage to read these letters of mine. I must be getting stupid. Can't spell, sentence structure going from bad to worse, writing becoming more illegible, words left out, and what's worse the same sentence or word written twice. I'm sure glad I don't have to read them. Guess I'm about due for a trip to the States to recuperate. Don't know what I would recuperate from seeing as how I haven't done anything, but it makes a good excuse for the state of the letters.

September 18, 1944

I have some good news for you this evening. In the continuing saga of the radio—it is working perfectly! We talked one of the fellows with radio maintenance into working on it for us. Now it works just like a charm and doesn't give us any trouble. It seems good to lie in the sack and listen to good old American jive. What a life! It comes in handy too to listen to the newscasts, and right now we're all very much interested in what is going on over the Channel.

Today was spent flying around all over the English countryside again. Cap has nothing on me as I'm getting to be quite an instructor myself. Lately we have been spending about three-fourths of our time breaking in new crews, getting them used to flying formation again and how to navigate in a combat theater. It does them a lot of good and also gives me practice leading. All in all it isn't bad but it slows down my missions. But I have learned one thing—"take things as they come and don't volunteer for anything," also "that everything happens for the best." That's the outlook we take on everything, good or bad.

No mail today for anyone in the hut. That's the first day we've had a complete shut-out for a long time. But that makes our chances better for a big haul tomorrow. Oh yes, today we were awarded another Oak Leaf Cluster for wear with the Air Medal. Same citation and all such stuff as goes with the Air Medal. I'll enclose the cluster in the letter so you may have it too.

September 20, 1944

. . . We have initiated a new regime—no more lying in the sack until noon. We decided that we were getting lazy and, besides, it is a bad habit. So now everyone gets up before nine, or if you can't make it then, at least by eleven fifty-nine! No kidding, since we've been getting up earlier on our days of leisure we've been feeling better. Maybe it's because we're getting more exercise by volunteering for the little odds and ends jobs around the Group. At least we're happier when our minds are occupied. Yesterday we took a short hop in the morning—kind of a weather check—then went to a show in the afternoon. It was one of those Peter Lorre mystery thrillers entitled The Mask of Dimitrius. *It was a waste of time and money when they produced it, but it didn't cost me anything so why should I gripe about it? . . .*

Here's the payoff—this is one for "Can You Beat This." Since our radio speaks German better than any other language we find ourselves listening most of the time to German stations. Last night they were playing "Don't

Sit Under The Apple Tree With Anyone Else But Me"—German words and all! That beats me! Can you imagine them playing our victory songs to their troops? Oh well, I guess they have to have some good music occasionally.

If it weren't for you and David I couldn't do the job I'm asked to do here. I'm not here because of patriotism to any ideals. I'm here to do what's expected of me only because I feel that in some way I'm aiding and protecting my little family. That feeling alone gives me the courage to keep on trying to do my part and just a little more. We all want to come home but we'll do our best before we do. Sometimes we get pretty discouraged, but that's only human nature, and usually comes as a result of loneliness for our loved ones. In the face of things here dreams of the past and future are about all that keep you going.

September 24

Doc Doxon, Copilot

Came back from London on a very crowded train. Buzz bomb went very close over the barracks. Fletcher really went under the bed.

It was after dark and the eight officers were gathered in Nissen hut #10 along with two visitors. A lively bull session was underway when we heard a buzz bomb coming our way.

The buzz bomb (or V-1 or Doodle Bug) was a strange instrument of war, somewhat like a small airplane. Buzz bombs were powered by a rocket engine mounted high on the tail and the fuselage was filled with high explosives. They were launched from ramps in Germany and France and headed in the direction of England. Their range varied by the amount of fuel the Germans pumped into them. When the fuel supply was exhausted the motor would stop. There would be absolute silence as the rocket plunged approximately 1,000 feet to the ground. A tremendous explosion would occur as these were strictly flying bombs.

The V-1s had short stubby wings and weren't particularly fast. In fact, the Spitfires and other fighters would, sometimes, try to intercept and shoot them down over the English Channel. Once they made landfall this process became more difficult because of the low altitude at which they flew. But the fighters would try to shoot them down over the farm country before they reached the major cities.

Since our airfield was located in East Anglia in the heart of the farm country we were not generally considered a prime target, al-though there were airfields located about ten miles apart all over the countryside. The buzz bombs didn't pose any particular problem to us unless they happened to run out of fuel while they were in our vicinity.

We had learned to respect them on our previous trips to London where we had seen the demolition even one could cause. We were all very conscious of them, and as long as we heard the engine run-ning we didn't take any particular precautions. By this time a lot of people were smart enough to head for shelter when they heard the things coming. But this meant running outside in the rain, fog, or snow. You wouldn't have your coat on, and you'd have to go down and stand in the shelter—even wondering whether the thing would fall before you got to the shelter. So finally we just stayed in our Nissen hut and took our chances.

On this particular evening we stopped our visiting when we heard the bomb coming and, of course, everyone had the same idea in mind—"please keep that engine running!" When it sounded as if it were very close to us, all of a sudden there was dead silence. This meant you had better seek whatever cover you could—it was too late to head for the bomb shelter.

The beds we had in the quonset at this time were all singles and on one level, so the safest place would be under the bed. At least you'd have the mattress and bed covers over the top of you. If the building should blow in you'd have a certain amount of protection. When the engine stopped my immediate thought was to crawl un-der my bed, and since I had a friend there visiting me he also looked around for a place. But that was his problem—I had solved mine. When he saw me under the bed the first thing he did was grab the mattress and all the blankets from off my bed. He flopped down on the floor and pulled them over him. It left me wide-eyed staring up through the springs on the bed with absolutely no protection. You can well imagine the thoughts going through my mind and what I thought of my friend.

When the big explosion came the building rattled and shook, but luckily there was no damage to our Nissen hut, and when we got our wits gathered about, everyone was laughing at my predicament because they had seen my protection disappear over the top of my buddy.

As Doc tells the story, there was a WAC in the barracks with us who was visiting the navigator on the other crew. And, as his story goes, all the rest of them jumped under the bed where the WAC was seeking protection.

Anyway, the moral of the story is: If you are going to seek protection from the buzz bombs, don't have company in your room at the same time.

The buzz bomb landed just a few hundred yards from our barracks and, as good luck would have it, it was in a farmer's field and did not cause any damage on the base. These little incidents made you want to strike back even harder. Fear has a way of making you mad.

September 25

Doc Doxon, Copilot

Flying practice mission—high squadron lead. Lots of new ships on the field. They left plenty of B-17s in Russia.

September 26

Doc Doxon, Copilot

Another practice day—2 practice missions, one at night, and on the list for tomorrow. Looks like we've had it.

September 27, 1944

You haven't had a letter from me for six days. The first three days were spent in London on pass—saw a lot of the old buddies and did some traveling on the London subway, affectionately known as "the tube."

London has an extensive subway system. It is very modern and clean. Many of the underground stations are finished in white ceramic tile. In some of the cars there is a map of the system. The routes are a line of light tubes. You push a button of where you are and a button for where you want to go and the route lights up on the map. The stations are round circles of light with names like Charing Cross, Marble Arch, etc. These will indicate whether you need to change cars at a particular station. It is all very simple and you can go almost any place in London without having to ask directions. Just pick out the station nearest to where you want to go, go to that station, get off, climb the stairs to street level and start walking. If you are lucky you might find a cab, but don't count on it.

There is one thing that is very important—you want to know when the last car runs because you could be stranded. These cars or trains do not run all night, so don't miss the last one. It's probably a good thing that they stop running because many of the stations are filled with people who are trying to sleep. These are people who are using these stations for bomb shelters and are seeking safety from the buzz bombs, the V-2 rockets, or an occasional bombing. When you see people actually living in stations, whole families of them, with no privacy, you just have to feel sorry for them, this world, and the state it is in. The people at home have no idea at all of what it is to have a war fought over or on your own country. There are a lot of things that I don't understand about the English people, but I do know one thing, from the privations they have suffered they are a brave lot!

These last three days I have really been running in circles—more work than I've ever had to do. Guess I'm about caught up now, or will be just as soon as I put in the sack time which I'm behind on. Have managed to get four hours in the sack in the last thirty-six. But in just a few minutes I intend to average that out.

Yesterday marked the ninth straight day with no mail from the States, but today I had ten letters from you. We found out only a few days ago why our mail was being held up. We should have pretty good service from now on.

Incidentally, number nineteen is over with so you can chalk that one off. I may have some good news for you tomorrow when I write. At the present I'm not quite sure about it but will double check in the morning.

Mission #19, Mainz, Germany, September 27

Frank Dimit, Bombardier

Due to a night practice mission after 2 hours sleep we briefed at 3:15 a.m. for our target at Mainz, Germany, just a few miles west of Frankfurt. Our target was the marshalling yards. The ground forces wanted it K.O.'d because reinforcements for the Siegfried Line were being brought through there.

We flew lead in the high squadron of the low group of the 13th combat wing. Was our first mission as deputy group lead. We carried 10 500-pound aimable cluster incendiaries. Bombing was PFF so we didn't see the results. Somebody goofed up because the wing lead PFF ship was not carrying smoke bombs, and we didn't know when to dump our load.

Also raised hell when we came back, because upper and lower turrets of every ship in the group were stowed most of the time. If fighters had hit us, we would still be over in the Fatherland. Maj. Fitzgerald and Lt. Schwartz promised to raise hell about it.

Our wing was last one in and last out of Germany. So we caught plenty of prop wash. Caught flak several places besides target area. None of it accurate and most of it light. Saw no enemy fighters— glad of it. Escort not as good as usual. Think we missed rendezvous.

Chalk up another one for us. *[End of mission notes by Frank Dimit]*

September 28, 1944

The good news that I was going to tell you about was that if I make good as a Squadron Lead I probably won't have to fly over thirty-one. I'm not positive about this yet so as soon as I get some time off I will get some confirmation on this rumor. It's positive on Group Leads, but we're in slight doubt on Squadron Leads.

In the meantime you can check off number twenty as another one gone by.

Mission #20, Merseburg, Germany, September 28

Frank Dimit, Bombardier

Today was a pistol. Briefed at 5:15 a.m. for a target at our old friend(?) Merseburg, Germany. It was the third time we have been briefed for this target, but we didn't get there the other two times. We did today. Target was an oil refinery, and they wanted the thing K.O.'d. The entire 3rd Division (9 Combat Wings) hit the same target. We were the sixth wing in.

We flew lead of low squadron of lead group, and had the hell shot right out of us. Carried 10 500-pound G.P. bombs. Bombing was PFF—results unobserved.

No enemy fighters—damn good support. Flak worst I've ever seen or hope to see. Our ship looked like a sieve with between 45-50 holes. Nobody was injured, but I almost stopped a slug. A small hunk of flak came through the plexiglass panel just above my seat. It clipped the back of my head, but it didn't hurt me. I didn't have my flak helmet on, but it didn't take me long to get it on. The extra radio man we carried collected two flak holes in his helmet, one going in, the other coming out. It scratched his skull but that was all. A hunk of flak knocked out our right waist gun. Fletch was saved

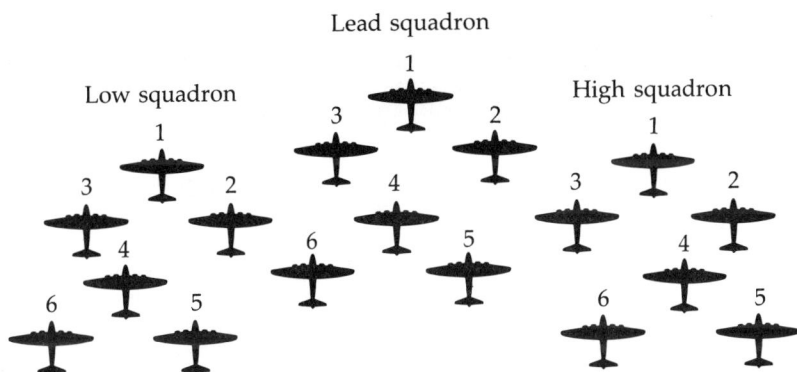

Top view of a group formation. The lead ship of a lead squadron was the group lead and was a PFF Mickey Radar ship. As a lead crew we flew squadron lead, leading either the high or low squadron as a backup or deputy visual lead to the group leader.

from death or serious injury by the bullet-proof glass on his window. Number two engine was K.O.'d.

We came back alone again, but this time we followed a formation out and didn't have to sweat out the navigation. Work always does a damn good job, but when you come back over an overcast, the element of chance has a lot to do with it. Sometimes the weather information leaves a lot to be desired.

Our entire group was hit hard. Our right wing man had his co-pilot killed. Our left wing man lost an engine, and the prop and cowling flew off the damn thing over France. Major Pomeroy (Squadron C.O.) was in the wing lead ship and it was hit bad also. (Major Pomeroy was hit in the face.) Wounded at least one man, and #1 engine was smoking very badly. They crash landed near Brussels.

It was the roughest we've seen. Don't think we'll fly tomorrow—battle damage too great. *[End of mission notes by Frank Dimit]*

In a combat formation a normal group was made up of eighteen planes. These were divided into three squadrons of six ships. Each squadron had two three-ship elements. The first element had a lead ship and two wingmen. The second element had a lead ship in the

Side view of a group formation: three squadrons, eighteen ships, 850 feet in depth

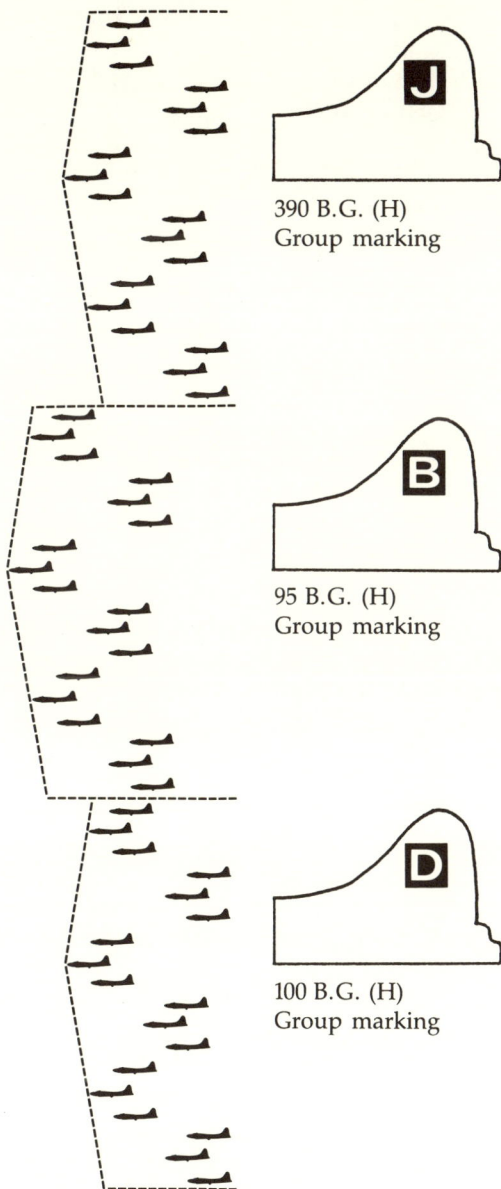

390 B.G. (H)
Group marking

95 B.G. (H)
Group marking

100 B.G. (H)
Group marking

Side view of the 13th Combat Wing formation comprised of the 390th, 95th, and 100th groups, showing the 95th as lead group; 3,000 feet in depth. Three groups constituted a wing and consisted of a lead group, a high group, and a low group stacked very similar to the squadrons within a group. We now had a formation of 54 aircraft.

diamond of the first element along with two wingmen. Each of the three squadrons had this same makeup.

The lead squadron had the group lead ship, a PFF Mickey Radar Ship, flying as the lead of the first element, with the second element in trail. The low squadron flew below, slightly behind, and left of the lead squadron with the lead ship slightly behind the left wingman of the lead element of the lead squadron. The high squadron flew above, slightly behind, and to the right of the lead squadron with the lead ship slightly behind the right wingman of the lead element of the lead squadron. From above the formation looked like the diagram on page 159.

In our case the three groups were the 95th Heavy Bombardment Group, the 390th Heavy Bombardment Group, and the 100th Heavy Bombardment Group. These three groups made up the Thirteenth Combat Wing and flew together. All wings going to the same target constituted a task force. This was the purist form and was used solely in the beginning.

As the groups continued to grow and received more aircraft and crews, it eventually became possible for a group to put up enough aircraft to make up two groups in a wing, or even a complete wing. As time went on even the number of aircraft in a group formation occasionally changed from eighteen to twelve, or any number in between. Squadrons became elements, groups became squadrons. But the eighteen-ship group was the most common.

The wings would fly in trail with a three-minute separation toward the Initial Point. At the IP the lead group of the wing would fire two flares five seconds apart and then turn for the target. The low group would continue on for twenty seconds, then turn in trail on the lead group and head for the target. The high group would continue on twenty seconds after the low group, then turn and start their run to the target in trail of the low group. This would put a maximum of eighteen aircraft over the target at any one time and was considered the maximum for a good bomb pattern, as all eighteen aircraft would drop simultaneously with the lead ship when his smoke bombs emerged from the bomb bay.

After "Bombs away" the lead group would fly straight ahead for at least another twenty seconds, then start a descending right turn losing 1,000 feet of altitude to the Rally Point. The low group would then cross the target and bomb, continue ahead for about ten seconds, then start a descending right turn inside of the lead group, losing 1,000 feet, and wind up back in position under the lead group on the left side at the RP. The high group would cross the target and bomb, then start an immediate descending turn to the right,

Perfect formation as the 95th heads for battle over greater Germany *(Boeing Archives)*

Wingman flying perfect formation for protection against enemy fighters. "Tuck it in tight!"

On the bomb run *(Boeing Archives)*

inside the low group. Upon losing 1,000 feet the high group would now reach the RP above and to the right of the lead group. The wing had now been re-formed for the best fighter protection and would head home.

The rest of the wings would complete this same maneuver until the entire task force had crossed the target.

General Curtis E. LeMay was the originator of this box-type formation, and it was considered a very formidable force, giving maximum firepower to ward off enemy fighter attacks.

Not all tactics are 100 percent effective and many casualties would result. But this was considered the very best that could be devised. The 100th Bomb Group was probably the best-known group in the Eighth Air Force for its many casualties, a rather dubious honor. There was one occasion in October 1943 when they sent out thirteen ships and only one returned!

On our twentieth mission our crew was leading the low squadron. Since the low squadron is always stacked below and left of the lead squadron it was much easier to fly this position from the right seat, which is the copilot's position. This was our third time to lead the low squadron. The first time I had found it difficult to see and maintain position for a long period of time from the left seat. I had a stiff neck from all the bobbing and weaving. So I requested that Doc fly from the left seat and I would fly from his position where I could have an uninterrupted view of the lead squadron. It would not only be easier on me but also on our wing and trail aircraft because in this position I could fly a more stable aircraft with fewer power changes. I could keep the lead ship in view at all times and detect any change in his position immediately.

The time before I had made this same switch and everything had worked fine, with the exception of a harmless case of vertigo on my part which was quickly pointed out by Doc, so it seemed logical to try again.

The bombardier had just called "Bombs away" when a loud explosion and shock wave rocked the ship violently. The huge shell had exploded on the right side of the ship just aft of the wing and beside the window of the right waist gunner. Instantly shrapnel from the burst filled the airplane. My windshield was like a spider web with lines radiating out from a hole near the top in the bulletproof glass. I immediately called for a damage report on the interphone. There was no answer. The interphone had to be dead. It was obvious that we had suffered major damage—we needed to communicate.

In this instant Doc grabbed the control column and patted the top of his head, indicating that he had control of the aircraft, and started his turn and 1,000-foot descent to the Rally Point.

Suddenly I was very mad—angry at the Germans—but more so at the lack of my ability to communicate with the crew, who at this time should need some leadership. In frustration I depressed what I thought to be a dead mike button and vented my emotion with a string of oaths. This was abruptly halted by the heat near my ankle and the smell of smoke. I looked down and saw that my flying suit on my right leg was smouldering and smoking, but there was no blaze. As I leaned over to grab the smoldering area and smother it with my gloved hands I heard two words—"Pilot hit," then after a couple of seconds, "Brownie." It was Doc's voice.

Immediately Brownie came out of the top turret. I knew then that some of the crew had communication. Brownie immediately grabbed me and pulled my head up from my bent-over position and was trying to find out where I was hit. I had squeezed out the glowing embers on my ankle and realized that the red-hot shrapnel had blown a hole in my flight suit, but had not hit my leg. It had also severed the wire in the cord leading to my headset, but it was still partly held together by the insulation around the wire. When I leaned over the broken wire made contact long enough for me to hear those few words. My string of oaths had been transmitted to the crew, then all was silent from my position since I assumed the interphone to be inoperative. This in turn caused the crew to believe I had problems, even more so because I had a standing order that no profanity would ever be used on the interphone.

In a theater of war the language would become somewhat salty on occasion. Our communication system was vital and I did not want it cluttered up with oaths or idle chatter. Up until now this order had never been violated, so it must have been quite a shock to the crew that the rule was violated by its originator.

In the meantime Brownie was still trying to find my injury. I, knowing that I had no physical problems, was trying to get him to get back up in the top gun turret because we were now at the Rally Point and could be subject to enemy fighter attacks at any moment.

In the course of our wrestling around in the copilot's seat Brownie discovered the severed wire on the interphone and quickly hooked up another to put me back into communication with the rest of the crew. It was then that I noticed that the hose leading to Brownie's oxygen mask had been cut by the flying shrapnel and he was receiving only a partial oxygen supply. This was remedied immediately and the cockpit crew was now back to normal. Thanks to Doc our low squadron was back in tight group formation and we were headed home. The #2 engine was losing oil pressure rapidly and had to be feathered. We dropped out of the formation and started the long journey home alone at 130 mph. Frank reported that there was a hole in the plexiglass nose.

I was then told that the men in the radio room and waist position had reported extensive damage and that it might be wise to make a visual structural check. Grabbing a portable oxygen bottle I went back to the radio room. It was almost like walking into a giant sieve, but all damage was confined to the skin and all structural members appeared to be okay.

Two days before this mission I had been contacted by a "specialty" radio operator who had requested permission to install his radio and recording equipment in our aircraft. I asked him about his specialty. He said he spoke German fluently, that his radios were tuned to the German fighter frequencies, and he would monitor and record all fighter activity from the time of their takeoff till their return to bases. He would record several different frequencies and return this information to Intelligence for whatever use they might be able to make of it. It sounded like a worthwhile project and one we would like to be associated with.

I asked him why he had picked our aircraft. He said Operations had told him we were a good, stable crew with plenty of experience. He also said that he knew Hinman, our radio operator, and George had assured him that this was the best crew on the field. Discounting individual prejudice, he had decided to go with us if I approved.

We had the ground crew install a table for him in the radio room at the forward bulkhead on the right side of the ship. Hinman was stationed just opposite on the left side.

While assessing the damage in the radio room, Hinman pointed to the other radio operator. Some of his equipment looked as if it had been hit by a hammer, and his eyes were as large as saucers. He handed me his steel flak helmet and I noticed two jagged holes near the top where flak had entered and exited. I looked at the top of his head. His leather flying helmet was split for about two inches with his white scalp showing and four little drops of blood interspersed along the crease. One look was all I wanted. Words weren't necessary—he knew how lucky he was. I gave him a pat on the shoulder and headed for the waist compartment where there was a rather large jagged hole in the right waist gunner's position. The right waist gun had been hit and rendered useless. This was Joe Firszt's position and he had just been dropped from the crew to comply with an order to change from ten-man to nine-man crews. I don't think anyone could have survived in that position—I gave thanks that Joe wasn't aboard.

Since we were flying the low squadron our left side was the one that was exposed to enemy fighter attack. For this reason Lynch was manning the left waist gun, which was staggered away from the right gun position. Flak had sprayed around him, but he hadn't been hit.

I called Smitty, the tail gunner, on the interphone from the waist compartment. He said his position was okay and that he was well wrapped in his cocoon of flak suits. I refilled the portable oxygen bottle and headed back to the copilot's seat, secure in the knowledge that the aircraft was structurally sound, maybe more so than its occupants.

On the way home it dawned on me that the crew had functioned perfectly during the time I was isolated—they could survive and continue without me. This is a terrible blow to one's ego, but it gave me a feeling of pride that these men knew their jobs and could perform them under any circumstances, with or without me.

What should have been a time of fear became a time of anger and sheer, cool determination to do the job and complete the mission. I had noticed many times that fear for some people sparked a very deliberate and deadly desire for survival. They functioned even beyond what was thought of as a brave or heroic capacity.

When we landed at the base the "specialty" radio operator had his equipment removed from our aircraft and never asked to go with us again. In fact, he never asked anyone else either. He decided flying was not his first desire and they could gather this information in some other way, such as automatic equipment which didn't require an operator.

For myself, I vowed never again to fly in the copilot's seat—that could be a dangerous place. From now on I would sit on the hallowed left side!

Then there still remained the matter of discipline for breaking the rule of profanity on the interphone. I thought about giving up the shot of whiskey which was provided each returning crew member just before interrogation. But that idea didn't sound too good—it should be a punishment more severe. So I decided to prudently ask for two shots and give up dessert at dinner that evening. I was sure the crew would understand and accept this as a reasonable sacrifice!

September 29, 1944

Have just finished logging fourteen hours of sack time and a couple hours of classes, so I'm back in pretty good humor.

I hardly know where to begin, but first I'll tell you more about my pass since that was the start of the non-letter days. We started out to go to Cambridge to look over the English colleges and universities. There are about twenty colleges there, I believe. We got our tickets, hopped on board a train and were to change trains in London. When we got there we loitered around the station for awhile waiting for the other train to come in and who should show up but Geagan, remember him? He talked us into staying in London and spending our pass together. . . .

After we got back from our pass things were happening pretty fast so we got quite a little work out before we knew what was going on. When the rush was over and the smoke cleared we wound up with two missions. Now that we've had a good night's sleep everyone is happy and we're all sitting around catching up on back correspondence.

The pictures I promised you still haven't come back. The negatives were developed but there is a shortage of paper to print them on. We lost one complete roll due to the fact that the Limey filing system was screwed up.

We may get them back but I doubt it. We returned the ones they gave us in place of ours. . . .

I'm not sure as yet but I'm becoming more convinced by the day that the thirty-one deal was pure rumor and pertained only to group leads. I was asked to become a group lead but I turned it down because I didn't want to break up the crew. Oh well, it was a good rumor anyway. Besides, when you have to do thirty-one, four more won't make any difference, I keep telling myself!

We will probably get a new airplane one of these days and get to name this one. Our good friend, Knock Out Baby isn't with us any more.

The radio is still working but I'm afraid we don't get to listen to any of the good radio programs. The German stations are so much more powerful than the English that they blanket the whole frequency band. Occasionally we get to hear an English station but the music they play isn't as good as the German. The Germans play most all of the hit tunes that were popular when I was home. We have a German condenser in the radio so we use that as the reason we can't get anything but German stations. . . .

On September 18 the 95th Bomb Group left on the third shuttle mission to Russia. This mission was called "Frantic Seven." Our crew did not go because Doc had a wisdom tooth pulled and was DNIF (Duty Not Involving Flying). However, *Knock Out Baby* made the trip, and she was shot up on the ground at Poltava by the Luftwaffe during the night and could not return with the group.

September 29

Doc Doxon, Copilot

Rested today. Rumor has it I will get Layl's crew. Hate to think of leaving Fletcher's gang.

September 30

Doc Doxon, Copilot

Fletch checked out a new plane #7783. Guess it is my last flight with them—don't even want to tell them about it. They're sure a swell crew. They are going on Flak Pass.

October 2, 1944

This is a note to let you know that I'm at one of the rest homes for combat personnel. We were released to come down here a few days sooner than I had expected. A whole week with nothing to do but relax and enjoy life! So far today we've played tennis, badminton, ping pong, and walked all over town. The rest of the day will be spent taking a shower, eating dinner and hitting the sack. Fiess and Pipkin and their crews came down with us and we're all having a real time.

October 3, 1944

This morning was spent playing tennis—three solid hours of it. The afternoon was passed with several games of ping pong and then an afternoon matinee. The picture was The Song of Bernadette. *It was wonderful and I highly recommend it to be put on your "must see" list. To describe it would detract from the picture so I won't try.*

Doc didn't come to the rest home with us. We truly miss him. It looks as if he's going to get a crew of his own so he had to stay behind to look after his interests. His leaving the crew will be felt by all of us for he was a swell guy and a darn good copilot. I won't feel bad about it, though, because I told him in the beginning that if he had a chance to get ahead I wouldn't stand in his way, in fact, I would do all I could to help him. Like I say, I hate to lose him, but at the same time, it makes me feel good to think that he was picked for the job. Maybe the little things that I showed him and hollered at him about were okay after all. Incidentally, Joe got a very good job when he left the crew. We all did our best for him but, mainly, it was up to him. He was a darn good kid and I know now that I should never have let him go. But I guess we all make a few mistakes. . . .

Now let me tell you about a little incident that happened here today. We don't get very much fresh fruit so today as we were passing the grocery stores downtown we spotted some peaches, grapes, and a few scraggly looking apples. The peaches, though, were first-grade and really looked delicious. My mind was made up—I would have some peaches. Frank decided on the grapes. Fiess took a fancy to the apples. Now comes the part I don't expect you to believe. I bought $3.60 worth of peaches and ate all three of them myself. I'm not kidding or trying to exaggerate. The peaches cost me $1.20 apiece and that was the legitimate price. Frank paid eighteen shillings, or $3.60, for a pound of grapes so you know how many he got. Fiess got a bargain. He got four apples and a half pound of grapes for $4. As you can see, foodstuffs are not plentiful here and there is a slight trace of inflation.

The average Englishman with wartime wages makes less than twenty dollars a week, so you can see how much fruit his family enjoys. . . .

October 4

Doc Doxon, Copilot

Fletch still on Flak Pass at Bournemouth. Our practice mission was called off so swung compass for him on his new aircraft, #7783. *Knock Out Baby*, #7257, came back from Russia today.

October 6, 1944

It is Friday so I'll pen my last letter to you from the rest home. We'll leave here early tomorrow morning. . . .

As you know we've been visiting the rest home on what is known as a "flak leave." Now we want to find out whether their sending us here was a matter of routine or whether they actually thought we were "flakky" enough to deserve it. Whichever the case, we've had a marvelous time and the rest has really been worthwhile. . . .

October 8, 1944

We got home late last night—didn't stay overnight in London as we had planned but came straight on home. The reason was that we were all anxious to get back and read the mail that had accumulated in our absence. And believe me, none of us were disappointed. Including today's mail I had sixteen letters! One was from my cousin in Italy that I wrote about. . . .

You know I told you about the Captain, who was one of my instructors in Ardmore, that came over here? He's now our Squadron Commander, and will probably be sporting shiny new oak leaves soon. That's good. We get along together swell so I'm glad he has the job.

Doc got his crew all right and they're flying together now. As yet I haven't been legally assigned a copilot, but the fellow I'll probably get is a swell fellow and was originally a first pilot. He has about the same number of missions that I have, so you can see that he's had plenty of experience and knows as much about his job as I do. So the crew hasn't suffered any by Doc's leaving except that we were good buddies. There's a long story that goes with all this, but I can't tell you about it until I get home.

Braund has moved and the hut is a little dead with them not around. There are only about six of us old buddies left around—the rest have finished up. It's getting to the point where I hardly know anybody around the outfit anymore. Most everybody seems to know us and they refer to us as "Permanent Party"! . . .

Now about our quarters—there are two crews of officers to the hut and our enlisted men share a hut with two other crews. Since Braund has moved we have the whole place to ourselves. As for the hut itself, it was just a tin shed with a concrete floor when we moved in. But now with all the little things we've done it is fairly livable. We built shelves, got some linoleum for the floor, and fixed up all kinds of little things. It's just as comfortable as a barn can be made and we're quite proud of our shack, even if we are sharing it with a good-sized family of rats.

I'm trying to write with the hubbub of conversation going on and it was just mentioned that we have another Battle Star. I guess I have never mentioned them. It's this way—you know we are all entitled to the ETO ribbon. Well, we now wear four battle stars on it. To tell what the stars are for would involve military information so we won't go into that. In addition to this ribbon and stars plus the Air Medal and clusters, we also wear a Presidential Unit Citation ribbon plus a cluster. Every member of the crew has the same awards, which is as it should be—we're all in this together. Gosh, when we dress up we look just like a Gypsy wedding going some place to happen!

One of the fellows just came in and said we had to work tomorrow so I'll stop writing and start sacking it.

Battle Stars were awarded for participation in major battles or campaigns. Our crew participated in five major campaigns: Normandy, North France, Rhineland, Ardennes, Air Combat Balkans.

October 9, 1944

Have just finished with the day's work and feel in a retiring sort of mood but first will pen a few short lines. In the meantime, you can cross off number twenty-one—that's another we won't have to do again.

Bob Layl has been assigned as my new copilot and he flew with us today. He's a very good pilot and the fellows all like him so we'll get along swell. He was the fellow I was telling you about who used to be a first pilot. Personally I like him and like his flying technique so that's about all there is to say.

Mission #21, *Mainz, Germany, October 9*

Frank Dimit, Bombardier

Briefed at 9:00 a.m. for target at Mainz, Germany. Target was to be an ordnance depot if it was visual bombing, but it was PFF, so the "Mickey" tried to pick up the marshalling yards at Mainz. Don't know if we hit the target, it was a 10/10ths [total] undercast.

We led the low squadron of lead group of 13th combat wing. We were the last wing into Germany today. Carried 5 1000-pound G.P. bombs.

Fighter escort was good. Were supposed to have 3 groups of P-47s and one of P-38s. But didn't see any P-38s. Didn't see any flak in range. Saw about six bursts, 1,000 yards away. Were afraid we would be hit by fighters when we didn't see any flak, but they didn't show, thank goodness.

Would like to see several more missions like this one. . . . Doc was on the Leipzig trip last Saturday, his first mission as first pilot, when the group was hit by fighters. Was a rough go. Our group lost three planes, and the outfit flying the low group lost eight. They are definitely getting rougher.

The ship we took to Merseburg on our 20th mission is back on operations again. It has been out for ten days. The line chief says he never saw so many holes and so little blood.

This was our first mission without Doxon as copilot. He's got a crew of his own now. Our new copilot is Bob Layl. Fletch is well pleased with him. Seems like a good boy. He used to be a first pilot, but cracked up a ship. Doc has Layl's old crew.

We just got back from the flak shack, and are feeling in pretty good shape.

We fly again tomorrow. *[End of mission notes by Frank Dimit]*

October 9

Doc Doxon, Copilot

Fletch goes to Mainz—a milk run. Sure hate to see Fletch take off without me. He didn't even have 1 hole.

On September 9 Billy Bob Layl and crew took off on his tenth mission to Dusseldorf. Immediately upon becoming airborne they lost

Billy Bob Layl's airplane crash

an engine. They left the area to let the rest of the group take off. When all of the takeoff activity was over with they came back to the base and attempted a three-engine landing with a full gas and bomb load, a procedure that was not unusual. During the flareout for landing another mechanical failure, real or imagined, was reported by a crew member. This caused Billy Bob to attempt a three-engine "go around." The attempt was unsuccessful because of the weight factor. The ship hit the runway with full power and the landing gear collapsed. The ship was completely destroyed, but the crew members walked away with only sprains and bruises. Thus Billy Bob became the victim of a system which required that the first pilot must accept full responsibility for everything that happens aboard his aircraft. He was removed from first pilot status and became our co-pilot.

October 10, 1944

I got up early this morning to work but for some reason didn't have to at the last minute. Instead, I spent practically the whole day flying around the countryside checking out an instructor, who used to be at Roswell when I was there, in the art of flying a lead squadron. Believe me I was in the height of my glory and I chewed on him just like he used to do on his students.

He's a good man, though, and realized that his students could teach him plenty about flying over here. We had a nice chat about life back in the good old days when we were in the States.

October 12, 1944

The events of the day were quite uninteresting. No practice—it was the real McCoy. So now chalk off number twenty-two as that's another one over. Things look brighter with the closing of each day.

Yes, our radio is working nicely these days, and it seems as if most of the music we hear are the tunes that were popular when I was home. We have some trouble picking up the good programs from the States because Jerry has a few stations with the same frequency and blocks them out. Give us a little time and we'll have Jerry blocked out in more ways than one.

Mission #22, *Bremen, Germany, October 12*

Frank Dimit, Bombardier

Briefed at 5:25 a.m. for a target at Bremen, Germany. Target was an aircraft components parts factory for FW-190s.

We flew the lead of the low squadron of the low group of our wing—really down in the cellar today. We carried 10 500-pound incendiary aimable clusters. Don't know how we hit today—cloud coverage of two to three tenths and a very effective smoke screen.

Escort was good. No enemy fighters and flak wasn't bad. There seemed to be a terrific barrage over the target. But when we got there, nobody was hit bad. The groups peeled off beautifully at the IP, and we hit the target at just the right intervals. Also think the chaff worked today. Anyhow, something had those flak gunners balled up. They didn't know where to shoot. But I'm not complaining—they can do that all the time.

With Fletch's O.K., Doc flew the lead of second element of our group today. That makes him 22 also. . . .

Heard that the missions have been lowered to thirty for all of us. I hope so. *[End of mission notes by Frank Dimit]*

Our twenty-second mission was to Bremen on October 12. The weather was good and we bombed visually. Our target was an aircraft factory that was also suspected of producing armored vehicles.

On this day the German Luftwaffe returned to the air in great numbers after a period of relatively little activity. Our gunners did not get a chance at the enemy fighters, nor did we receive their death-dealing massive attacks. Our escorting fighter squadrons gave us almost complete protection from the enemy guns.

When the dogfights in the sky were over our visual bombing showed good results. The cost to our task force was three bombers and six fighters, but eighteen enemy aircraft were shot down, with four being bagged by First Lieutenant Charles E. Yeager, a P-51 squadron leader from Hamlin, West Virginia. He was later credited with five to become an Ace in one day.

October 13, 1944

It's Friday the thirteenth and I've spent most of the day just puttering around the Squadron Area. Not that I'm superstitious, but just being cautious. With twenty-two missions chalked off I'm taking no chances at this stage of the game. It would have taken a whole company of MPs to have put me on board an airplane today!

Spent the whole afternoon cleaning up my end of the barracks, throwing away a lot of odds and ends that have collected and have my things ready to move. We're still staying in the squadron but tomorrow we move to a different barracks—just something to keep us from being contented. . . .

October 14, 1944

It's a beautiful Saturday night. The air is clear and crisp, thousands of little stars are winking at a great big red-faced moon. The wind is gently rustling through the branches of the trees breathing a sigh of contentment, and here I sit like a bottle of milk on somebody's front porch six thousand miles away from my loved ones, smoking my pipe and spinning idle dreams. . . .

October 15, 1944

. . . As of today we no longer have a radio. We gave it to Braund's boys. They had a stronger claim on it than we did, although the initial idea of obtaining it was ours. We're just about lost without it, but they were the same way so it's just rough on us. Maybe we can find another around someplace, but I rather doubt it because it took months to locate that one. Besides, we don't need a radio anyway—Frank can sing while Work whis-

tles and I can M.C. the show! What we will miss will be the sultry voice of Axis Sally telling us what our wives and girlfriends are doing at home, and what the American fighting men are doing in England and over Germany. She can even tell us our losses by groups. The information is much too accurate to be all propaganda. She also dedicates certain songs to certain groups on certain occasions.

We haven't moved as yet but the papers have been served on us. We're waiting now for them to find us a shack to move into. Our minds are made up that we aren't going to like it wherever they put us be it shack or palace. Could be that we're getting slightly stubborn.

October 17, 1944

The events of yesterday were practically nil. We took a short hop during the afternoon over the wilds of England. Then last night when we should have been writing letters the crew got together for a little bull session which lasted way past our bed time. Today, however, was just a little different and you can now mark up number twenty-three. What a day! Remind me to tell you about it sometime when we have nothing else to do—by that time we'll probably be old folks and I'll have forgotten it, anyway.

There was no mail for me yesterday but did receive one from you today dated September 28th. It always happens—every time I work I get a letter from you. So the moral is if you want more letters you gotta do more work, and if you do more work the sooner you get home, and when you get home there's no need for letters. I have it all figured out and am turning into an eager beaver.

Mission #23, *Cologne, Germany, October 17*

Frank Dimit, Bombardier

Briefed at 3:20 a.m. for our target in Cologne—right in the middle of the Ruhr Valley. Target was a marshalling yard about a mile from the center of town.

It was a screwed up mission from the start with a night, overcast takeoff. We started out leading the high squadron of the low group of our wing. The 95th led the 3rd Division today and also the 8th A.F. Carried 34 100-pound G.P. bombs and 2 500-pound aimable cluster incendiaries.

Right after we departed on course the lead PFF Ship of our group aborted. We tried to re-form the group, take over the lead, and catch the lead and high groups of our wing. Our wingmen stuck with us but the rest of the group fell behind. We tried to catch our outfit and indicated 160–165 mph all the way, but no soap. Finally, we tacked onto the high squadron of another group (it turned out to be the 100th) at the IP and flew the 2nd element of the high squadron. Dropped our bombs and started back. Found out why the 100th loses so many planes. They damn near had a collision between two groups just after bombs away. Fletch had enough of that, and we tacked onto another group.

Shortly after that we found two more elements of our group wandering around over Germany so we picked them up and led them back home.

Enemy fighters—escorts good. Heavy flak barrage over target but not very accurate as far as we were concerned. Entire 8th A.F. hit the same target (PFF bombing through 10/10ths undercast) today. I think there were too many ships in the air for those flak gunners to shoot at. They must have been very sadly confused. Caught some very accurate flak over Koblenz coming out. But we didn't pick up one hole all day.

Maybe it was a good thing that our PFF lead had to abort. When we got back we learned that the other two groups had been badly shot up—our wing lost three ships. And neither of the groups had dropped their bombs. We were the only group to get rid of them.

Chalk up another one. *[End of mission notes by Frank Dimit]*

When making deep penetration into Germany we always flew north or south of the Ruhr Valley. The Ruhr Valley was truly Germany's industrial area—manufacturing and steel. It was an area to be avoided at all costs, unless the target was there. It was very heavily defended by anti-aircraft guns, many of which were mobile. If a target was known ahead of time more guns could be brought in. Consequently, our routes were altered. Additional turns and legs were added, not only to miss known anti-aircraft guns, but also to confuse the enemy, hoping that they might get their fighters airborne while we were flying a diversion leg.

German fighters were quite limited in their air time because of high fuel consumption—probably forty-five minutes to an hour at most—although they could refuel quickly and come back to hit other groups. They could fly much faster than the bombers, but the idea was to get them off the ground on a feint toward a target, then turn and head in a different direction, hoping they would expend a good part of their fuel before they could reach us. This could cut down the time they could actually spend fighting, but it also meant that we would spend more time over enemy territory, and be vulnerable for a longer period of time and from more places.

October 18, 1944

We had sort of a hard day today, which sends me to bed early. While I'm dreaming of you and little David you can cross off another one—number twenty-four is now behind us. Hope you don't mind these short notes but can't seem to do any better after a long day—know you understand.

Mission #24, *Kassel, Germany, October 18*

Frank Dimit, Bombardier

Briefed at 4:30 a.m. for target at Kassel, Germany. Target was an aero-engine factory about two miles south of town. The crew considered this a "grudge" target, because we figured we had a little score to settle with the flak gunners there, after the bad time they gave us when we were coming back from Merseburg alone on the 28th of July. So we went back today and took a few of our friends (the entire 3rd Division and part of the 1st). I don't think we made them very happy over in that part of Germany.

We flew lead of high squadron of low group of our wing. Carried 5 500-pound G.P. bombs and 5 500-pound aimable cluster incendiaries. Bombing was PFF.

Flak wasn't bad today. Used the new anti-radar equipment today for the first time—that may have been the reason. Escort was excellent and no enemy fighters seen.

Weather was our worst trouble today. Had to rendezvous at 24,000 feet this a.m. because of clouds. Then ran into the soup on the way back over France. Gave a bunch of Frenchmen the "willies," I imagine, because we were only about 500 feet off the ground. Thought for a while we were going to be weathered-in in France. Saw a little of France today when we were doing the buzzing. Gave us a chance to see the results of bombing at close range. Things have really been plastered over there. [*End of mission notes by Frank Dimit*]

We were inbound to the target at 25,000 feet and about thirty minutes from the Initial Point when I was alerted by the gunners that we had a strange B-17 flying along with us at nine o'clock—level and the same airspeed. This aircraft had come from behind us, and it was close enough that we could see that the gun stations were manned. They appeared to be watching us. I cautioned the gunners to watch this ship and move our guns so they could see that our guns also were manned. I could have saved my breath. These gunners were sharp and they watched that bird like a hawk trying to find out what he was up to. Immediately they flashed the "color of the day" with the Aldis lamp, but got no response.

After approximately five minutes the aircraft accelerated and I noticed that his trailing wire antenna was extended. The trailing wire antenna has a pear-shaped weight on the end and could extend out the back of the airplane a hundred feet or more. This would increase the range of transmission. In formation flying it was never extended because of the danger of someone flying into it. After the bomb run the task force commander used this system to relay to Eighth Air Force that a particular target had been bombed, and the time. The antenna was then retracted into the ship—this was its only use in formation. A ship returning home alone might use it, but the occasions would be limited.

After the aircraft accelerated he flew to the group ahead of us, but he still didn't join formation. He flew along for a while, then moved to another group. This seemed very strange to me. He obviously didn't have a bomb load because of the speed at which he could accelerate and move around from group to group. The group markings on the tail of the aircraft and the serial number appeared genuine, but it was not a group I was familiar with. Why would anybody leave the protection of a formation and go from one group to the other unless he was gathering data of heading, altitude, airspeed, and numbers, and passing it along to someone? It was a puzzle and the crew members kept watching and commenting on it.

I signaled the copilot to switch back to the interphone, and asked if he thought he could contact our fighter escort. He said that radio silence had already been broken—the leading groups had dropped and were heading home. It would be just a matter of calling and using the right call signs.

The fighters answered on the first call and we asked them to check out a suspicious-acting B-17. We gave the location, the group identification symbol, and the serial number. They replied that they would try to locate him.

We had now reached the Initial Point and the strange B-17 did not show any indication of going on the bomb run. After the bomb run when we were headed home, the fighters called and said they had located the B-17. His trailing wire antenna was still out. By now he was headed west and was still moving about the bomber stream. The guns were manned and were aimed at the "Little Friends" if they moved in too sharply. A friendly fighter would always fly parallel to you and slip over to you, keeping his nose away from you, and request identification. The gunners were apt to start shooting at any aircraft that came in nose first.

The fighters called again and said they could not make radio contact with the bird. But then, not all ships had fighter crystals so that didn't prove anything. This was our last wave of fighters for our unit and they were the ones to escort us home.

"What do you want us to do now?"

"We don't trust that airplane and we would like to see it cross the Channel."

"Roger, we have him in a box [a P-51 on each side and one behind]. Don't worry, he's going home or down—it's his choice."

"Roger, that's all we ask."

We never learned the ending to this aerial drama. But we do know that by this time the Germans had flyable B-17s pieced together from our many losses. It was later rumored that a German-manned B-17 landed in England. But this was only rumor. What happened to our bird was to remain a mystery to us. Only the Little Friends know the answer.

That mission saw another first for us. On October 9 we had been assigned a brand-new shiny airplane, a B-17G, every pilot's dream. After our second mission in her, while we were down on the line, the crew chief came to me and told me about a new device that had just come into the group. It was an electronic radar jamming device called "carpet." It consisted of a small black box and an antenna about eight inches long enclosed in a glass tube that would protrude through the underbelly of the ship. He said there was only one on the base, that he had access to it and could install it on the airplane for us if we would like it.

We asked him whether it was effective and he answered, "Who knows? It's an experimental device." He need say no more because in combat a man will clutch any straw that might provide hope, whether it be useful or not. The installation was completed in time for our mission on October 18.

Thus it was that *Lucky Sherry* was the first airplane in our group to be equipped with "carpet." I don't know whether it was ever installed on any other airplanes in the group, or whether it was really effective because, somehow, we still managed to attract enemy fire. But it was fun to see the expression on the faces of the other pilots and crewmen when we told them that our new aircraft had carpet installed. In fact, a few even went so far as to peek inside and comment on our color scheme. Who was kidding whom! But our presence was still tolerated and we were to be humored. After all, we had been around a long time. Maybe just too long.

October 19, 1944

When I said last night that I thought today would be one of rest, little did I realize that I would spend the whole day moving to another barracks. . . . It's just a little hut called the "Quacks' Shack," but room aplenty for four men, much warmer and more ideal than our old place. Things are still pretty much scattered around and there's a lot of work to be done, but when it's all over I'm sure we'll all be reasonably happy with our hut.

The mail situation is worse, that's for sure, because all the fellows have been commenting lately that their folks haven't heard from them for at least ten days or more. The situation probably won't improve because the boys on

Work, Dimit, and Fletcher in front of their new home, the Quacks' Shack, awaiting assignment of a new copilot. Notice the coke-stealing shovel, which sometimes doubled as a broom.

the Continent now have priority over us on the mail service, both coming and going. While our mail means everything in the world to us we also realize what it means to the boys in the foxholes on the front lines. That's the reason we've quit squawking when our mail is delayed. It used to be the mail came here and was then shipped over there. Now it all goes over there and ours comes back. This causes the incoming mail to be delayed, and also causes a transportation shortage on our outgoing mail.

Shortly after our twentieth mission we moved from Nissen hut #10 to the small Nissen hut which was our home for the rest of the time we were with the 412th. This was a little building that had formerly been occupied by the medics.

We spent considerable time fixing it up—building shelves, desks, etc. We even went so far as to acquire a portable wash basin which stood up on four legs. It would fold up like a camp stool that had a canvas seat. When you unfolded the legs you put the wash basin between the legs where the canvas top would be on a stool. Then the basin was held in place by installing two screws in the top. A drain at the bottom extended down only two or three inches from the bowl, but we had acquired some oxygen hose and some hose clamps so we made a drain. Then we cut a hole in the Nissen hut wall and shoved the hose outside. This was to be used only to wash your hands and face, or to shave. Since there was no heat whatsoever in the washrooms, shaving could be a rather cold event. So we were tickled to be able to heat a little water on top of our stove during the evenings when we were burning our coke rations—then we would use the hot water to shave.

When no one was looking we borrowed some aluminum and made some shelves plus some coat hangers so we could hang our clothes under these individual racks. We also cut into the wiring and ran a single wire down to each of the writing desks. You could have the individual light either over your desk or over your bed. The light was held in place in either position by hooking it to some wire we had attached to the building wall. All in all we were living, comparatively speaking, in the lap of luxury.

Most of the things we had came from salvage, but a few items couldn't be acquired from salvage so we just told people we'd like to have them and they'd turn their backs. This is how we got the oxygen hose to make the drain and a few other things.

Lo and behold, something was going to happen that hadn't happened before in all the time I had been on the base. We were going to have a stand-by inspection. The Group Commander would inspect the barracks of the 412th Squadron.

By this time Doc had his own crew, but he hadn't moved out of our barracks yet, so he was standing by with us. Each man was required to stand at the foot of his bed. There was a knock on the door. I opened the door, summoned the men to attention. The Group Commander, the Squadron Commander, and the First Sergeant entered. The First Sergeant was carrying a clipboard and paper, which in Cadets we called the "gig sheet." I don't know if they were actually going to give people demerits. Maybe they just wanted us to realize we were still in the Army.

The colonel became very interested in all the modifications he found in our room—the wires running to the individual lights, the wash basin, the shelves, the table desks, and all the other goodies. As he looked around the room it was hard to tell whether he was pleased or angry. Most colonels have a way of giving you a very noncommittal blank look. But he turned to me on his way out and said, "Lieutenant, I want the man who is responsible for the condition of this hut to report to my office within the hour."

"Well," I thought, "he obviously wants to know where we got all this stuff and by whose authority we had cut a hole in the building for the drain." The only thing I could visualize was that somebody had to be in trouble. It seemed to me that I was always before these people trying to explain our actions. Our encounters were always on a high plane, however, with mutual military respect. But I would not face them today. While I had contributed to the work, all the ideas were not necessarily mine. "So," I thought, "since most of these ideas were Doc's, if somebody is going to catch the devil for it, it might as well be him."

After the entourage had gone I told Doc, "You heard the order. You'll be the one to present yourself to the colonel's office." And Doc, with his usual big grin, said, "Fine. I'll go up and see what's on his mind." "Incidentally," I added, "you might prepare yourself for a good chewing out because many of the things we have in here are not necessarily contraband, but they haven't been assigned to us either."

He made his call on the colonel. When he came back to the barracks we were all anxiously waiting to hear what his reception was like and how long did we have to return these items—with good luck maybe the usual twenty-four hours. When he came in the door he still had a big grin on his face, but he didn't say anything. So I said, "Okay Doc, tell us about your experience." And he answered, "Well, frankly, the colonel had nothing but praise for our barracks

and our ingenuity. The reason he wanted the man who was responsible for it was so he could congratulate him and have him make the
same modifications in his living quarters."

The one time I could have been praised I turned it down. Anyway, we all wished Doc well on his new enterprise. None of us had
courage enough to help him out, but as I understand it, he did a
good job and now the colonel was able to have the same amenities
that the former crew of *Knock Out Baby* were enjoying.

October 20, 1944

. . . *Our new copilot moved in with us today so now the four of us are all
together. Brown and the rest of the boys pitched in both days and gave us a
hand on the moving and building. A better bunch of fellows couldn't be
found. As long as we've been together I've never heard one of them give the
other a harsh word. I was certainly lucky when they passed out the fellows
to make the crew.*

October 22, 1944

. . . *Didn't write yesterday—instead we held a big celebration for the crew
in our new hut. In the morning they gave us a pass but our financial status
was too low to take advantage of it, so we're spending it here on the post.
We had some very good reasons for the celebration. First, we were on pass;
Doc, Work, and Dimit made 1st lieutenants; it was my birthday #23 (and
can you imagine being called "The Old Man"!); and with the new hut we
had to have a housewarming. So we took care of all those things last evening.*

*I'm anxiously awaiting a letter telling me all about your little trip to
Dayton—who you saw—and what all you did. Hope you got to go to Walla
Walla and up to the college. I don't imagine there are too many kids there
now that we know, but hope you were able to see some. Would sure like to
see the old campus on a clear, crisp fall night, see the big moon, and hear
the clock strike twelve.*

October 23, 1944

. . . *We're really an antagonistic bunch tonight. We've been reading about
the strikes in a few of the aircraft factories. Our thoughts and words, as you
can guess, are not fit to write. How some people can quibble over a few*

dollars in times like these beats me. I only wish each and every one of them could be with us for a little while. I believe they would be content to go back and do a better job than they have ever done. But some people will cut off their nose to spite their face regardless. They have a point, though—the cost of living is high; it's pretty high here too, only we don't measure it in dollars and cents!

October 24, 1944

The fellows are always asking about you and David—wondering how you are getting along, and I sure puff up when I tell them how big he is. George is next to be a papa, the date sometime the first of January. Then Brown with the fifteenth of January. I sure give them a hard time with mine all over and a great big husky boy to brag about. They get quite a kick out of it, though, and know I'm only kidding. I have to get those guys home in time for the big event, that's for sure. It looks bad in a way but I think I can do it. I know what it's like to be away from your wife when that time comes and sure don't want it to happen to them. I may fail them, but if I do no one will feel any worse about it than myself. . . .

October 25, 1944

Here's some good news for you. You can mark up number twenty-five as water under the bridge. Things look better each day and with good weather I should be able to turn in some pretty good work for a while. I'm going to turn in for the sandman has me in his clutches.

Mission #25, Hamburg, Germany, October 25

Frank Dimit, Bombardier

Briefed at 6:30 a.m. for a target at Hamburg, Germany. Target was an oil refinery.

Flew lead of high squadron of high group. Carried 19 250-pound G.P. bombs. Bombing was PFF, but think we hit something. Two big clouds of black smoke were boiling up through the undercast when we left the target area. Entire 3rd Division hit the target and part of the 1st Division.

Was a little doubtful whether this anti-radar equipment was really working until today. When we hit Hamburg the last time, the group

was shot to hell. Today we didn't have a feathered prop in the outfit. The outfit ahead of us really caught hell today, but when we hit
the target, those flak gunners didn't have any idea where we were.
They were just throwing it up and hoping to hit something. We
came back without a hole.

Good fighter cover—no enemy fighters.

From now on we'll be working on Doolittle's missions. [Reference
to extension of the missions from twenty-five to thirty to thirty-five]

The PFF lead of our group aborted as soon as the bombs were
dropped and we brought the group back. *[End of mission notes by
Frank Dimit]*

October 26, 1944

*I thought I was tired when I sent you that short note last night, but this
evening I'm doubly so. I'll hit the sack in a very few minutes, but first just
a few lines to let you know you can get out the pencil and chalk up another
one. Number twenty-six is over!*

Mission #26, *Hanover, Germany, October 26*

Frank Dimit, Bombardier

Briefed at 7:15 a.m. for our target at Misburg, Germany. It's a sub-
urb of Hanover—one mile east of Hanover itself.

Target was an oil refinery if it was visual, but bombing was PFF,
so the aiming point was the marshalling yards in Hanover.

Flew lead of the high squadron of lead group of our wing. Carried
20 250-pound G.P. bombs.

Target area had 150 guns, but the carpet and chaff were working
and we brought our ship home without a hole again. Very little
damage done to the group. Good escort and no enemy fighters.

Weather was our worst enemy today. That and prop wash. We
followed an outfit (the 390th) into the target pretty close and some
of the boys had a rough time. Had a bad time getting into the base.
We went up and down through an overcast. The visibility was so
poor after we got down through the clouds we could not find the
field or anything else. And to top it off, the RAF and our Little Friends
were in the area. We were damn near run over several times. But
we got back. *[End of mission notes by Frank Dimit]*

October 28

Doc Doxon, Copilot

Group went on a mission. Fletch and I both stayed home. Gordon Braund had a wing fire and Futoma, his ball turret gunner, bailed out over Germany.

Periodically we had a pilot's meeting. During these sessions we discussed everyone's gripes and suggestions that would make us a better fighting force. This included all things from rendezvous, execution of the mission, to conclusion.

One thing that bothered our crew was the fact that many times we observed other aircraft in our formation with gun positions which were not manned. At these meetings we were informed that these guns were inoperable and they didn't feel it necessary to have a gunner in these cramped, cold positions when they were powerless to react to enemy action.

It was always my contention that these people were the eyes for all of the formation, and at least they could look and give information to the unit, whether it be enemy action or a mechanical emergency. If the guns were moving, even though unfirable, they still represented a deterrent.

These repeated violations were my pet peeve. My views were always reinforced and upheld by our squadron and group people, but I don't think I won any friends among the other pilots, who by now I thought were getting a little careless.

It wasn't too long before the wisdom of my contention was borne out as the enemy introduced airborne rockets into the fray. These rockets were fired from just outside the range of our fifty-caliber machine guns—they were crude but deadly. In the initial point of their flight they were quite slow and their trajectory somewhat erratic. But a watchful gunner could spot the release of the rocket and determine its flight accurately enough to have the pilot move the plane slightly up or down to avoid being hit.

From this point on it was no problem keeping the gunners in their positions for it was now proven that a warning given in time could save their own lives. A better incentive would never be found!

October 29, 1944

Today being Sunday we got up and went to church as usual. Then this afternoon we ground swung the compass on our airplane. After that we just fiddled around, going over the ship fixing any little thing we found wrong, and in general, giving it a good once over. Incidentally, the airplane wasn't named Knock Out Baby. *Instead it was called* Lucky Sherry *and a picture is now in the process of being painted on the side which is quite apropos to the title. When the job is complete I will send you a picture of it and let you pass judgment.* . . .

October 30, 1944

Put in a good day's work today and it may turn out even better than I think. Destination Tokyo *was playing at the picture house so after supper I went up to see it. We saw it together, I believe, in Salt Lake City, but I enjoyed it again.*

Mission #27, *Merseburg, Germany, October 30*

Frank Dimit, Bombardier

Briefed at 6:15 a.m. for our old friend (?) Merseburg. Same oil refinery that we have been trying to knock out for so long. This was our fourth attempt at this target.

Didn't climb through any overcast during assembly for a change. But we ran into weather over the continent and we had to turn back. It was the same kind of soup we ran into on the way to Berlin. It was high cirrus above 20,000 feet. We got a little east of the Zuider Zee in Holland before the entire division turned around. And I was mighty glad to see them do that 180.

Found out later that Jerry fighters had already formed and were waiting for us. The radio man that monitors German frequencies could hear the ground stations giving the German fighters bearings on us. We were mighty lucky.

Were flying lead of high squadron of lead group. We were to be the last ones over the target. Carried 20 250-pound bombs and brought them back. Expected bombing to be PFF.

Don't know for sure if we get credit for this one. Sure hope so. *[End of mission notes by Frank Dimit]*

October 31, 1944

Here it is Halloween with no outhouses to push over and no pumpkins to make jack-o-lanterns. It would be a perfect night for fun-raising because it's just as black as coal outside.

It was also payday today and I collected my usual sum of twelve pounds. I paid back the four I had borrowed so I'm in pretty fair shape to start out the month. This should be a big month coming up and I don't figure on having too much time off to spend a few pounds.

Now I have some good news. Yesterday's work lived up to my best hopes so you can chalk up another one—make this number twenty-seven. Thought I was going to get another today but it didn't work out, which is very good. There are times to go and times not to go—this was definitely the latter!

October 31

Frank Dimit, Bombardier

Just got the good news we received credit for yesterday's mission.

Briefed this a.m. for the target at Politz, Germany, near Stettin. Target was oil refinery. 320 flak guns in target area. Last time the group hit it they lost 5 planes.

Mission scrubbed before we took off. Thank God.

November 1, 1944

. . . It's beginning to get hard to write letters for I don't know what's going on. I've had one letter in the last eight or nine days—drew a blank again today—haven't heard from anyone. Could be that I've got combatitis as the patience is worn kind of thin at times and I get rather irritable over things here. The cigarettes go by the pack and nothing seems to satisfy. Worries pop up everywhere about nothing.Well, it'll all be over soon. Then I can sit down and figure everything out and forget about it. This last part is the worst when so much hangs on so little!

November 2, 1944

This is just a short note to let you know that I'm in a much better mood this evening and am sorry for the bad humor last night. Could be that I was sweating out a rough one. Anyway, it's all over with and I feel like a new man. By the way, get out the pencil and mark up another one—number twenty-eight is over!

Your letter of October 23rd was waiting for me when I finished. Was glad to hear you enjoyed your visit to Dayton—only wish I could have been there with you.

Mission #28, Merseburg, Germany, November 2

Frank Dimit, Bombardier

Briefed at 5:15 a.m. for the same damn target—Merseburg. We're getting mighty tired of this target. It was the same oil refinery (Leuna) as always.

The 3rd Division and part of the 1st hit the same target. We were the fifth outfit over the target. We led the 13th Combat Wing. We were flying lead of high squadron of high group. Carried 10 500-pound G.P. bombs. Bombing was PFF and from 29,000 feet. But we weren't half high enough.

Flak was the worst I have ever seen. Saw more flak today than on any other two missions. It was terrific. But thank goodness for that carpet. The anti-radar equipment is definitely working. Flak was strictly barrage today and certainly not up to the true Merseburg accuracy. Battle damage was very slight compared to the last raid there. We came back with one small hole in the trailing edge of left wing. The group lost one plane. The Jerries were waiting for us with railroad guns and they threw up everything they had. It was terrible.

We expected to be hit by fighters, but we weren't. Some of the outfits were hit that went over the target after us. Our escort was excellent—never better. We even had a group of P-51s and P-38s from the 9th A.F. They were all over the sky.

One more for us. Not many more to go, I hope. *[End of mission notes by Frank Dimit]*

Forty heavy bombers were lost on this day, but the Eighth Air Force shot down a total of 130 enemy aircraft. This broke the record that was set back on September 11 when we went to Ruhland, a mission that cost us forty-four heavy bombers in exchange for 116 enemy fighters. Another twenty-five Nazi planes were destroyed on the ground.

The Mustang squadron led by Major George E. Preddy of Greensboro, North Carolina, who at this point was the top active Eighth fighter pilot in the ETO, shot down twenty-four Nazi craft to cop this day's squadron honors.

The 55th Fighter Group, a P-51 outfit, led by Major Eugene E. Ryan of Darien, Connecticut, tangled with over seventy-five single-engine Jerries which were "ganging up" on one bomber force over Merseburg. They claimed nineteen enemy planes shot down for the loss of one Mustang.

The *Blue Streak,* based in Sudbury, Suffolk, with the 486th Bomb Group, piloted by Lt. David Paris and his crew; went down November 2, 1944, on the raid to Merseburg, Germany *(8th Air Force photo, from Ian Hawkins)*

Doc in the cockpit of *Kimmie Kar*

The heavies' gunners reported getting their share of additional "kills," shooting down fifty-three.

November 3, 1944

Had an easy day with nothing to do and that's exactly what I did—absolutely nothing. Got a haircut this morning and spent the rest of the day playing cards, reading, and participating in a bull session. The day of rest was welcomed, though, because yesterday's work really tired us out. It was a long, hard day. . . .

Doc got an airplane of his own awhile back and he has named it Kimmie Kar *after his daughter as her nickname is Kim. I'll send you a picture of it—it's very cute. . . .*

November 5, 1944

The mailman was good to me today for your letters written the 23rd and 24th and one from the folks were waiting for me when I finished work. Will answer your letter tomorrow, but in the meantime, you can chalk up an-

other one—number twenty-nine is now in the list of has-beens. Nothing like making hay while the sun shines. Will enclose a few more negatives tonight and will continue to do so until you get them all.

Mission #29, *Ludwigshafen, Germany, November 5*

Frank Dimit, Bombardier

Briefed at 5:00 a.m. for a target that was northeast of Metz, France, and east of Thionville. Target was a German fort that has been giving our ground forces in that sector some trouble the last few weeks. The entire 3rd Division was hitting four fortifications in that area. But we had a 10/10ths undercast, so we had to go on to the secondary.

Secondary was at Ludwigshafen, across the river from Mannheim. Nobody knows what the target was. New buildings had shown up on some PRU [photo reconnaissance] photos. So somebody said let's blast them out of existence. That's what we did.

Briefed for 280 guns at Ludwigshafen and they have every one of them there. Bombing was visual through a smoke screen, so carpet

A classic bomb drop, the bombs falling in trail (*95th B.G. photo*)

didn't work so good. We had some of the closest flak today that we've had since our 20th mission. Picked up 10 or 12 holes—hardly bother to count any more.

Flew lead of high squadron of lead group of second wing over target. The 100th led the Division today. Carried 6 1,000-pound G.P. bombs. Didn't see the results of our bombing, but we hit in the target area.

Had first serious damage to our new plane today. Some of the holes caused a wing change. One piece of flak hit the main spar of left wing. Piece of flak came in the left side of waist and went through ammo box of right gun. It hit a cap on one of the cartridges and it exploded. Tore up the case and projectile went out the right side of the waist. Bob Lynch has cases as a souvenir.

Enemy fighters—Bob Work saw a German jet-propelled job. Escort was good.

Had a helluva time getting into field tonight. Don't see how one country could have so much bad weather. They didn't expect us back tonight, thought we would be "weathered-in" in France when we left this a.m. But we beat the cold front back to the base. Damn near got killed in the traffic pattern several times. Getting so the weather we fly in is worse than the actual mission.

Not many more to go. Expect a pass soon. *[End of mission notes by Frank Dimit]*

We had just released our bombs at 27,000 feet but had not had time to close the bomb-bay doors. The formation had loosened up and was making the turn to the Rally Point when there was a tremendous explosion at the top of the bomb bay and then another off the left wing. The acrid stench of burning powder and smoke permeated the ship immediately. A shell had come up through the open, empty bomb bay and had exploded on contact as it was exiting through the top of the fuselage. Fortunately most of the force of the explosion was diverted upward. But in this instant the plane nosed over into a vertical dive. In an attempt to correct the nosing over I pulled back on the control column. The column came right back into my stomach—the elevator controls were gone and the aircraft was out of control. It was a time when you wanted to be on good terms with your Creator.

I called for the copilot to engage the autopilot, but it wasn't necessary for his hand had already reached the master bar which controlled all systems relating to elevators, ailerons, and rudders. As he engaged the master bar it was apparent that everyone on board had reached the same conclusion—short of a miracle we had had our last ride. In a few seconds, ever so slowly, the nose of the aircraft began its return to normal flight.

Our miracle came in the design of the aircraft. The manual control cables were mounted near the ceiling and the elevator control cables were completely cut in half. The electrical cables that supplied energy to the servo motors, which were located at each of the control surfaces, were positioned on each side of the ship in the walls at the bottom. This dispersion of the two systems saved the day for us. The backup system, which in our case was the AFCE (autopilot), now allowed us to control the aircraft.

Since we were flying the lead of the high squadron we were still able to maintain our position, albeit not with perfection, as our wingmen were working hard to stay in formation with us for maximum protection. We would be fine as long as we were airborne, but it would not be possible to land on autopilot. The manual controls would have to be fixed or else after bringing our squadron home to the base we would head the airplane back toward the Channel and bail out while still over land.

With all these things going through my mind, only a few minutes had elapsed when I was informed by the waist gunner that his ammo box had been hit by a piece of flak and several 50 caliber shells had exploded in the box, creating a weird fireworks display in his position. He had not been hit but I'm sure he had plenty of cause to worry about his life expectancy in all the excitement.

Immediately I called the engineer and asked if he thought it would be possible in some way to splice the cables together—although I had no idea of what he would use to do the job. He said it not only was possible but he was already working on it in conjunction with the radio operator. Everything he needed—cable, cable clamps, and a few tools—was in his emergency kit. All he would need was time, because at each movement of the control surface the broken cable ends would jerk fore and aft. It would not be easy, but he could do the job.

I had seen him carry his "goodie bag" aboard at every mission and it appeared to be a little heavier each time we flew as the ground crew cooperated and kept supplying him with more gear.

Long before the Channel was in sight I received a call that the cables had been reconnected, but they would not have the same tension as they would have had if the job had been performed on the ground with the proper instruments. No mind—let's unhook the autopilot and see what kind of control we have. It was sloppy, but we could control the aircraft and I felt comfortable that we could land it when we reached the base. The landing was sloppy, but the empty B-17 was a very forgiving aircraft.

We had a crew that had experienced some very terrifying moments, and knew it is of fear that heroes are born. But we also had an engineer who could take pride in the knowledge that he had saved an aircraft from certain destruction.

November 6, 1944

. . . There was no mail for me today so I'll read yesterday's letter again. . . . Even when your letters are behind schedule it is a small matter. The thing that counts is getting a letter. I live for the letters and the date makes little difference. Reading your letters is just like talking to you, and, believe me, I need those talks. They give me strength and courage where everything else fails. They keep my thinking straight and jar me back into reality when I get off on a tangent. . . .

November 7, 1944

I fixed the boys up last night so they could go on pass this morning. Much to my surprise only two of them left the post. The other fellows decided to spend their pass on the base too when they found out I wasn't going anyplace. We'll just spend the time chewing the fat, playing some pinochle, and reading a few magazines which we've been lucky to get ahold of. . . .

Tonight is the night that the election returns come in. The election is kind of a minor thing over here. There are too many more issues of greater importance—I'm sure you know what I mean. I don't think the outcome of the election will have much to do with the outcome of the war. The main idea is to get the war over with. Then we'll argue over other things—one thing at a time is enough. I frankly hope Roosevelt beats Dewey by a wide majority, but that's only personally, of course. I have never liked Dewey or his campaign. He hasn't near the experience with foreign affairs, personalities, and policies as does Roosevelt, and we are definitely going to need a continuance of cooperation between nations when this is over. But that is not for me to say. Besides even Hitler wears a mustache.

November 8, 1944

. . . I'm glad to hear that you and Velda [Redfern, a Tekoa friend] enjoy each other's company so much. Friendship is a wonderful thing to pass the

time and ease the moments of loneliness which pop up. It gives you someone to talk to who has the same problems you have.

Now we come to the favor you asked of me—"please don't ever change." I will admit that in some ways I have changed. First, my outlook on life has changed greatly due only to circumstances here. This is probably a temporary change only. We have to take into consideration that our life and our purpose here is different from anything we have ever experienced, so naturally our views are changed to meet the need of this existence, just as furniture is moved about the house. Never fear. The basic structure does not change a bit.

Your friends who are having difficulties are probably too weak to face the facts, or maybe they made a mistake in the first place. They quite possibly may have never had a deep understanding of one another, or a mutual love strong enough to carry them over long periods of separation. It isn't real love if it won't stand up under the test. You are the ray of sunshine in my life. It's you who gives me the courage and the determination to keep going. The thought of my little family at home waiting for me leaves me with a burning desire to keep going and not stop until we're together again.

Have I changed? Does that sound like a man who has lost everything that was dear to him and would return to his wife a total stranger, bearing only the physical looks of the man she had bid good-bye? I think not. Rest assured that I will come back just as I was when I left with the exception of a gray hair or two and a few minor things. Perhaps my letters have sounded to you as if I might be changing—I hope not. Before judging them too harshly remember that they are written in a world of nervous tension and sometimes the pen does not put the real meaning across the page.

I don't know whether I can keep our date by Christmas or not. I'll do my best, but if I fail it'll only be by a week or two. This evening brought our pass to an end so now we're back at the old grind of sweating the war again. We've been reading the election returns in the daily Stars *and* Stripes. *The election went as many of us thought it would, so it caused very little concern over here. Of course all the papers carried huge headlines, but other than that, there was no display. Could be that there are other things more important which occupy our minds.*

Now to tell you more about Billy Bob, our copilot. He is from Piggott, Arkansas, a very likable sort of person with a remarkable sense of humor. He isn't married and claims he has given up all hope, but judging from his correspondence, I would say he's still trying to make them all happy instead of concentrating a maximum effort on one. He's twenty-two years old and reminds me very much of my cousin, Hallie. He gets along very well with the rest of the fellows and they're quite attached to him, so everything is running smoothly and there is no lack of cooperation. In the negatives I sent were several pictures of him. Just look for the strange officer in our midst and you have him spotted. . . .

Crew of *Lucky Sherry* with new copilot Billy Bob Layl, after returning home from a mission. Layl: back row, second from left, wearing service cap

November 11, 1944

This is just a short note to let you know that everything goes well with me. It's past my sack time, that's my apology for the short letter. But wanted to let you know that you can now chalk up number thirty—it has come and gone.

Again the postman forgot to bring me any letters, but he compensated somewhat by bringing me a Christmas package from Cap and Sis. It was a very nice package full of the little things we can't get here. You can imagine how it was appreciated.

Mission #30, *Koblenz, Germany, November 11*

Frank Dimit, Bombardier

Briefed at 5:45 a.m. for our target at a point about three miles south of Koblenz, Germany. It was a marshalling yard.

We used the new Micro-H [an improved radar bombing system supposedly better than H2X which we had been using] to bomb with today, and it looks as if we might have done some good. Bob Work got G-fixes all the way. At "bombs away" he got a fix that put us just short of the target.

Flew lead of high squadron of high group of our wing. Carried 12 500-pound G.P. bombs. Complete undercast—didn't see bombs hit.

Flak was light and inaccurate. No fighters seen. Close fighter escort. This could very easily be termed a "milk run" and hope we have two or three more just like it. Didn't pick up any holes.

Climbed through the usual overcast this a.m., but we had good weather when we got back to the base.

Our target was to be Politz today, but it was changed just before briefing. Thank goodness. Politz is going to come up one day, and I hope we're not on it. *[End of mission account by Frank Dimit]*

It was 7 in the morning and the crew was still sound asleep. We had finished a long, arduous, nerve-wracking mission the day before. Everyone was completely pooped out and had no intentions of getting up until 11, this being in plenty of time to reach the mess hall at 11:30 for dinner.

But here I was being shaken by the shoulder, and a voice was saying, "Fletch, wake up!" I opened my eyes to see my grinning ex-copilot standing over my bunk. "Why should I?" I asked. "Hey, I've got a big deal for us." "Go away," I said. "We're all dead tired—we had a long, hard day yesterday." "Ah, but today will make up for yesterday and give you a new lease on life—no shooting, just a nice flight with lots of pleasant female company."

"What are you talking about?" I queried. "Well, this big war bond drive that they're having on the base . . ." "Yeah," I interrupted, "I heard about it. I know fighting a war isn't enough now. They want us to buy bonds so we can pay for our own airplanes."

"Naw, you've got it all wrong. They're bringing in a USO troop or something for a big performance called *Petticoats* to kick off the drive. They need two airplanes to fly down to one of the bases near London and bring the troupe up for the show. I told the squadron commander that you and I would fly the airplanes down and bring them back. How about it? Let's go!"

"Everyone around here is dragging. I don't think the boys will want to fly." At this Work rolled over and mumbled, "Count me out. I'm not going anywhere except back to sleep." "Well, that ends that," I said. "I don't want to fly without a navigator."

"Mine is flying," Doc countered, "so all you have to do is take off, climb up on my wing and fly formation to the base."

At this Billy Bob roused up and said, "It sounds like fun." I countered with, "We still don't know whether the radio operator or the engineer want to fly. They may have other plans—like sleeping." "You guys get dressed and I'll go down to see them," Doc said. "But hurry up because I have a truck and driver standing by to take us out to the airplanes."

In a few minutes Doc reported, "Yeah, they will go, but they weren't overjoyed. I promised them that you would let them adjust the parachute harness for the girls and instruct them in the use of the parachutes. That seemed to sell the deal."

With this we went out to the truck to await Brownie and Hinman. Doc's skeleton crew was already on the truck.

The weather was typical for England—a real gray day, slight mist, ceiling about 800 or 900 feet, visibility in the vicinity of one mile.

Upon reaching the airplanes we made a hurried ground check. With everything in order, and a lot of extra parachutes and harnesses in the waist position, we fired up the engines. When the last one sputtered to life Doc came taxiing by on the perimeter track. We fell in behind and taxied out to the runway. After the engine check Doc headed down the runway. We gave him a twenty-second head start and took off after him. As he headed back over the field we swung into position on his right wing and headed southwest at about 700 feet in poor visibility.

Billy Bob unfolded his map and asked the name of the base that was our destination. I had to confess that I didn't know. Doc hadn't said, so we would just have to stay on his wing until he landed. The weather didn't improve any and we would be right on top of an airfield by the time we could see it.

Finally after an hour and a half in the air, in which we seemed to be flying in circles since I had seen the same smokestack go by on three occasions, I asked Billy Bob to call Doc and see if he had a problem. He reported that they had been disoriented, but the navigator had the Gee Box working and now had a fix. In a few minutes we would be flying down the runway where we would peel off for a landing. This was good news because everyone was tired and grouchy—this was supposed to be a twenty-minute flight.

We finally settled down on a nice air base, not your usual bomber base with everything dispersed. We taxied up to Base Operations and cut the engines. I could hear Billy Bob, Brownie, and Hinman saying, "Bring on the girls!" as they were busy unloading the parachutes and harnesses in neat piles near the tail of the aircraft.

I thought, "Well, at least they will enjoy the flight back. This will compensate for dragging them out of bed when they were bushed."

Doc had already gone into Base Ops and I explained to Brownie if he happened to find a good-looking blonde it would be all right to put her in the engineer's seat between the pilots, because we would probably be crowded for space and I knew he would rather spend his time making everyone comfortable.

About this time I heard Billy Bob's slow Southern drawl muttering something about Doc's ancestors—maybe there was something wrong. I turned around to see what appeared to be an endless line of GIs filing out the Operations door and lining up beside the two aircraft. There had to be a mistake!

Then Doc announced, "These GIs are members of the Thirteenth Service Company and they will be performing in the show *Petticoats* to kick off the Eighth Air Force War Bond Drive at the 95th. I'll take half, and Fletch, you get the rest."

I turned to Brownie and said, "Prepare the troops for boarding and if you need me I'll be up in the pilot's seat going through the checklist." I heard him say, "Men, this is a parachute harness and this is a parachute. Grab one of each and get on board. Don't worry about how to use it because we won't be above the tree tops anyway. Just hurry it up because the taxi driver is ready to head for home."

In about two minutes Brownie called on the interphone and said, "The troops are loaded, the hatches secure, ready to start engines." I gave Billy Bob the signal, he started winding them up, and we went taxiing toward the runway. Just as we lifted off Billy Bob reported that Doc wanted to know if we were going to circle the field until he could get off. "Tell him that we know a shortcut home, a single heading with no turns, and we will be there in thirty minutes. He can follow us if he can catch us. If not, he can fly in circles with his navigator." Billy Bob said, "Sounds good to me. I think we have been had. But by whom, Doc or the Squadron Commander?"

"I can assure you there is only one culprit and he is on our tail right now laughing away."

Hinman requested permission to go back and man the tail guns, but I suggested that he had better wait until we were on a regular combat mission. We would have a better excuse and not so many personnel would be involved.

As it turned out the show was pretty good—but I didn't buy any war bonds. My wife was already doing that at home.

November 13, 1944

Thanks to Roco we attended church at ten yesterday as we do almost every Sunday. Apparently he has more faith in Divine Guidance than he does in

Russians following progress of the war *(Paul Fiess photo)*

his pilot! That boy likes to cover all bases, and we'll take help wherever we can get it. It's a good insurance policy for all of us. . . .

November 19, 1944

I have neglected to write you for the past four days as I have been on pass. As you can guess I didn't spend this one on the post. We went into London again so we could sleep in a good bed with clean sheets and have breakfast in the sack. The change was welcome. I didn't really want this pass because it only slows me down, but I didn't have any choice in the matter. When the Big Boys say you need a rest that's the final word and no amount of argument will change their judgment. The weather has been too bad for very much work lately. . . .

I'm in a good mood because when I got home there were three letters from you. The box of Christmas cookies arrived and they came through without a one being broken, not even the ones with David's footprints, and just as fresh as if they had been baked yesterday. Boy, are they good! We're all convinced that the design of trees and stars also add to their flavor. Packing

Pin-up girl, Russian style, Poltava, Russia *(95th B.G. photo)*

Russian soldiers. The women had front-line duty for one week alternating with one week of KP duty behind the lines. *(95th B.G. photo)*

them in popcorn was a good idea. The fellows join with me in thanking you for them, all hoping there are more packages just like this on the way.

We got up early this morning in order to work, but nothing came of it so we stayed up and went to church. Finished dinner just a few minutes ago and am writing this while waiting for mail call. Now to get back to answer a few of your questions. Yes, the picture is of a Russian pin-up girl. Boy, those guys sure have a lot to go home to, and I do mean a lot! I'm afraid I don't envy them in the least. The reason I sent the picture home was because it gave me the jitters and was shaking my faith in feminine delicateness. The soldiers were of the same descent and are my prize pictures. . . .

Now then to answer your question about the missions. Yes, I've had my share of the rough ones and also I've had my share of the easy ones. There's no reason for me to believe that I won't have more of both. Don't worry, though, we'll do all right. I much prefer not to write about them, but will give you the highlights when we're together again. I know some fellows do write home their experiences, but somehow, I just don't see it that way. . . .

So our little man has already laughed out loud. He's learning fast. Dog-gone, I sure would like to be home to see all these little things as they happen, but I guess there will be plenty more when my time comes.

November 22, 1944

I have certainly been slipping on my letter writing. You no doubt are wondering why. Each day I have started a letter to you, but somehow they don't get finished and eventually wind up in the stove. I wish I could explain it, but I can't understand it myself. When things are going good and I have plenty of work to do and my mind is occupied it's very easy to write. But when things aren't going so well, there's nothing to do, and you can't do anything about it, that's when you get so disgusted you can't write a decent letter. Things have been pretty discouraging of late—maybe I had too many eggs in one basket. I'm not complaining, but trying to give an explanation for my laxity in letter writing.

When we lie around the war on nerves starts and fighting that is worse than any job we've been called on to do. You get that started, then get a few setbacks, and it leaves you pretty low. I've been fighting a battle of time lately. At times everything looks pretty rosy like I might come out on top. Then the picture changes—I start lying around, get behind schedule, and realize I can't possibly win. I won't give up, though. As long as there's a day left I'll keep trying, but, believe me, it's discouraging. I can hardly bring myself to write when I haven't some good news for you or am in a bad humor. I know how much you had planned on my being home for Christmas and I realize how much I had counted on being there. But, at the present, it looks as if that's one dream that won't come true. I'm pretty morbid about the whole affair so let's change the subject, besides, to explain it would involve a certain amount of military information. . . .

In the course of our thirty-five combat missions we received three direct hits from German flak guns. One exploded while exiting the top of the open bomb bay. Another was in the right wing, narrowly missing a fuel tank, but severing a part of the main spar. This one should have blown the wing off in a terrible explosion of fire, eliminating another bomber crew and making way for a new replacement crew in the barracks. But that did not happen. The shell entered the bottom of the wing and exited the top, leaving a jagged, ragged, expanded top edge surrounding a near-perfect round hole. The shell was a dud. We were very lucky and hoped that the Germans would not improve their quality control.

The third one came through the waist compartment—it also did not explode. Many other crews reported the same experience—a direct hit and no explosion. Was it just the nature of German mass production that so many shells were defective? Divine deliverance? Sloppy production? Who knows?

After the war another possibility was introduced. We began to read stories of the many workers who were pressed into slavery in German munition factories, and how they would occasionally, when not being watched, forget to put in powder or sabotage the fuse, or in any way they could hinder the German war effort.

So, to be on the safe side, we will credit and give thanks to all possibilities, knowing that someone or something sheltered us from certain death.

November 26, 1944

Why do I delay so in writing? I tried to explain part of it in my last letter. This time there were also two other reasons. First, I kept hoping each day that I might have some good news to write. In this I was wrong for each day brought more disappointment and less hope. Secondly, I kept hoping that each new day might bring me a letter from you which would give me something to grasp hold of and write about without boring you again with the problems of lonesomeness, blues, and homesickness of a fellow in my predicament. The postman has failed me in this respect, so now I've decided that I've let things go almost too far and regardless of the outside influences you must have a letter from me.

As you have gathered by now, this bum English weather hasn't let us work as much as we'd like. How long can a man stand idleness, away from everything he dearly loves, before cynicism will penetrate his character and outlook? The boys are fit to be tied. They sweat this thing far more than I do and I take it too seriously myself. The result is a bunch of nervous, agitated, and irritable individuals looking for one way or another to blow off the steam caused by the presence of this existence.

As usual, though, the crew is still one happy family and we air our thoughts freely with one another and depend more upon one another as time goes by. My part in this goes without saying—the man in charge, the guy who will lend a sympathetic ear to the most chronic of all gripes. Then give a little pep talk, keep your chin up and all that sort of thing, offer a few words of sound advice, then wind up with an assurance that everything goes well, be not short of patience, let nature take its course, and, in the end, our reward will be more than we had dared realize.

That brings a sort of satisfaction and they go off wondering whether I have any feelings at all. I'm the "Old Rock" they can cling to to keep their thinking straight while being unnerved by their existence here. Yet little do they realize that the guy who scoffs at their fears and finds humor when they are blue is probably more homesick and more lonesome than they ever thought of being. But it's my job, and since my neck depends on their actions they will never know my feelings. But I make no pretense with my wife—she will at least know the truth. While I'm endeavoring to keep my chin up, she will know that I haven't escaped the heartaches and the deep-down-inside hurt of being apart.

Now that we're discussing the future it's only fair to assume that sometime the day will come when Uncle Sam will no longer desire my services. Along with that goes a supposition that civilian clothes will be in vogue and a man will, no doubt, have to resort to work in some form of occupation to support a wife and family. Since you have told me that my future job will be one of my choosing, and in no way would you attempt to sway my judgment, I have given it considerable thought in order that my choice might be a wise one. Accordingly, I have sought some advice in this connection from those older and wiser than I. The words of wisdom which I have gathered when condensed down mean about this: for a man to succeed in any gainful occupation he must dearly love his work and put his heart and soul into it. I trust the judgment of that statement and thoroughly agree with it. Now it becomes only a simple matter to think of something which I'll love to do and can put my heart and soul into. At this point no real choices have been made, but a lot of possibilities have been eliminated! The good things in life come only after hard work and perseverance so if we will both be of good cheer I know our day will come soon.

November 27, 1944

We're on pass again. Yes, they decided that we should rest again, but I haven't done anything since the last pass! We can gripe all we want but it doesn't do any good. . . .

Our pass ends tomorrow night. Then with good weather maybe we can get a little work accomplished. I surely hope so because there's nothing more discouraging than just lying around. I've read more books, magazines, and newspapers this past month than I ever have before. My poetry books are all dog-eared from this siege of lonesomeness and inactivity. . . .

It's going to be hell spending Christmas over here but it can't be helped, so we'll just have to make the best of it. I hope we can finish operations by then—that will be the best Christmas present any of us could wish for. . . .

November 28, 1944

As the day comes to an end so does my pass. That puts me back in the old grind again taking my turn and my chances. Sure hope we can get a few good breaks during the next couple of weeks. Couldn't get any worse I don't think. We certainly have had plenty of weather both above and underfoot, and all of it has been bad. Did I tell you we had some snow here about a week ago? It did melt as soon as it fell, though. I have never seen such rain and mud in all my life. It rains twenty-four hours a day, seven days a week. Webs are beginning to grow between our toes—beats anything I've ever seen and I've seen six county fairs, a corn husking, an election, and a quilting bee! . . .

Fiess came over to bid me "so long"—the lucky guy! Well, in time that joyful day will come for all of us. . . .

November 30, 1944

It gives me great pleasure and satisfaction to send you this short note this evening. Why? Because it means that I have finally put in a good day's work. I'm really worn out because it has been a long, hard day, but, somehow, I feel much better than usual. I know I can hit the sack in a few minutes and rest well for a change, with a feeling that I have actually ac-

*complished something. While I'm sleeping soundly you can chalk up another
one. Number thirty-one has come and gone.*

Mission #31, *Merseburg, Germany, November 30*

Frank Dimit, Bombardier

Briefed at 5:30 a.m. for the same damn target—oil refinery at Merseburg.

Flew lead of high squadron of high group. Carried 20 250-pound
G.P. bombs. Bombed from 28,300 feet and it was a visual run. Very
effective smoke screen at target; best I've seen, so can't say how
much damage we did. Hope to hell we creamed it.

Flak was the usual terrific Merseburg variety. But we were lucky
and only picked up one hole. They routed us in differently today
and we were only in range of 270 guns. But every one of those were
firing at us.

Fighter escort was splendid. Had little friends around us all day.
Expected to be bounced by Luftwaffe, but didn't see any.

Felt pretty low when I went up to war room this a.m. and saw
the target. I've had just about as much of this target as I can stand.
Politz will probably be the next move. Was damn glad to get back.

The 1st Division went to Zeitz and Bohlen today. Half the 3rd
Division hit an oil refinery just north of ours. They really caught
hell. Saw about six planes down in flames. Convinced flak is wicked
stuff. Gordy Braund's crew led the 13th Combat Wing today. Four
more to go.

December 1

Strike photos show that we didn't hit Merseburg after all. Lead navigator goofed up and we unloaded them a couple miles north of
Zeitz, which is south of Merseburg. Dumped them into a smoke
screen and I think it was nothing but a potato patch, at most. *[End
of mission notes by Frank Dimit]*

More than 1,250 Eighth Air Force heavy bombers and more than
1,000 Eighth and Ninth Air Force fighters made the attack against
German oil plants at Bohlen, Zeitz, Merseburg, and Lutzendorf, all
in the Leipzig area. Our group lost two aircraft—eighteen men. Ini-

A ride through Flak Alley

The group sandwiched between two layers of clouds—the sun breaking through the top layer and Jerry's calling card through the bottom layer *(95th B.G. photo)*

tially the Eighth Air Force reported losses of fifty-six heavy bombers and thirty fighters. The heavy bomber losses were later revised as it was determined that some of these aircraft landed in occupied territory. Enemy flak was so heavy, according to some of the returning bomber crews, that they could hardly see the bomber formations in front of them.

December 1, 1944

Happy December 1st to you.
Since I worked late yesterday today was pay day for me, and that's always a happy day. I was paid early this morning so the rest of the day was spent settling up with my creditors. As the day comes to an end I find all debts paid and I, myself, am the proud possessor of a ten shilling note, which, believe it or not, I own outright. Oh well, I'll probably lose it in a card game and be broke as usual. But don't worry, the approximate value of a ten shilling note is only two dollars, so I can't do much heavy playing. Roco makes a pretty good banker. Someday me thinks he will make a good Shylock. At least he doesn't charge a pound of flesh—just a pound. . . .
Incidentally, I sent more newspapers to you today, but don't let the headlines worry you because I think we've seen our worst ones. It shouldn't be too long now—just a question of weather. Four more to go.

Late afternoon of December 2 the group was alerted for a mission the next morning. In the wee hours of the morning we were awakened by the "alert runner" and told to prepare for briefing. We headed for the ablution shack in the early morning chill to splash cold water on our faces to wake up and shave. We liked to fly clean-shaven because it made the oxygen mask fit better and was less irritating. We then went to the combat mess hall to get our special mission breakfast of "fresh" eggs. These eggs would probably cover eight inches of the grill when the shell was broken, but the cooks would do a good job of folding them back together in order to get them on a plate. The smell of burnt grease permeated the air, and the smoke from the grill, plus that from the cigarettes, created an eerie light.

There wouldn't be a lot of chatter in the mess hall on mission morning. People would usually speak only for a greeting or a nodding of the head. The crew would visit quietly, nothing boisterous. It was almost as if we were afraid we might wake up the enemy. Besides, it was a time when everyone wanted to be alone with his own thoughts.

After a light breakfast, which everyone picked at, and several cups of coffee, we headed for the briefing room. I always liked to have my crew there early—preferably in the front row, or at least in the first two or three rows. On this morning we were in time for the front row. The briefing room was rapidly filling up when the briefing officer from the Intelligence Section, Major Clyde Bingham, walked by. He stopped and inquired what in the world we were doing there. Well, it was pretty obvious we were going on a mission.

The major was a very low-key, likable man. His briefings were good and he was very sincere with a keen sense of fair play. If it was going to be rough he would tell you so—he didn't want anybody to be surprised. In this manner he commanded a lot of respect. Briefing for him was very serious and he would not be the one to tell a joke to lighten the tension—leave that to one of the other briefing officers. His business was Intelligence and this was serious. He would cover everything he could to help you.

After a short pause, during which he just looked at us, he said, "I refuse to brief you to go on this mission." I became somewhat embarrassed. I didn't like to cause controversy and I didn't know what the problem was. At least by now most of the crews were assembled in the briefing room and there was enough visiting going on among several hundred men that our conversation was confined to our own area. So I cautiously asked, "What do you mean?" "Just what I said, 'I refuse to brief you for this mission.' "

At this time Colonel Jack Shuck, our Group Commander, came over and asked what the problem was. The mission curtains were still closed and we didn't know what the target was or where the group was going. Major Bingham turned to the colonel and said, "As you know the target is the Leuna Oil Refinery at Merseburg. I have briefed this same crew to go there six times already."

Merseburg, the most dreaded target in all of Germany—one of the very last oil refineries still operating. Every day more flak guns were being moved into the area. Every time we flew against it we had trouble—our bombing record against this target was poor. On October 30 our whole group had been shut out because of weather, but not until we were involved in enemy action and had flown around in clouds, which in itself presented a terrible hazard because of the number of planes involved.

"Now there are a lot of crews on this base who have never been to this target, and a lot of crews who have been there only one or two times, but this is a crew that has been briefed every time and I don't think it's fair." All of a sudden I was on Major Bingham's side. You don't ask to fly and you don't refuse to fly, but if someone is trying to help you, you don't turn him down either. Colonel Shuck said, "Well, let's check into this."

By this time our squadron commander, Major James Frankosky, could see that some controversy was going on and he came over to join our group. Subconsciously our minds were starting to revolt against this mission. I'm sure that we were not content to just put in our two cents worth—we felt we had better join the ranks of the big spenders and really unload. The colonel turned to the squadron commander and said, "You've heard a part of this controversy. Now why are these men here?"

Major Frankosky, not one to be flustered by controversy and a very sincere man with whom we had developed a good relationship, looked at the colonel and replied, "Sir, my orders were to supply the best crew I had. This is the ranking crew in number of missions flown in the 412th Squadron, and on that basis I have to assume they are the best." Somehow you just can't argue when you've been paid that kind of compliment, even if it only involves the number of missions you've flown.

At this the colonel turned to me and said, "We all have our jobs to do. You know why you have been chosen, and it's obviously too late to make any changes. But I promise you one thing—you fly this mission today and you'll never have to fly to Merseburg again. Agreed?" "Yes, Sir, but please be aware that I didn't start this controversy." (I hadn't done anything to stop it either.)

Major Bingham mounted the platform and pulled the curtain to reveal the mission board, then intoned, "Gentlemen, your target for today is the Leuna Oil Refinery at Merseburg, Germany." Immediately the room was filled with groans, oohs, aahs—obviously many of the others had been there too.

But I was not paying any attention to the groans. I was busy scanning the board to find our place in the formation. We had been flying visual deputy lead to the Pathfinders, but our usual slots were already filled. I couldn't find my name in the regular formation— what was all the controversy about anyway? Then way up in the corner of the board I saw my name—Fletcher (lead) with two wingmen and a diamond man. Radio call sign "Fireball Black." Somehow I thought that ominous call sign was very apropos because this mission would involve even more danger and responsibility than I had imagined.

The intelligence officer went on—the 95th would lead the task force for the groups bombing Merseburg for the Eighth Air Force, and so on. The rest would be a blur until he finally announced that Fireball Black would tack on to the lead squadron of the 95th Group. This way we could use the Pathfinder ship for navigation. But at five minutes before the IP we would break away from the group, increase our speed, and head for the target. We would not have any bombs. Our bomb bays would be loaded with chaff to confuse the radar that was aiming the flak guns. There would be approximately 300 in the area. We were to precede the group, and when over the target open the bomb-bay doors and allow the chaff to fall free.

I did not think that four aircraft could fly over that target. With four aircraft to shoot at, the flak gunners would use tracking flak, and they were good with this as we had found out over Kassel. They could save the barrage box firing for the main group. We would have one advantage; without the bomb load we could fly a little higher and a lot faster than the group. But not much higher because we wanted the chaff below the group where it would do some good for the whole task force, and they wouldn't have to fly through it.

The briefing went on and then it became time to break up for specialized briefing. I turned to my crew and probably told the biggest lie of my combat career. I don't know what the crew thought, but I suspected that like me they felt like men condemned to the gallows. But fear will feed on fear, and I was not going to let that happen. "Men, if there is a crew in the Eighth Air Force that can fly this mission then we're the ones that can do it. See you at the hardstand." The Squadron Commander was watching us and I don't know whether he heard what I said, but almost immediately he flashed the thumbs up sign. If he thought we could do it then we had better believe him.

After the specialized briefing when the airplane was ready to go, we gathered the flight crew in the ground crew's tent beside the airplane for our final preparation before boarding. The attitude was tense, a little more so than on most missions, but our thoughts were well concealed—*four aircraft with one hell of a backup!* We had no desire to be dead heroes or, for that matter, live cowards, but merely to fly the middle line between the two. It now appeared that circumstances were going to bounce us off the perimeters of each. We boarded the aircraft—our flight check complete. All eyes were on our watches counting the seconds to start-engine time.

Near each airplane was a loudspeaker mounted on a pole. This system was called the "Tannoy." As the seconds were counting down, the loudspeaker crackled to life and a single word boomed out— "Boston"—a code word which meant the mission had been scrubbed.

The weather had deteriorated over the Continent. We crawled out of the airplane amidst shouts of joy. The cares of the day were left behind. We could now start worrying about tomorrow.

This crew would not fly to Merseburg again, and neither would
the 95th Bomb Group. We had a perfect record—six for six. Over
the years I've always wondered, "Could we have really flown that
mission and survived?" But maybe that was the omen that neither
the 95th nor we should return.

December 3, 1944

*. . . This evening has been taken up with a bull session. The main topic
was "What does tomorrow mean for us?" We argue back and forth, never
reaching a decision. The four of us have argued a point all day long sometimes and the next morning started all over again. You'd think we'd run
ourselves down but we seem to have plenty of wind and never at a loss for
something to discuss. About an hour or so each evening we get serious and
discuss the possibilities of the next day. It's a good idea and I've seen the
time when a little pre-planning or meditating, I should say, has come in
handy.*

*I've just been informed that I have some little details to look after. That's
what I like about this job—you never know ten minutes ahead of time what's
cooking.*

Immediately after writing this letter I was alerted that we would
brief at midnight in order to fly a weather reconnaissance mission
for the Third Air Division. This could be very hazardous because a
single aircraft flies the mission and there wouldn't be any fighter
escort. You were strictly on your own.

We were briefed to fly a course which would approximate the one
to be flown that day by the combat crews of the Eighth Air Force.
We would fly until we reached the enemy lines, then turn south and
fly parallel to the lines, recording temperatures, winds aloft at various altitudes, cloud cover, icing conditions, and on through a whole
weather checklist. This information would be transmitted back to
headquarters in code at regular intervals. It would be given to the
aircraft crews at their briefings, but its primary use would be in
planning the mission—which targets could be hit visually, what the
winds would be like, and so on.

We took off shortly after 2 a.m. with a full load of fuel. We felt
very apprehensive, as this was to be our first time heading toward
the enemy all by ourselves. We had returned home alone, but you
could always see other aircraft. This was a big sky, and a long flight
for a lone plane. The weather mission was flown before every combat mission and was rotated throughout the Air Force groups so that

a crew would fly this mission only once. Because of the danger involved this would normally count as a combat mission, so if the tour was thirty-five the crews that flew the weather route would fly only thirty-four combat missions.

The night was especially black. There was no horizon—we made an instrument takeoff. The runway lights were turned on only when we were ready to take off and they were extinguished the minute we were airborne. Why advertise to Jerry where you are? On our way out we knew we would be a sitting duck for any night fighters that wanted to give chase. The four exhaust stacks were cherry red and they made a good target.

I was still fretting about these things when the navigator called and said we were getting close to the enemy lines and he would soon be giving me a new heading. I expressed amazement that we had covered so much ground so quickly. He replied that we had one heck of a tail wind, and at our altitude cruising at 150 mph indicated air speed, it was probably the fastest ground speed we would ever encounter.

I knew the radio operator would be monitoring his own frequency and would not be on the interphone so I asked the navigator, who was responsible along with the bombardier for gathering the weather data, if this information had been received at headquarters. He said the radio operator had been transmitting regularly. His messages had been received and each time they asked him to verify and repeat. So we knew they were getting through.

The navigator called again to give me the new heading. We now headed south and would hold this heading for about forty-five minutes. He told me we had made our turn a little late and were now a little ways over enemy territory. But he added that we had enough correction in the new heading to bring us back over our own lines and still make good the track that we had been briefed to fly. The thought of enemy action had now started to recede from my list of worries. If they hadn't hit us by now they probably wouldn't.

The winds were coming to the forefront as my number one worry— you have to keep your mind occupied. While I was still mulling this one around the navigator called and said it was time to turn to a northwesterly heading that would take us home. The whole crew heaved a sigh of relief. The journey home is always more pleasant.

After a time the sky was just starting to let a horizon form—in a few minutes I could barely make out the English Channel. Oh, happy day! The sky continued to lighten and I could see the outline of the coast of France. I checked my watch, scanned the instrument panel— the altimeter was on 27,000 feet, the heading was right on, and all engine instruments looked good. I fiddled with every knob in the cockpit that could be wiggled or jiggled, anything to pass the time. I looked out the window again. There was the coast, and there was the Channel. Nothing had changed. It was as though we were suspended in air and everything was at a standstill.

I called the navigator and asked him what was going on—we should be getting somewhere. His reply was that the tail wind we had going out was now a head wind. "We're still indicating 150 mph airspeed," I said. "Give me a true ground speed reading and ETA [estimated time of arrival] for the base so we can check it against the fuel supply." "I'll have it for you in a couple of minutes," he answered, "but it might interest you to know that in the past six minutes you have made good five miles." Forget the ETA—even I can figure out that we have a head wind of approximately 100 mph, and at this altitude we can't get home on the fuel we have left.

I called the waist gunner and told him to tell the radio operator I wanted him on the interphone, but to make sure he didn't interrupt any communication he might be sending or receiving. In a few minutes the radio operator called. I asked, "Have you been getting all this weather information into headquarters?" He answered, "Yes, and every time I send the message they keep asking me to verify, which I do, so they know the score." "Okay, that's fine. Now please radio headquarters that we have to descend because we can't reach the base at this altitude and we will descend until we get a more favorable ground speed. But I want them to notify the Coastal Command that we are coming in under the assigned altitude and we don't particularly want to be shot at by our friends." To this he answered, "Roger. Will do. Shall I give them an altitude?" "Not in this first message because I don't know how far we will have to descend. We will descend at 2,000-foot intervals, allowing the navigator to get a ground speed at each altitude. When he finds one that looks as if it will get us home that's the one we will use. But I want the ground speed at each altitude radioed to headquarters." "Roger. Will code and start sending immediately."

By now it was broad daylight and we could see the first bomber groups starting to form into wings over the splashers and heading for Germany. "My God," I thought, "is somebody crazy? We have risked our necks to supply information and no one is paying any attention. They must know something we don't."

At 14,000 feet we were happy with the ground speed and headed on to our base where we made a quick landing. There wasn't any air traffic as our group had already taken off.

We headed immediately for interrogation and were very curious. Why would a mission be scheduled with the upper level winds reaching almost unheard of velocities? Our questions were soon answered. Headquarters had received our messages, and when decoded, they looked bizarre. Obviously such wind conditions did not exist. Consequently, we must be using the wrong code or we had something fouled up. This was the reason we had been asked to verify each time.

By now the lead crews on the mission were confirming our reports. The groups that were still on the ground were ordered to stand down. Those just taking off were recalled. The early birds would have to continue on—they were committed—but they could not return to England. After "Bombs away" they were diverted to tactical bases in France.

All of this was understandable because in that day and age not much was known about the jet streams. This was obviously an early encounter with the shifting winds. We were very irritated that no one saw fit to believe us. We felt we had the knowledge and the expertise to do our job and do it right—certainly we could read the "code of the day." We were gently reminded that our job was to "do"—the planning phase belonged to others.

We did not receive credit for this mission. It would be easier for all to just forget it and fly our thirty-five combat missions. We did, however, have the satisfaction of knowing that we had done our best.

December 5, 1944

Since I've had only five hours sleep in the last forty-eight and very little the day before that I deem it time I turned in. We'll probably sleep for the next twenty-four anyway. Get out the chalk now and mark up another one. Number thirty-two has joined the list of has-beens. Sure hope I don't get bogged down again. Can't make any predictions, but I can wish, hope, and dream, and I'm making an all out effort to finish as soon as is humanly possible. I know we can't make our holiday date, but I'll try not to be too late.

Mission #32, *Berlin, Germany, December 5*

Frank Dimit, Bombardier

Briefed at 4:15 a.m. for two targets. It was one of those Plan A and Plan B jobs. "A" was an oil refinery at Politz. "B" was a tank and flak gun factory at Berlin. We used B, thank goodness.

Had another one of those night takeoff and rendezvous. Think my nerves and those of most of the crew are about shot. Be glad when this tour is finished. We dived and climbed all over the sky this a.m., like a P-51. Most of the time we were dodging flares. The red-green jobs look just like the wing lights of a B-17. Thought several times we were dead ducks for sure. Looked like planes coming head-on. I haven't stopped shaking yet.

Flew lead of high squadron of lead group and our group led the wing. Carried 20 250-pound G.P. bombs. The load was meant for Politz, but then we used B plan. Bombing was PFF.

Flak was pathetic. Really expected much more from Berlin. They have moved a lot of their guns to Merseburg. Didn't pick up a hole.

Expected to get a lot of trouble with fighters today, but we didn't see any. Had splendid escort.

Smitty, our tail gunner, missed today's mission. Has been in the hospital for several days. Out now, but not on flying duty. E. J. Kolbush replaced Smitty. He taught me aircraft recognition at Kingman, Arizona.

Was colder than hell up there today. Damn near froze my hands and feet. Trouble with bomb-bay doors. Brownie and I cranked them open and closed.

Doc goes on flak pass tomorrow.

Three more to go.

Yesterday we flew weather ship for the Division. Up at 12 a.m., takeoff at 2:00 a.m. Flew to Rennes, France, and sent back several weather reports. Landed about 9:30 a.m. Thought we might get a mission for it. But no luck. *[End of mission notes by Frank Dimit]*

The 357th fighter group, a P-51 outfit, led by Major Joseph E. Broadhead, of Rupert, Idaho, shot down twenty Nazi aircraft December 5.

If there was anything that struck fear in the hearts of the air crewmen, even more so than the enemy, it was the thought of a fire on board or a midair collision, mainly because you couldn't fight back. These two things resulted in many lost aircraft and claimed the lives of many crew members. These thoughts were never out of our minds and they preyed on us constantly—the pilots especially because they were responsible for the safety of the crew, not to mention their own necks. From a safety standpoint our flight procedures left a lot to be desired on our climb to altitude in the soup. To say it was a harrowing experience would be an understatement of gross proportion.

We took off at thirty-second intervals with fifty or sixty planes involved. This would require approximately thirty minutes to get everyone airborne. Each plane had to take off at the precise second in order to maintain our required flight separation. Sometimes our takeoffs were visual and we would have several hundred feet of altitude before entering the soup and going on instruments. But there were times when we made instrument takeoffs with one pilot totally on instruments and the other pilot trying to watch the edge of the runway. This resulted in both pilots making corrections and required complete cooperation.

On reaching 200 feet of altitude "takeoff power" was reduced to "climb power," and the pilot immediately started a left turn with 15 degrees of bank. This turn was held throughout the "climb-out." At the same time our airspeed was held constant at 150 mph, our rate of climb at 300 feet per minute. Our radio direction finder was tuned to the Base Radio Beacon frequency and the needle was kept on 270 degrees, which indicated that the field and beacon were always off of the left wing tip. Between this reading and our degree of bank, our position in relation to the field was held constant, and we were now spiraling counterclockwise up to altitude. Our flight pattern was a corkscrew with the air base being represented by the point on the screw. We held this position until we broke out of the clouds. This could mean anywhere from a few thousand feet to, at times, over 15,000 feet.

Now, visualize sixty aircraft from one field going up this corkscrew at thirty-second intervals and knowing that ten miles in either direction other groups were doing the same thing in clouds and pitch-black darkness. This system could and did work, but only if every pilot did precisely the same thing and held everything constant. There was no margin for error.

In the soup visibility was almost nil, but we used our red-green running lights on these "climb-outs," hoping they would be detected to avoid a collision if someone were out of position. We were young, but we were still subject to stress, and many a combat pilot will tell you that by the time we emerged from the cloud bank our flight gear would be soaked through with sweat.

Our crew never saw a collision in the overcast, but we did see several while trying to join up in formation after breaking out of the clouds. There are two that still stand out in my mind. On our July 28 mission we saw two ships from the 100th Bomb Group collide head-on in a clear sky well above the undercast. On October 26 we saw another midair collision during assembly.

On this particular day, as we were climbing through the overcast in the dark, we saw the red-green lights and I immediately lowered the nose to allow the lights to go over the top of us and then resumed normal climb. In a matter of a few minutes Billy Bob eased back on the yoke and in a nose-high attitude we allowed the lights to go below us. Then we made an immediate recovery to keep from stalling out for our aircraft was loaded to its maximum weight and our controls were sluggish. After this happened several more times it was hard to tell who was spooked the most, the crew, who could only watch, or the pilots, who were trying to react.

About this time Billy Bob and I put our heads together and pondered the problem. If we were this close to a midair collision so many times, why didn't we feel prop wash from the other aircraft? But in our agitated state we could probably have flown through a brick wall and never noticed. This was a conundrum that we think was solved when we broke out of the clouds. There was our lead ship flying in a circle above us firing red-green magnesium flares to identify his position so we could form on him. These were the colors that were assigned to us and he was doing his job, but did he have to do it so well? With tongue in cheek we told the crew that in all likelihood we had been dodging flares rather than airplanes, but who knows? We had already sweat blood, and no amount of explanation could erase what we had gone through.

I made a vow that if I returned from this mission somebody at group was going to hear about it. When we returned I was allowed to vent my steam, but there appeared to be no solution or alternative.

December 6, 1944

Just another short note before hitting the sack. I'm not a bit sleepy and I feel good—first time I've had such high spirits in a long time. Today I won a great moral victory on a matter which has been giving me trouble lately, so I have been quite jubilant since. Now I think things will go much better. It was the first time the crew had ever seen me mad. Little did they realize what I would do on their behalf if somebody started pushing them or us around. We really click together and we have an unbeatable team.

The reason for the elated spirits was that a problem had been resolved relating to our crew and the number of missions we would fly. There had been some talk of extending the number.

Our tail gunner had been in the hospital and had missed the December 5 mission. He was now one behind the rest of the crew. The group was now insisting that he fly a makeup mission by flying with a different crew. Since he was my tail gunner I didn't want him to fly with another crew and take a chance of losing him. Every crew had their own procedures and proven bond. (Our navigator had been two missions behind, but he had made these up by flying with other crews.) I was then reminded that Headquarters USAAF in Washington had recently said that crews would not be relieved from combat duty simply on the basis of number of missions or combat hours flown, but only after evidence of combat fatigue.

This meant that any crew could be asked to fly more than thirty-five missions. However, Headquarters of the Eighth Air Force knew that if the order were applied to everyone there would be some real serious morale problems. They knew that the flight crews had to have a goal to shoot for. So they initiated an order of their own which could be used to signify compliance with the order from Washington, but still give us a goal. The order simply stated that all flight crew members would be examined for combat fatigue by the group flight surgeons, and under no condition would this examination be put off beyond thirty-five missions. This meant that the group flight surgeons had the authority to set the actual number of missions flown. The flight surgeon and our group officers had no desire to see a crew fly more than thirty-five missions.

The discussion over the tail gunner became heated, but when I was dismissed I left knowing that all members of my crew, with the exception of the copilot, were fatigued enough to be able to finish upon the completion of *my* thirty-fifth mission.

December 7, 1944

How's my little family this dreary evening? Me? Oh, I'm in a pretty good mood for a change. No particular reason, just things in general. One of the reasons for our good spirits, I think, is because one of the fellows went to a rest home so he let us have his phonograph and collection of records to use while he was gone. It sure seems good to hear some good music. It kinda brightens up the day and puts a little atmosphere in our shack.

No mail for me yesterday, but today I received a letter from my cousin, Virgil, who is in Italy. He has been overseas 30 months and he's getting lonesome for the gal he left behind. I know just how he feels—today marks my six-month anniversary here. I know I could never stand it that long with the worries and trials of this life.

Received another Oak Leaf Cluster to go with the Air Medal this morning. This makes the fourth one—when I get them all on you can't see the ribbon. But they can take all their awards and decorations. All I want is a ticket home for a live passenger, and I may be getting that pretty soon. As you know, we have thirty-two in now. Not many more left, but it still seems like a long ways to go. This sweating every day in and out begins to get old after so long a time. . . .

December 10, 1944

*. . . Want to buy me a couple of records? If you do here are the ones I would like—*The Kerry Dance *featuring Connie Boswell, and* Don't Believe Everything You Dream *with the Ink Spots. Both are Brunswick records, and, of course, they are made in England. . . .*

We have had some cold weather lately. The temperature doesn't drop too low, although it is below freezing, but the air is so damp it goes right through you. I don't know how long it has been since there was a day when it didn't rain, sleet, snow, or something. It gets pretty chilly up where we work— many times around fifty below—that all adds to the comfort of flying. When I get home I'm going to buy a cat and just sit by the fireplace where it is warm. This flying racket is for the birds, and I don't have a feather on me.

Our rooms were heated by a little old stove which was probably twelve inches in diameter and maybe eighteen inches tall. We had a coke ration every three days, but if you had a fire for several hours a ration would last only for one evening. If your ration was used up, the minute you came in from the outside the logical thing to do was go to bed or else put on a lot of extra clothes because it always seemed colder inside the quonset than it was outside.

The English weather is very, very damp and all the time we were there I don't remember ever putting on clothes that were completely dry. Things would mildew fast; consequently, most of our clothing was wool. Wool could be wet and still keep you warm—the only thing wrong with it was that it would smell a little musty. This may have contributed to our reluctance to take a bath—we were never positive where the odor came from. Knowing that we had only a choice of being cold or staying in bed it seemed much more logical to make a midnight requisition to the coke pile and load a couple of shovelsful into an old wheelbarrow.

We used to draw lots to see who would go up and raid the coke pile. In the beginning, as the ranking officer on the crew, I refused to put my name in the list. But after a while this got old for the rest of them and, as I was enjoying the heat too, it seemed only fair that my name should be put in along with the rest of them. Sure enough my name was finally drawn.

The coke pile was located up a gently rolling hill probably 200 yards from our barracks. Some nights there were two sentries at the pile, but generally there was only one. In order to keep warm he spent his time walking around the perimeter of the coke pile, or maybe he'd walk back and forth, then stop and listen, light a cigarette, stomp his feet, and rub his hands. It was usually cold and very black.

On this particular night I took the old wheelbarrow up the hill and managed to get about three shovelsful in and was ready to start back. The sentry had his back to me and was 100 feet or so away. I thought, "Now is the time to get out of here." The sentry carried a flashlight, but he wouldn't turn it on unless it was absolutely necessary to locate somebody, because of blackout restrictions.

There was only one problem with this wheelbarrow. It had an old iron wheel with a bearing that hadn't been greased in all the time the group had been there. It let out a little high-pitched squeal every time it hit a certain spot on its rotation. Of course the noise was always louder once a little weight was added.

Now all the members on the crew, myself included, were somewhat mechanically inclined, but it had never dawned on us to bring some oil or grease from the flight line and grease the bearing. If there were two of us, we might carry the thing rather than push it.

After ascertaining that the guard wasn't paying any attention to me, I started back down the hill, pushing the wheelbarrow along with its squeaks and creaks. About this time I heard the guard say, "You know, I really don't mind turning my back while you filch the coke, but I certainly wish somebody would grease that damn wheel before we all get in trouble." Needless to say, that shook us up. Here we thought we had been executing a coup, and all these times we were being watched by the sentry.

In all the time we were there we wished that just one time we could have enough coke to start a fire, run it all day, and completely dry out our barracks and our clothes. But such was not to be the case. Even at that we probably had a larger ration than any of the civilian people, and maybe even more than some of the military personnel.

This wasn't a particularly big problem for our flight crew. They had converted their little stove into an oil burner. As the engines on the B-17 required an oil change occasionally this old oil would pile up at the dump. So with their friends amongst the ground crew, the boys could always figure out a way to get some used oil which would otherwise be thrown away. Their ground crew also supplied a few gallons of gasoline, which they would use to ignite the initial drips of oil going into the stove. Once the fire box was hot they could cut down on the gas and burn almost pure oil. So they didn't need to steal coke, but they were never completely warm either. At least their problems were different, because they had to spend their time figuring out a way to get oil and gas.

I can remember a couple of occasions when the boys invited me down to their barracks to get warm and it was rather pleasant to be next to an oil-fired stove. But it wasn't right or possible to do this every evening.

December 17, 1944

Another week gone by and a new one just beginning. Maybe this week will bear more fruit than the last. Last week was a pretty hard one, though, as we did quite a bit of work. None of it was the kind I wanted to do, but it was work that had to be done and someone had to do it. Lucky me, if there are any odd jobs lying around I get them. Asking the Squadron Commander to keep us busy really paid off. There's one consolation; they can't keep this up much longer, I hope.

We missed church this morning. We were going to the evening service but changed our minds. They are having a choir come in and sing Christmas carols and no sermon. The reason we decided not to go was that the place will be crowded and I don't think any of us could stand to listen to the carols without getting a good solid case of the blues. We have them enough without bringing any atmosphere in it and asking for them. . . .

As you've probably guessed we're all pretty well disgusted with life over here. It's not because combat is unbearable, it's just because of certain events and happenings. Things have changed considerably since we first arrived. We're the "Old Timers" now—the "Remember When" boys!

In late November and December our crew had a pretty rough time. We were subconsciously suffering from stress and battle fatigue, but we were still very capable of doing our missions and any other job that was required of us. By now our experience had placed us at the very peak of our combat capabilities, but internal changes would now play a role.

We were a proud crew and we had extended the time of our tour by taking lead crew training. We felt we were making a real contribution to the welfare and success of our group. We had seen many crews finish, some of whom had spent much less time in the group than ourselves. We had been present at the awards ceremony when these men finished their tours and were awarded the Distinguished Flying Cross. It made us proud because we knew that you could not complete a tour of twenty-five, thirty, or thirty-five missions and not exhibit the outstanding heroism and exceptional performance to win this award—the old timers knew!

But we were to receive a new group commanding officer and this would no longer be the practice. A crew finishing their missions would not be recognized for what they had done in the past or would do in the future. Flying against the enemy would be just a job. Apparently the art of preparing citations had now become a far too *difficult task,* or simply too dangerous in the European Theater of Operations.

Previously when a crew finished their last mission they would depart from the formation after making landfall on England. They would pour on the coal and reach the base ahead of the formation, and fly down the runway at 200 feet firing flares in a victory celebration. There would be cause for joy both in the airplane and among the crews observing on the ground. This was tangible evidence that a crew could live to finish a tour and it was a real morale booster. This practice was ordered to cease.

Another honor accorded a crew when this big event arrived was the "Lucky Bastard Club" dinner. The whole crew would dress in Class A uniform and come to the Combat Officers Mess Hall, where they were seated at a table of honor with a white tablecloth and given a steak dinner with a bottle of wine. During their dinner they were given a standing ovation from the combat crew officers in the mess hall. It made them feel good and we felt good. Besides, it would be the only time a combat officer and crew would receive a steak at the 95th. The staff officers ate in a separate dining facility and I doubt if they knew what this little ceremony meant to the men who were to fly and go, *if* they survived.

They were also given a certificate stating that they had joined the Lucky Bastard Club. A 1st pilot who flew as a deputy lead or squadron lead, along with his crew members, was given a certificate signed by the group commanding officer and by the Third Air Division Commander, Major General Partridge, stating that they had been a crew leading combat formations.

It was all trivial in a sense, but it meant somebody cared. All of these practices would cease immediately—a new regime had come into being. I thought at first this was an Air Force–wide decision, but soon discovered that it pertained only to the 95th.

When these orders were given our crew still had four missions to fly, and we had just gone through the last scrubbed mission to Merseburg. There was even some talk of extending the tour. I would now have to relay all this information to my crew. The new C.O. obviously did not realize what impact these orders would have on the morale of the seasoned crews. The new ones wouldn't know any difference. A wise and fair man would have instituted a "grand-father clause," because the most important things in a combat group were morale and loyalty, but loyalty had to be a two-way street. All of a sudden the changes were coming so fast that we felt we were back in Cadet Training. We were no longer entitled to the respect and recognition that comes with having done your very best.

The day I told my crew of these new rules I played them down as best I could, and reminded them that I knew what they had done and I was proud of them even if they didn't get any goodies. In their hearts they knew they were good and had done their best—this would have to be their reward. The most important thing, with God willing, was that we would get home with something more meaningful—our lives!

I dismissed them in a hurry because I didn't want them to see how much it hurt to relay these orders. I wished the colonel could have seen the consequence of his orders mirrored in the eyes of all of us. Our crew had been let down by a man who would never know, or care, what we had contributed. I wouldn't be able to fly those last missions fast enough.

December 19, 1944

Happy Days! Only five more shoplifting days until Christmas! Why all the jubilation? Yesterday I had seven letters! Besides I was pretty busy most of the day, then went to bed early because I figured I would be routed out pretty early this morning. I wasn't disappointed, because I was awakened at four a.m. What an ungodly hour to get up. That's just the right time to be going to bed. Nothing like getting up early so you have a long day to loaf. That's our new policy.

I'm feeling halfway human and I don't think I'll ever get down in the dumps again like I was a short time back. I'm not saying that I won't have the blues—they're practically chronic. But morale will never slip as low again as then. That's a fact and a promise. Some mighty bleak and despairing days have passed, but I seem to have my thinking cap pretty well in hand now and have resolved my mind to a few things.

You may want to know what made me so irritable and hard to get along with awhile back. Well, I'll tell you. It was the culmination of a mistake I had started earlier. The mistake was trying to live each day as it comes. You just can't do that—it's impossible in the long run. Why? Because if you have bad luck every day for a period of time you gradually become dejected and finally destitute. No, you have to live more than each day as it comes. Life and happiness are more complex than the momentary elations of any one day. You must live each day as it comes and also live the treasured memories of the past as well as the exotic dreams of the future. Only in this way can you balance the mind over a continued length of time. That's the story.

Now to answer a few questions which appeared in your letters. Yes, you might say that Lucky Sherry *is a much better airplane than* Knock Out Baby. *It's our real pride and joy and we sure baby it along. The picture is quite unique and pretty hard to describe so I think I'll keep you waiting on this point until you can see the picture. We have quite a color scheme. The picture is painted on the back of all our leather jackets. Boy, are we flashy! I'll send you a picture of all of us with our dress battle dress on. The dress battle dress is what we wear when we want to impress the recruits. . . .*

We were awakened at 4 a.m., had breakfast, and attended briefing. Everyone was elated because we were finally going on a mission to aid the ground troops. But the weather didn't hold up and the mission was scrubbed at 9:30 a.m. It was a very disgruntled flight crew that piled out of the airplane to go back to the everyday grind.

December 20, 1944

. . . It has been pretty chilly here lately, and fog—I've never seen the like of it. It gets you soaking wet just walking in it. It's so thick you have to cut it before you can walk. At times you can see almost ten or fifteen feet in front of you, but most of the time you don't know whether you are walking on the trail or across the fields until you run into a fence or fall in a ditch. Funny people these English. They dig a ditch instead of building a fence. But far be it from me to point out their mistakes.

Now comes the subject I've been wanting to talk over with you. I've been wondering how you felt about my flying. I don't mean my flying ability, technique, or anything like that because I think you know that I can pilot as safe an airplane as there is flying. No, I just wondered how you felt about my job here. There was a time when I loved flying in civilian life, but like everything else, the Army has taken all the joy out of it. Flying now is just a job and the worries and responsibilities are far too high for the compensa-

tion. It wouldn't necessarily have to be that way, but I think too highly of the men under me to endanger them through any shortcomings, fault, or ignorance on my part. . . .

Now let's do some supposing or wishing. Say my tour here was completed. In a couple of months I would be on a train looking forward to three wonderful weeks with my wife and son. At the end of that time I would find myself at a Reclassification Center being interviewed for reclassification.

One of the first things he would ask would be, "What are your objections or attitude toward another tour of combat?" I would say that I don't like it and I don't want to do another tour. Why? Because any man who has been in combat once is afraid of it and wouldn't ask for any more. It's a story he has heard a thousand times in his job. So he would say, "Other than that, what other objections do you have, physically or mentally?" To this I would have to answer none, for they haven't brought out the Army physical yet that I can't pass. And mentally I'm just as sane as I've ever been.

No, I know these two factors wouldn't keep me out of combat. At the end of this interview the verdict would probably be, "You've done a good job, but there is still a war to be won. With your experience you would be valuable in the South Pacific. We'll give you three or four months training here to rehabilitate you and get started with a new crew, then back to battle." To this I could probably refuse—then after the court martial I would undoubtedly find myself in the walking Army with the rating of Private. As you know that would never happen. First, because I have a sense of duty, and, secondly, there's a war to be won and somebody has to do the fighting. If one tour of combat were to exempt all from further combat there soon wouldn't be anyone left to fight on our side.

Now that you have that picture, let's say the reclassification officer had said, "Well, you've done your part in combat, so now we'll give you a job in the States. Let's look at your records and see what you are qualified for. Hmmmmmmmm Pilot, specialized training only, good experience, would make a good flying instructor." He's right. There's no choice. The only thing I could qualify for would be duty involving flying. I'd be the low man on the totem pole, the guy who has to do the work. No administrative training and no chance of getting any in the States. It would mean flying day in and day out hoping you can catch a student's mistake before he smears you all over the runway. It's okay if you love flying and are content to remain a throttle jockey all your life. While I'm in the Army I would like to get above just being a pilot. I would like getting on the inside and help run things while somebody else does the actual flying.

Now let's see—I have the qualifications and experience of flying which are necessary for a job like that, but where can I get the administrative training? If you have enough rank you can get it in the States or anyplace. Everybody wants an administrative flying job so that puts it out of reach of the junior *officers regardless of how much grey matter they might have. At this point it looks as if I'm stuck with flying even though I want to quit.*

Now let's go further. What would happen if I stayed with this outfit when my tour was over. Of the several jobs that have been offered in the Group, what would they lead to? On one of them I could get a jump in rank, learn operational duty and at the same time fly a few more missions. Well, that's out! When this one's over I've had enough combat flying. There isn't anything that will force me to do any extra missions. Suppose I take one of the other jobs—fly as an instructor, no more combat, but plenty of flying. No thanks, if I have to fly as an instructor I'll take a chance of doing it in the States where I can be with my wife and family. Another job I could take here would be just monkeying around flying just enough to get flying pay, serve maybe six months or a year, and maybe make Captain with good luck. But yet I wouldn't learn anything that would benefit me or help me get the job I want. It would just delay my coming home and then when I did get there I would still be just a pilot and wouldn't have any better chance of staying in the States than I would right now. That's out. I can't get what I want by staying with this Group.

What I really want is to stop this everyday flying and come home. But I can't realize both of those dreams right now and still help win the war, a little matter which I have to do. If I come home now I can be with you for at least six months chasing around the country, and with half a miracle I might get to be an instructor and remain indefinitely, wondering each day if I will be called back to combat duty. That was exactly what I was going to do and what I might still do. But when I come home I want to live the life we've always planned.

Here's what I'm getting at. I was interviewed yesterday by a Colonel from higher Headquarters offering me a chance to train and take a staff job. No more combat flying—just the four hours a month for flying pay, as the job requires a flying man with combat experience. This would be a chance to work toward a job which I've always wanted since coming in the Army— the planning end. I think I've had my share of the doing end. I would like to try to use my brain for a change and see how that works. If I make good at the job it would mean staying here at least another six months after my tour is over. If I don't make good or don't like the work I could quit and come home. If I do make good and come home my chances of staying in the States are greatly improved and the hazards of everyday flying are overcome.

I was very much impressed by Colonel Huglin. I felt that here was a man who would give me some responsibility and expect me to do my best. I had the feeling that I could learn a lot about administration by being on his staff. I have spoken with the Squadron Commander about this move and he thinks it is a wise choice. As you know, I have a lot of faith in his judgment. During the interview I kept seeing similarities between these two men. Of course, Colonel Huglin is much older, but both are real quiet, firm, sincere, and command respect. I wonder if this is what "The Point" does for you, but then, maybe it is just their nature. Anyway, I was pleased to be asked to be on his staff even in a junior capacity. Something tells me that Frankosky has had more to do with this than he is letting on. This man had to get my name from somewhere. Anyway, I am thankful to both and will be happy to get out of the pipeline and learn something different while still contributing to a just cause.

While you are reading all of this I'll be trying to finish this tour I'm on. I don't know how much longer it will drag on. With good luck and weather it wouldn't take long, but you see how things are going.

December 24, 1944

'Twas the night before Christmas and all through the house not a creature was stirring—everyone was just plain tuckered out. But there wasn't a man that wasn't thinking of home and his loved ones. It's pretty quiet tonight, only an occasional sage remark about this time last year. On close inspection you can see that the eyes glisten with a little water when home is mentioned. We'd give darn near anything to be home tonight, but since we can't we'll just make the best of it.

I hate to miss our son's first Christmas, but the best present I can give the two of you is that you can chalk off number thirty-three.

Mission #33, *Biblis, Germany, December 24*

Frank Dimit, Bombardier

Briefed at 5:45 a.m. for our target, an airfield on the Rhine River about 20 miles south and a little west of Frankfurt, or about 5–10 miles southwest of Darmstadt.

We flew high squadron lead of the lead group of our wing.

Carried 38 100-pound demolition bombs—used tail fuses only. Wanted to dig holes in their field. Had a bomb rack malfunction. Formation slid under us before I had a chance to salvo them. Got over Rhine River before I could get rid of them. Bombing was visual, but bad haze and we flew into the sun. Visibility was poor. Don't think bombing was so good.

Flak was very light and inaccurate over target. But we caught hell going over the front lines. Used to be a few corridors there, but they are definitely closed up. Picked up several holes.

This was a maximum effort for the 8th A.F. today. The 95th contributed 60 aircraft. Germans have been playing hell with our ground forces, so today we did a little playing. Everyone was hitting airfields or tactical targets.

Luftwaffe was probably up, but we didn't see it.

Two more to go. An alert on now, may fly tomorrow. *[End of mission notes by Frank Dimit]*

The month of December was hard on the nerves of the flying crews of the 95th Bomb Group. On December 16 the Germans staged a surprise counterattack, and troops of the 101st Airborne Division, a part of the First Army commanded by General McAuliffe, were caught and trapped in the forests of the Belgian Ardennes. Our group flew only one mission from December 12 to 24, to Stuttgart on December 16, the same day as the breakthrough.

Our crew did not fly from December 5 until the 24th. We had nineteen days of nonproductive work with our minds working overtime. The weather kept the group grounded and nerves were raw and on edge.

Meanwhile, the ground troops who were encircled at Bastogne and trapped in the Battle of the Bulge were hungry, tired, and cold. Their casualties were mounting. Their ammunition and supplies were running out. The supply depot at Antwerp was placed under intensive bombardment by German V-2 rockets. The First and Ninth U.S. Armies were attacking from the north, and the Third Army from the south. The snow and cold were making rescue difficult.

The weather was horrible. We couldn't get an airplane off the ground. This bothered us as we were helpless to do anything but worry. We were fighting men and we wanted to fight. We had flown in support of the ground troops before, both bombing and dropping supplies, and we wanted to again. But Mother Nature had us caught in her grasp. In a sense we were being held captive just as the troops were in the Bulge. Yet we were still warm with plenty to eat, in civilization, and this is what hurt. Our conscience was making life miserable for us.

But on December 24 the weather broke and we flew with a vengeance. That day we put over 2,000 heavy bombers in the air at one time in support of our people in the Ardennes. As our first echelons were bombing the enemy the last ones in the bomber stream were leaving England, a truly magnificent sight. Jerry caught it that day and he paid dearly for the misery that had been inflicted upon the ground troops. This was the largest bomber mission of the war to date, and it was supported by 900 fighters. Our frustrations eased, we could think clearly again. Our morale soared, we could now fight back!

December 25, 1944

Here it is Christmas Day come and almost gone. There wasn't too much time to think and really get homesick today. But I will admit that there was a more prominent loneliness today than usual. I sincerely hope I never spend another Christmas like this. When we finished our work we had a wonderful dinner, but everyone was almost too tired to enjoy it. We were so hungry we would have eaten the usual chow and pronounced it good. . . . Now then, get out the chalk and scoreboard and mark up number thirty-four while I sweat out the remaining one.

Explain to our little man that all Christmases aren't like his first and that it will be different when Santa Claus gets out of the Army.

Mission #34, *Bad Münster, Germany, December 25*

Frank Dimit, Bombardier

Briefed at 6:15 a.m. for our target. It was a marshalling yard at Bad Münster, a little town just south of Bad Kreuznach, which is about 20 miles southwest of Mainz.

Flew lead of high squadron of low group of our wing. Carried 10 500-pound G.P. bombs and 2 500-pound aimable cluster incendiaries. Bombing was visual and think our squadron did a damn good job. Other two squadrons hit the town of Bad Kreuznach. Four boys in our squadron goofed up a bit and dropped early, but still think we creamed it.

Our Division and the 2nd Division were the only ones to fly. 1st Division was stood down. The 2nd hit tactical targets and we hit marshalling yards. Fighter escort was good. Didn't see the Luftwaffe, but expect they were up.

Were not in range of any flak except coming home. Picked up a little in the Ludwigshaven-Mannheim area. No holes. Wasn't too accurate. Went across the front lines about 8 miles south of the place we did yesterday. Didn't get any flak today.

Was sweating out weather on return. Division said there was a 50–50 chance of having to land in France, because of fog at the base. Fletch didn't go much for landing away from our base and missing

Bombs exploding on the target at Bad Munster, Germany. Strike photo taken from ship #7783, *Lucky Sherry*, Christmas Day, 1944 *(95th B.G. photo)*

our Christmas dinner. Fog was just on the edge of the field when we came in. Finished our roll-out in zero visibility. We were the last plane to land. About two-thirds of the group got in, the others landed at another base in England.

Whatta way to spend Christmas!

Telegrams arrived from Generals Doolittle and Partridge congratulating us on our part in yesterday's big mission.

One more to go!! *[End of mission account by Frank Dimit]*

Lack of good judgment or mistakes in identification always seemed to result in tragedy whether it be bombs dropped on friendly troops or on friendly territory. There were occasions of our own fighters being fired on by bomber gunners. There were also instances of the ground troops firing on one another and creating chaos. Fighting in combat is a very fluid situation—identification and action have to be taken simultaneously or there will be no tomorrow for him who hesitates.

Christmas Day was one of those days—a flight of three low-flying P-51s were mistaken for ME 109s and were fired on by our own ground troops on the Continent. Two planes were shot down and the Eighth Air Force Fighter Command lost one of their top scoring aces and squadron leaders, Major George E. Preddy.

December 27, 1944

I have some good news for you! Now sit down and lay David in his crib because I wouldn't want you to drop him. Here it is. It's all over with now—I'm an ex-combat man!! You can chalk up number thirty-five, the last one, as of right now. Don't worry about me any more because the danger is over. Don't know as yet when I'm coming or what, but will get something definite within the next few days. But don't look for me home very soon.

Mission #35, *Fulda, Germany, December 27*

Frank Dimit, Bombardier

Briefed at 4:15 a.m. for our target—a marshalling yard at Fulda, Germany, a town about 30 miles northeast of Frankfurt.

Flew lead of high squadron of the lead group of our wing. Carried 12 500-pound G.P. bombs. Bombing was visual, and think we creamed it. Made two runs on the target. A squadron from the 390th flew a collision course with us on the bomb run. We were looking up at bombs and it was just about time to drop. We got out of there quick and came around again.

Didn't see much flak today. Caught a few bursts at several different places. Saw some at the front lines going in, but only meager coming out.

The Luftwaffe was up but we didn't see it, thank goodness. We were without fighter escort for a good while after that second pass at the target. Except for that, escort was good.

When we were awakened at 2:00 a.m. thought sure we were going to enjoy a night takeoff and a mission to Politz. But things worked out pretty good. We were going to take off in the dark, but they changed takeoff time.

FINISHED AT LAST!!!! *[End of mission notes by Frank Dimit]*

Intelligence photo. Last mission of Fletcher's crew. Target is a marshalling yard at Fulda, Germany. Photo shows route in, primary target, secondary target, and target of last resort, December 27, 1944. *(95th B.G. photo)*

On our final mission there was more nervousness and trepidation than usual. It had appeared to all of us that more crews were lost on their first several missions and on the last two or three than at any other time during their tour. There were no statistics to reinforce this view, only a feeling which permeated all bomber crews in combat.

All of a sudden this feeling was brought home when on the bomb run to the target a squadron from the 390th came over the top of us on a collision course. As we stared up into the loaded bomb bays our normal breathing pattern quickly changed as we gulped for more oxygen to alleviate fear.

Our group lead immediately broke off of the bomb run and made a tight circle to get in behind the errant group. We were able to execute the turn and give the bombardiers the time they needed to synchronize on the target and still stay out of the way of the following groups of the task force. But, somehow, we couldn't pass it off as just another mixup in the target area. The mental jinx was work-ing overtime, but we were fighting to overcome it and regain our composure.

As we flew through the flak at the target our nerves were ragged; the tension was building. One way or another, as a crew we were on our final ride. The flak bursts were not too close, but who knows where the next bursts will be. As Dimit called "Bombs away," some relief spread throughout the ship as we were now flying for our-selves. On the way in we flew for Uncle Sam, but going home was different, we'd done our job, we were now flying to save our own necks and to keep our group intact.

But the mission wasn't over yet. We still had about four hours of flying before we even dared to relax—almost two hours of it over hostile territory, not knowing when we might be hit by fighters or accidentally fly over some unknown flak batteries. There was always the possibility of mechanical failure which could spell disaster.

All the way back from the target I had a wrestling match with my conscience. The colonel's orders were still ringing in my ears: "No more DFC's on finishing a tour, no Lucky Bastard dinner, no more victory flyovers." *Obey the orders.* Don't violate the rules. This was ingrained in us from the first day we entered military service. My conscience was fighting hard and it appeared to be winning the bat-tle. But my heart was revolting. What's a court martial compared to the dangers of what we had faced in flying thirty-five combat mis-sions against the Third Reich, plus the countless training missions in poor weather over England?

I thought about my crew and the disappointment we had to face when these rule changes were made known to us—the misty eyes, the choked voices. I owed these men something. They had given me and the 95th Group their very best throughout some very trying times. No aircraft commander could ask and receive more from his crew.

We were leading the high squadron of the lead group and the battle went on—conscience versus heart. While the wrath of a colo-nel is not to be taken lightly, a 105 millimeter shell exploding under your tail is no great pleasure either.

As we made landfall on the coast of England I called my right wingman, Lieutenant Metzinger, and requested he bring my for-mation home. He wiggled his wings and verified with a very happy "Roger." I switched back to interphone and asked Billy Bob to give me 2100 rpm and monitor the manifold pressure on the engines. My course had now become clear. My conscience and the military were thrust into the background as I shoved the throttles to the fire wall, lowered the nose, and called Roco to give me a heading that would take us straight down the runway at the base.

The crew now realized what was happening and each one let out a big "Yippee!!" We may be reprimanded, but orders or no orders—*we're going for it!* This was one thing they couldn't take away—I was in command of the aircraft. I told the crew that anyone who wanted to fire a flare should come on up to the flight deck and start firing when we reached the runway. I would make two passes to give everyone a chance, but cautioned them not to fire any red-red flares which indicated there were wounded on board.

Brownie immediately locked the Very pistol in the mounting bracket on the top of the fuselage on the flight deck and started breaking out the cartridges. As we went roaring down the runway on the victory flyover at full high rpm, *Lucky Sherry* looked like a giant roman candle gone mad, erupting the brightly colored magnesium flares—red-green, red-blue, red-white. Old "Fireball Red Leader" was coming home for the last time and our presence was being announced with great hilarity. I was sure I heard Billy Bob's drawl on the interphone, "Y'all be sure and fire one for the colonel, now."

In the middle of our second pass the group lead came over the field and requested permission to start their landing peel-off. The tower (code name Bezel) requested that they circle the field once as there was a ship in the pattern with wounded aboard. As the group went around we pulled up, made a real tight turn, and settled down on the runway where we made at least three good, hard bounces. It was a landing that Airplane #7783, *Lucky Sherry*, and the crew would not forget. The Tower responded with "Good Show," and I with "Roger, Bezel, good to be back!"

Our tour had now been completed, and that was our "thank-you"—the only time I ever knowingly failed to heed an order. To this day I have a hard time forgiving the Group C.O. who denied my men the decoration they risked their lives to earn and so richly deserved!

As we cut the engines after taxiing to the hardstand we were congratulated by the seldom-praised and often forgotten true heroes of this war, the crew chief of the airplane and his ground crew. Without their dedicated service, many times twenty-four hours at a stretch in cold and inclement weather, these airplanes would not have flown. The flight crews were an extension of their aircraft, and the pride they exhibited toward both the crew and airplane made you feel like something special. It was good to report no battle damage today.

The hilarity now put behind us, we had to get on with the serious business of interrogation.

As the interrogating officer went through his checklist of questions, Roco mentioned that Smitty, our tail gunner, had reported flak while we were over Belgium—somewhat meager, about thirty bursts, pretty small stuff. They couldn't quite reach us, but they were trying. This was a surprise because we thought we were over territory that had already been liberated, yet as we flew across this little town someone was objecting.

The interrogation officer said the area was being held by the Germans, a small enemy pocket completely surrounded by U.S. forces. It was felt that they would realize the hopelessness of their position and surrender as they ran out of food and ammunition. This would be better than assaulting the area and having casualties on both sides.

At the close of interrogation the interrogating officer called out to others in the room to see if any of the other crews had seen enemy action in this area. Upon receiving a negative report he said that the position reported was a known area of enemy resistance. Hostile action had been reported by a crew who had now finished their missions and it would behoove them all to be more observant because this group of eyes would no longer be with them.

This is the type of statement that really endears you in the hearts and eyes of those who will carry on! It was time to go!

December 27, 1944   V-Mail

The good Lord has led us home for the thirty-fifth time today. May we all give thanks for the answer to our prayers. Letter will follow.
NO MORE COMBAT!!!!!

Epilogue

December 30, 1944

How does it feel to receive a letter from your ground-pounding ex-combat husband? It sure seems good just to lie down and go to sleep with no worries to keep me tossing and rolling—most restful sleep I've had since my arrival here.

No, I won't be coming home for a while. I'm going to take a staff job with the Thirteenth Combat Wing. If I like the job and it pans out okay I'll remain here six months, that's maximum. The war isn't going so good right at the present and I would like to do just a little more than my part before departing here. Maybe I can make it a little easier for someone else. The good Lord knows I've had plenty of breaks and good luck during my tour. In fact, the whole crew came through well and happy without a scratch on them, even though they do feel as if they're living on borrowed time. Many of our buddies were not so fortunate, so I feel that I should do just a little more. All the boys except Work and myself are returning to the States. Layl has a few more to fly before he finishes up, but it won't take long. He'll get his old crew back when Doc finishes. Doc has several more to go but he'll come through okay.

Just got some good news. I've been picked to go to London to be on a broadcast Sunday afternoon. Must get started getting a few things in order. I think it's called "London Calling" and will be beamed to the U.S.

January 3, 1945

I got back from London just in time to go to work last night. They sure gave it to me. I was pretty tired after the trip, but when I finished a thirteen-hour tour of duty I was really dead.

*Now about the broadcast. I didn't make it after all. My orders were in-
correct and I got to the wrong place at the right time. By the time I found
the right place it was the wrong time and the big show was over. Oh well,
I had the satisfaction of seeing the New Year in London. Met some fellows
who had been at Douglas, Arizona, with me so we had a big bull session.*

*The fellows have all started for home except Work and myself. Work is on
a furlough and you know what I'm doing. I'm still living with the 95th,
but will move to the 13th Wing tomorrow. So far I'm very much pleased
with my new job. It's interesting and very vital—there's no room for mistakes. I think I can handle it okay but time will tell. Right now I'll have to
put in long hours and work pretty hard to learn everything, but in a few
weeks when I can handle things alone it will be okay. . . .*

January 5, 1945

*. . . If someone had told me that I had to stay here I would have been
awfully unhappy, mad as hell, and probably griped about everything. But
since I've done it on my own hook even the worst things have taken on a
rosy appearance and life is much more bearable. After people quit shooting
at you and the only danger you have to face is falling on icy sidewalks it
takes quite a bit to get one in a bad humor.*

*I'm very well pleased with my new job. The training and experience are
well worth my staying here a couple of extra months. It also gives me a
chance to rehabilitate myself after combat in my own way.*

*It seems funny going to work in "Class A" uniform, blouse, tie, and all
the trimmings. You, no doubt, wonder what the nature of my new job is
and I'd like very much to tell you, but there are regulations which prevent
it. As you can see, I'm with headquarters immediately higher than the Group
I was with. We coordinate the groups within our command and see that
they get the necessary info to carry on their operations. It's really interesting
and at the present I'm very enthused about it. Maybe the novelty will wear
off after a time. There's one thing about this job. It will occupy just as much
of my time as I want it to. That is, I can live it all day, eat with it and
sleep with it day in and day out, or I can forget about it any time and
things will go on anyway.*

*I hope it is easier for you knowing that I am safe, that my combat is over,
and all we have to do is wait a few more months before being together for
good. . . .*

*There were times in combat when I wondered if I would see my wife again
or ever see my son. That worry and that feeling are now gone. I know darn
well I will and it's just a question of time. I realize that it was only through
the grace of God that this was brought about, so I feel perhaps I should do*

just a little more in appreciation of our good fortune. We have more than either of us realize to be thankful for. I don't like being away from you, but I won't gripe about it now in the face of all our good luck.

January 9, 1945

. . . Darn near got injured this morning. The snow was packed hard on the sidewalk and was just like clear ice. I started walking down the hill with hands in my pockets, slipped, and before I could get my balance I had made a three-point landing and slid twenty feet on my undercarriage. It sure would be heck after finishing my missions without a scratch to slip and fall on the sidewalk and get hurt.

Here's something I'm very sorry about. I told you that I would get a picture of Lucky Sherry *just as soon as was possible since the last two bunches of pictures didn't turn out. Well, I've waited just a wee bit too long 'cause she isn't with us any more. But I'll say one thing . . . she was lucky all the way for everyone that flew her. . . .*

I received the fifth Oak Leaf Cluster to the Air Medal today so am sending it on. That's the last one I'll ever earn in this Theater and I hope it is the last one ever. I probably won't write again for a couple of days because I'm going to another field to attend to some duties. But I promise a long letter upon returning.

January 14, 1945

. . . Here's what I've done so far today, and will do later. Being Sunday I got up at eight for breakfast and was ready for church at ten. After church I stopped and talked to Work and Billy Bob for about an hour and then it was dinner time. After dinner I worked an hour so another guy could go eat—I shouldn't say "work" as it was just a question of having a guy on duty in case the telephone should ring. This afternoon I have to go to one of the groups for interrogation of crews and find out what happened in today's operation. That will probably be over about six—then I'll have dinner and go to work at seven and get off at eight in the morning. You see when we get started we really put in the time and usually get something done. . . .

January 15, 1945

In this new job I have a heck of a time trying to work out a sleeping schedule that will coincide with my working time. Did you ever stop to think that when you work twelve hours and take off twenty-four there isn't a plausible time to sleep? If I go to bed when I first get through work then I get up too soon and am tired before going to work again. But then I'm too tired to stay up after finishing work. Boy, I sure have problems to worry about. Notice how things have changed. Less than three weeks ago I was worrying about my neck. Now all I do is try to make my stay here just a little more comfortable. . . .

Had a letter from Smith today telling me all the news about the boys. They are still awaiting transportation home—hence are just lying around killing time and occasionally doing a few odd details. Sure hated to see them go, in a way. We had been through a lot together. I bid them good-bye in London, a rather touching ordeal. After all we've done it seemed kind of odd to see them with tears in their eyes—and in mine too—after everything was over and them with a train ticket home. A finer bunch of fellows will never be found again on one crew. I sure enjoyed having them with me. But every pilot thinks he has the best crew there is.

January 16, 1945

Here it is the middle of January and the way things look at the present I figure on tendering my resignation here the end of March. This is still subject to change one way or the other, but I think we're safe in planning on my leaving here in April.

Guess what happened this afternoon! Well, I won't keep you guessing any longer. They fell out the troops, had a big parade, band and all, and at the climax gave Work, myself, and a couple of other fellows the Distinguished Flying Cross. Are you interested in the citation? Okay, I'll copy it down for you since I have only one copy and it has to go in my 201 file. Don't believe any of it, though, just read it and forget it 'cause it does get flowery and all I was doing was saving my own neck.

"The Distinguished Flying Cross is awarded the following named Officers: Eugene R. Fletcher 0-759211 1st Lt. Army Air Forces, United States Army.

"For extraordinary achievements while serving as pilot on heavy bombardment missions to Cologne, Germany, 17 October 1944 and Hamburg, Germany, 25 October 1944. On both these occasions Lt. Fletcher demonstrated outstanding qualities of initiative and leadership by assuming lead responsibilities for his group when scheduled leaders were forced to leave formation because of mechanical difficulties. The superior airmanship, resourcefulness and devotion to duty displayed by Lt. Fletcher materially con-

tributed to the success of these important operations and reflect highest credit upon himself and the Army Air Forces."

I'll send the medal on to you as soon as I can get something to wrap it in.

No mail for me today, but I didn't expect any for lately we have only been getting mail from the States about once a week. I hope by now you know my tour is over. I'm anxiously awaiting your reaction to my decision to remain here awhile. I believe you understand what I'm trying to do so I'm hoping you won't be too disappointed.

January 17 was a rough but happy day for Doc. He had engine trouble, but managed to get home on 3 engines from Hamburg for his final mission #35. Billy Bob was reinstated as 1st pilot and would now fly his remaining missions with his old crew.

January 18, 1945

. . . We have our working schedule all messed up again. Some day maybe we'll get it worked out. Last night I worked at the job which I'm trying to get. It's a good deal, but will take some time before I can handle it alone competently. The job I have been doing is very closely coordinated to it, but is the junior position which must be learned before doing this. I don't know how I'll make out. There are six of us all working for the same job and only two of us will get it. Naturally our work is very closely supervised and when a mistake is made it stands out like a sore thumb. So far most of us have displayed just about the same ability and willingness to learn, so it's just a question of waiting to see who will mess up the worst first, or if that doesn't happen then I don't know how they'll figure out who gets the job and who doesn't. I'll just do my best and if that isn't enough I'll take my leave of absence and head for my little family.

According to your letters right now you are reading my late November and early December letters. We're each just about a good month behind in the activities of the other. One of these days we won't have to put up with this pony express system. When we want to tell the other something we'll just be face to face, one of the advantages of close proximity.

I feel sorry for the ground pounders I work with here. Most of them haven't seen their families in well over two years. I don't see how they can stand it, and they know they can't get home until the end of the war. When I compare my predicament with theirs I really can't gripe because I know I can come home in a few months.

January 22, 1945

In my spare time I have been doing a little flying. We have an AT-17 here like I used to fly in Advanced Training, and I've been getting a kick out of flying it. But I guess I'm just a land lover at heart because now that I have my four hours in and just a little more I've lost the urge to sail in the blue.

February 1, 1945

. . . Things are going to change a little bit around here—don't know exactly how yet. But I suggest you stop writing me at this present address. I'll let you know before very long what to do. If you want you can start a letter and add to it each day, then when you find out what goes you can send it on. Don't misinterpret this as meaning I might be coming home because I don't want any hopes up. It's just a suggestion which will improve the mail situation for me a little later on.

February 4, 1944

Really had a time yesterday! It was a beautiful day with sunshine and all so I decided to go flying. Flew up to Edinburgh, then over Loch Lomond just so I could say that I have seen the "bonnie banks." It was a nice trip and I enjoyed myself. The weather probably had a lot to do with it because it has been cold and dreary up until then. . . .

We had some bad news on February 6, when we heard that Billy Bob had failed to return from a mission to Chemnitz. I went immediately to the 95th Group Operations and was informed that he was okay, having landed at Brussels.

February 24, 1945   Telegram

Arrived in New York last night will be home as soon as possible will wire again from Tacoma and let you know details with all my love
  Gene

Postscript

When the war in England ended I was serving in a staff capacity at the air base in Hobbs, New Mexico, and was one of the first released. I left the service knowing that I had proudly been a part of a massive struggle that would surely end all wars, and that totalitarianism had been dealt such a defeat that never again would greedy men seek to covet another nation's territory and its people. I felt we had truly brought peace to a world which in the past had known only war!

It was on this note that I dearly wanted to end this book for this was, in truth, my belief at the cessation of hostilities. But the passage of time showed nothing could have been farther from reality. It was obvious that again I was spinning "idle dreams."

Who could foresee that Brownie would participate in two more wars, that Doc would continue flying in the Air Force Reserve and retire a lieutenant colonel? Or, for that matter, that Frank and I would be called upon to serve our country in one more war? So now it seems only fair to the reader that we muster for interrogation one last time.

I am happy to report that all crew members have lived a full and rewarding life with their families.

Doc is still working full-time with his brother operating automobile dealerships in Tacoma and Auburn, Washington. He and Margaret live in Tacoma.

Billy Bob Layl is now Dr. B. B. Layl. He and his wife Emma Jean live in Piggott, Arkansas, where he is a practicing eye specialist.

Roco has retired after a career in accounting. In 1947 he came to Richland, Washington, to visit his brother who was a nuclear phys-

The nine living members of "Fletcher's Gang," 41 years later. Back row, left to right: McQuitty, Lynch, Firszt, Brown, Hinman; front row: Fletcher, Doxon, Work, Dimit. "We miss you, Smitty."

icist at the Hanford project. He liked the state, and made it his home. He and his wife, Dottie, now live in Puyallup.

Frank Dimit has now retired from a management position of a subsidiary of a major steel company. He continues to serve on the Board of Trustees for a technical school. Peggy and Frank reside in Steubenville, Ohio.

Brownie was the only one of our group to make the military his career. After retiring from the Air Force he returned to Pittsburg, Kansas, where he purchased the farm which was his wife's family home. He has now retired and his son operates the farm. Mary passed away during the time this book was being written.

George Hinman has retired after a career with the United States Soil Conservation Service as a technician designing and overseeing conservation projects. Yorkville, Illinois, is home to George and Mary.

Ken McQuitty has retired from a life in the home building industry. Mac and Jane live in Columbia, Missouri.

Robert Lynch is working for an electrical company where he assembles motors. He will retire in January 1988. Muldrow, Oklahoma, is still home to Bob and Willie.

Joe Firszt operated his own dry cleaning business and has only recently retired after selling his business. He and his wife, Helen, live in Carpentersville, Illinois.

Martin Smith is the only deceased member of the crew, a fact which was learned when Doc attempted to locate the gang for our crew reunion in 1985. All we knew was his home was in Milwaukee, Wisconsin, in 1944. After many calls, a dedicated telephone company employee was able to locate his daughter. By strange coincidence she lived in Seattle and represented her father at the crew reunion.

Fletch, after a career in agriculture and many years of community service, retired in 1983 from the active management of the corporate family farm. This business is carried on by sons David and James. Sherry and Fletch live in Tekoa, Washington.

All members present or accounted for, Sir. Crew dismissed!

Eugene Fletcher
Major USAF Ret.

Appendixes

THE ODYSSEY OF TWO AIRPLANES
PLUS TEN

We were assigned two aircraft during our tour—both were Boeing built. We were especially pleased to be assigned *Knock Out Baby*, #42-97257. This aircraft was originally named by Lieutenant Roy W. Gielen and his crew. Their first mission was to Berlin on April 18, 1944. This was a premier target for the group because the 95th and 100th had the honor of flying the first U.S. heavy bombers over Berlin on March 4, 1944. This Task Force was led by H. Griffin Mumford of the 95th Bomb Group. For this mission our group received another Presidential Unit Citation.

On September 18, 1944, *Knock Out Baby* took part in the third Russia-Italy-England Shuttle Raid. She was shot up on the ground during the night in Poltava, Russia, and was not able to return with the group. But she was repaired and ferried back to England and was returned to the 95th Bomb Group on October 4, 1944.

In the meantime, we were assigned #43-37783, a brand new B-17G, which we named *Lucky Sherry*. This was the aircraft in which we flew our last fifteen missions. She did not return from a mission to Frankfurt on January 5, 1945, and I assumed at the time that she had been shot down. In September 1986 I was informed by Paul Andrews from information he had gleaned from the archives of the 95th Bomb Group that she made an emergency landing at Lille, France. She was repaired and returned to the group on February 15, 1945. Sometime after that she was transferred to the 335th Squadron where she was renamed *Temptation*. The last personal record I have of her is a picture taken from a mission camera on board which indicated that she was still flying combat on March 17, 1945, when the group went to Ruhland. A recorded entry in the archives reported that she returned early from a mission to Berlin on March 18. The final entry in the archives showed her last operational sortie

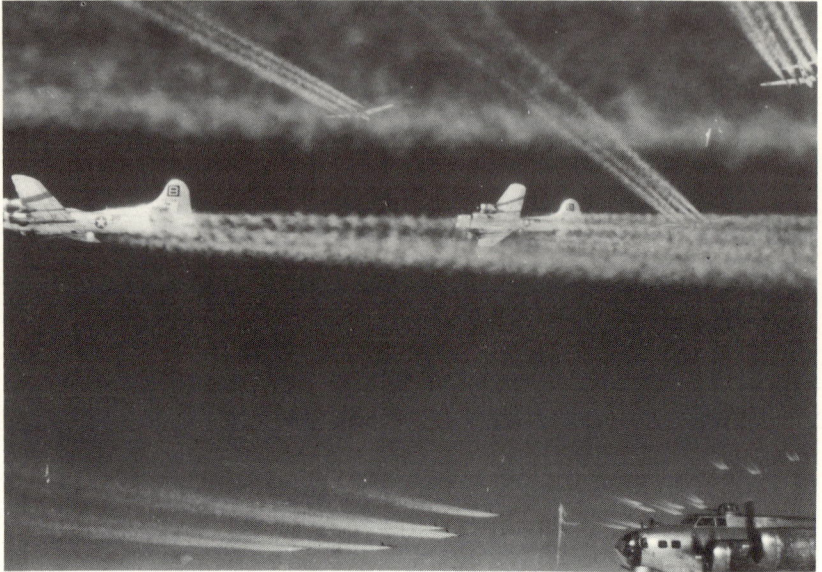

Picture taken from *Lucky Sherry*, March 17, 1945 *(Boeing Archives)*

was May 20, 1945, returning POWs from the continent to England. During her lifetime she was dispatched on sixty-two combat missions plus eight mercy missions after the war ended.

On March 28, 1945, on a mission to Hanover, *Knock Out Baby* landed at Le Bourget, France, with the #1 engine feathered. The crew was not credited with a mission. That same day she was earmarked for salvage, but the order was cancelled—she was repaired and continued to fly.

Additional information provided by Paul Andrews and our own diaries makes it possible to record the destiny of the other ten aircraft we flew in combat.

On August 6, 1944, aircraft #231999, *Chicken Ship*, ran out of fuel and landed short of the base at Poltava, Russia, on our "Frantic Five" mission. She was left there and was assigned to the Eastern Command.

On August 16, on a mission to Zeitz, aircraft #297797, *Full House*, received a direct flak hit to the left wing. The aircraft disintegrated, killing six members of the crew. The other four became POWs. We lost four aircraft on this raid including #231514, also named *Full House* because of the card hand painted on her nose. She left the formation over the target with the #2 engine feathered and #3 on fire. All nine members of her crew became POWs.

November 2, on the mission to Merseburg, aircraft #2102678, *Ole Worrybird*, left the formation with the #2 and #3 engines feathered. At that time she was under the escort of a single P-51 fighter. One member of the crew was killed and eight became POWs.

On November 29, aircraft #231675, *Berlin Bessie*, after returning from a mission to Hamm, was declared beyond repair and joined the bone yard.

On our mission to Merseburg on November 30, aircraft #2102560, *The Thomper*, received a direct flak hit in the bomb bay. The aircraft left the formation on fire and broke in half at the radio compartment. Six members of the crew were killed and three became POWs.

On December 16 on a raid to Stuttgart aircraft #297232, *Government Issue*, was destroyed, killing all nine crew members. Aircraft #232066, *Silver Slipper*, crash landed on the base the same day. The aircraft was demolished but all crew members were safe.

On January 20, 1945, aircraft #231462, *Roaring Bill*, landed on the continent and was declared beyond repair. Two members of the crew bailed out over enemy territory and became POWs. The rest, including one wounded, stayed with the plane until they crossed the allied lines.

On April 16 aircraft #237882, *Blues in the Reich*, was declared beyond salvage and relegated to the bone pile.

And thus it was that our two assigned ships survived the war intact. *Knock Out Baby*, even though destined for the scrap pile, became a survivor in the tradition of the crews that flew her. At the end of hostilities she had been dispatched on 113 combat missions and on June 6, 1945, she arrived back in the United States.

THE MISSIONS

Target	A/C No.	Name	Date	Group Mission	Air Time
1. Abbeville	7232	*Government Issue*	July 6	168	5:10
2. Merseburg	1462	*Roaring Bill*	July 7	169	4:15
3. Munich	2560	*The Thomper*	July 11	171	9:45
4. Maquis	7882	*Blues in the Reich*	July 14	173	9:30
5. Paris (RR bridge SE)	97797	*Full House*	July 17	175	7:00
6. Hemmingstedt	1675	*Berlin Bessie*	July 18	177	7:00
7. St. Lo	1999	*Chicken Ship*	July 24	181	6:35
8. St. Lo	1514	*Full House*	July 25	182	6:05
9. Merseburg	7257	*Knock Out Baby*	July 28	183	8:35
10. Maquis	1675	*Berlin Bessie*	Aug. 1	185	9:40
11. Hamburg	7882	*Blues in the Reich*	Aug. 4	188	7:15
12. Rahmel (Gdynia)	7257	*Knock Out Baby*	Aug. 6	189	10:35
13. Trzebinia	7257	*Knock Out Baby*	Aug. 7	190	10:10
14. Buzau	7257	*Knock Out Baby*	Aug. 8	191	9:00
15. Toulouse	7257	*Knock Out Baby*	Aug. 12	192	10:00
16. Ruhland	7257	*Knock Out Baby*	Aug. 24	197	9:10
17. Berlin	2678	*Ole Worrybird*	Aug. 27	200	6:05
18. Ruhland	7257	*Knock Out Baby*	Sep. 11	207	8:40
19. Mainz	2066	*Silver Slipper*	Sep. 27	213	6:40
20. Merseburg	2066	*Silver Slipper*	Sep. 28	214	8:20
21. Mainz	7783	*Lucky Sherry*	Oct. 9	221	6:30
22. Bremen	7783	*Lucky Sherry*	Oct. 12	222	7:05
23. Cologne	7783	*Lucky Sherry*	Oct. 17	224	7:00
24. Kassel	7783	*Lucky Sherry*	Oct. 18	225	8:35
25. Hamburg	7783	*Lucky Sherry*	Oct. 25	228	7:20

Target	A/C No.	Name	Date	Group Mission	Air Time
26. Hanover	7783	*Lucky Sherry*	Oct. 26	229	7:15
27. Merseburg	7783	*Lucky Sherry*	Oct. 30	231	5:15
28. Merseburg	7783	*Lucky Sherry*	Nov. 2	232	7:50
29. Ludwigshafen	7783	*Lucky Sherry*	Nov. 5	234	7:50
30. Koblenz	7783	*Lucky Sherry*	Nov. 11	237	6:25
31. Merseburg	7783	*Lucky Sherry*	Nov. 30	242	8:20
32. Berlin	7783	*Lucky Sherry*	Dec. 5	245	8:35
33. Biblis	7783	*Lucky Sherry*	Dec. 24	250	8:45
34. Bad Munster	7783	*Lucky Sherry*	Dec. 25	251	7:05
35. Fulda	7783	*Lucky Sherry*	Dec. 27	252	7:50

Bombardier's Note

My notes were written immediately after each mission. Needless to say, they are not literary masterpieces—just notes as recorded while I was still scared.

As usual my hindsight is 100 percent, but my foresight leaves a lot to be desired. I wish now that I had written a more complete record. However, I can assure you that I'm not going to fly thirty-five more missions just for a better record.

Frank S. Dimit

Navigator's Note

My writing had its beginning during the waiting part of many nights between the end of our tour and the end of hostilities in Europe. For the same reasons Fletch chose to take a staff job with the Thirteenth Combat Wing, I became a group briefing officer reporting to Major Bingham (who became so upset about our being assigned to fly to Merseburg for the seventh time). My primary task was to prepare and present to combat crews an overview of bombing missions. Typically these briefings included targets being attacked by the Royal Air Force and the U.S. Fifteenth Air Force in Italy in addition to what the Eighth Air Force would be doing.

Each mission's specifications were received by teletype at intervals during the late afternoon and night before. Invariably the intervals allowed far more time than was needed to prepare the briefing, so I filled the waiting time by commencing a narrative of the missions our crew had flown. However, the time required for the writing exceeded the waiting time.

I briefed the 320th combat mission flown by the 95th Bomb Group on April 18, and was on duty May 7 when orders were received restricting all U.S. personnel to their bases for an indefinite period beginning early May 8 (V-E Day). Luckily there was enough lead time for me to arrange a pass, since I greatly preferred to celebrate that event in London.

In June 1945 I was surprised to be assigned to navigate *Knock Out Baby* on its return flight to the States. Through rare good fortune the payload consisted of personal gear for the flight crew and our passengers, *ten crew chiefs.*

In exchange for publications rights to what I have written, Fletch has opened himself to gratuitous remarks from this member of his crew. Somewhat arrogant and excessively competitive as I was in

265

1944 when our crew was formed, I was prepared to follow orders and salute by the book—period. Everything else would be "wait and see." What I saw was an aircraft commander not much taller than my own 5 foot 5, weighing perhaps 130 pounds in full flight gear. Look out, Hitler!

Having read this far, however, you already realize how capable Fletch was. He was admired and trusted by each of us. We knew he was loyal and would fight to protect our interests. The longer I live and the more people I observe, the more certain I become that Fletch was an exceptional leader; he is an extraordinary man!

Robert "Roco" Work

Note on Sources

The main sources of information for this book were the letters I wrote to my wife, Sherry, and my diary. Also invaluable were the personal notes of the copilot, navigator, bombardier, and armorer gunner—along with information provided by Paul Fiess. I have also consulted the following secondary sources: the *Stars and Stripes, ETO edition,* and *Yank* magazine.

In all probability many of the facts and figures in our original diaries may have appeared in the *Stars and Stripes,* since this was the official newspaper for the troops during World War II.

In addition to our regular mission briefing, we had voluntary news briefings conducted once or twice a week which contained a lot of information. We were given facts and figures, and followed the progress of the war. These plus our first-hand knowledge and experiences made up the bulk of our diary entries. To differentiate one source from another after forty-three years would be impossible.

If the reader should wish to verify that some of these incidents took place, three sources would be invaluable: *Contrails,* the unofficial history of the 95th Bomb Group, published by the 95th Bomb Group Photographic section under the supervision of Captain David B. Henderson; *Münster: The Way it Was,* written by Ian Hawkins of Bacton, Stowmarket, England, and published by Robinson Typographics of Anaheim, California; *Mighty Eighth War Diary,* by Roger Freeman of New Colchester, England, a foremost authority on the Eighth Air Force and the men who flew the planes. This last book was published by Jane's Publishing Company Limited, London.